No 37

Editorial Manager	Chester Fisher
Senior Editor	Judith Maxwell
Editors	Bridget Daly
	Brenda Clarke
Series Designers	QED (Alastair Campbell
	and Edward Kinsey)
Designer	Howard Dyke
Series Consultant	Keith Lye
Consultant	Dr Charles Gullick
Production	Penny Kitchenham
Picture Research	Jenny De Gex
	Janice Croot
	Georgina Booker

© Macdonald Educational Ltd. 1980
First Published 1980
Macdonald Educational Ltd.
Holywell House,
Worship Street,
London EC2A 2EN

2081/3200
ISBN 0 356 07006 9

Designed and created in
Great Britain

Printed and bound by
New Interlitho, Italy

WORLD OF KNOWLEDGE

Peoples and Places

Arthur Butterfield

Ron Carter

Peter Muccini

Peter Way

Susan Wilson
1980

Macdonald

Contents

Part II

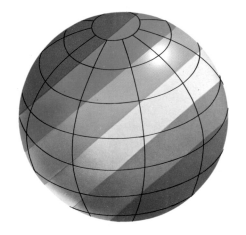

World of Knowledge

This book breaks new ground in the method it uses to present information to the reader. The unique page design combines narrative with an alphabetical reference section and it uses colourful photographs, diagrams and illustrations to provide an instant and detailed understanding of the book's theme. The main body of information is presented in a series of chapters that cover, in depth, the subject of this book. At the bottom of each page is a reference section which gives, in alphabetical order, concise articles which define, or enlarge on, the topics discussed in the chapter. Throughout the book, the use of SMALL CAPITALS in the text directs the reader to further information that is printed in the reference section. The same method is used to cross-reference entries within each reference section. Finally, there is a comprehensive index at the end of the book that will help the reader find information in the text, illustrations and reference sections. The quality of the text, and the originality of its presentation, ensure that this book can be read both for enjoyment and for the most up-to-date information on the subject.

World of Knowledge

Peoples and Places

Arthur Butterfield

Ron Carter

Peter Muccini

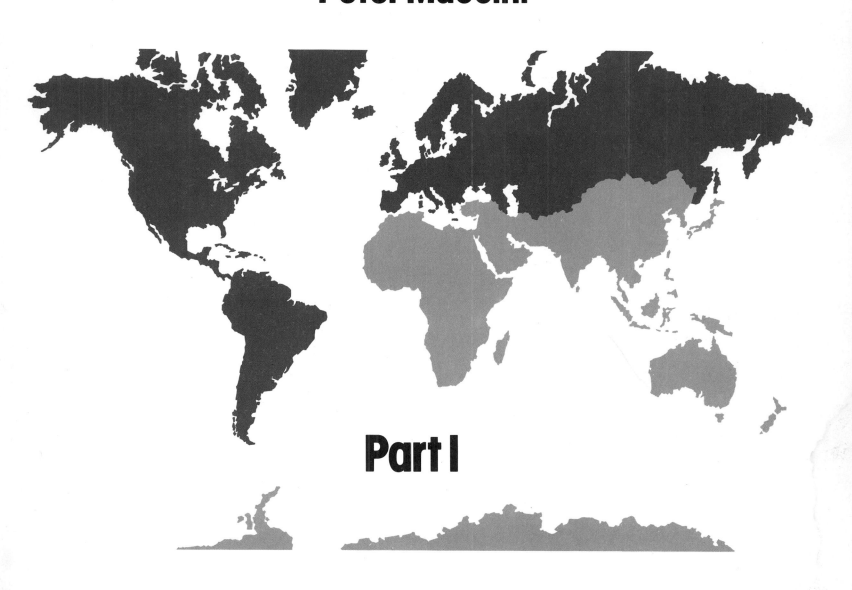

Part I

Introduction

We live in a shrinking world and up-to-date knowledge of other countries — their peoples, cultures and economies — is more important today than at any other time in world history. It is now essential for us to try to understand the aspirations of peoples in far-away lands, if only because actions taken on the opposite side of the globe increasingly affect our lives. **Peoples and Places, Part I** throws a spotlight on the Old World of Europe and the New World of the Americas, two regions which are closely linked by cultural ties which date back to the early days of the European Age of Exploration. It sets out the essential information we require if we want to comprehend the problems we will all face in the last two decades of this century. Except where otherwise stated, population figures for countries are 1980 estimates, based on United Nations' statistics. Populations of other political divisions, cities and towns are the latest available figures.

Western Europe's importance in world affairs is out of all proportion to its size. Its modern history has been marred by wars, but modern Europeans are seeking unity through economic co-operation.

Western Europe

Western Europe, as its name implies, is part of the European continent, which, except for Australasia, is the smallest in the world. Yet despite its size, it has played a leading role in the political, economic, scientific and cultural development of the rest of the world for the past 2,000 years.

Western Europe covers 3,686,000 square kilometres, about 35 per cent of the total area of the continent. It is a political entity rather than a definite geographical area and consists of those countries that are not part of the communist bloc in Eastern Europe.

The reasons why a small part of the globe has had such far reaching influence are due to a combination of climatic, geographical and social factors. Most of Western Europe has no great extremes of temperature. This has helped to make life in most of Europe less of a struggle than it is for people living in very hot or very cold lands. Much of the land is fertile and, through the development of social organizations, it was not difficult to exploit it.

These factors must certainly have proved most attractive to the various waves of settlers, who came from the east. The settlers seized upon the opportunities that the land afforded. They migrated throughout the region, inter-married and combined their talents and abilities. So began the process that eventually led to what we now call Western civilization. The impact that European values and ideas have had on the world has been tremendous.

The concepts of democracy, communism and fascism were born in Western Europe and these have affected the lives of practically everyone in the world. Natural curiosity also led to recent scientific and technological discoveries. Much that is associated with modern living has resulted from these. The influence of European literature, music, painting, sculpture and architecture, too,

Above: A key trade route in Western Europe, the Rhine is also a major tourist area.

is widespread, partly as a result of European colonization.

Western Europe was the starting point of the great voyages of exploration in the 1400s and 1500s. Consequently, certain nations came to possess vast empires in the Americas, in the East and in Africa. West European influences were thus extended to peoples in distant lands. Today, Spanish and Portuguese are the languages of Latin America, French is spoken in many African countries, while English, once simply the language of the inhabitants of a small island off the west coast of Europe, is now spoken by hundreds of millions of people of all races, creeds and colours.

Western European history has been scarred by continual wars and the apparent inability of the

Reference

A **Alps** are a mountain range extending from south-east FRANCE across SWITZERLAND, AUSTRIA and northern ITALY into YUGOSLAVIA. The highest peak is Mt Blanc (4,807 metres).

Amsterdam is the capital and largest city of the NETHERLANDS. It is a financial, business and industrial centre and world famous for its beautiful canal system. Population: 738,000.

Andorra is a tiny state in the

PYRENEES between FRANCE and SPAIN. Its government is shared by Spanish and French officials. The official language is Catalan and

Amsterdam canal

most of the people are Roman Catholic. Agriculture is the mainstay of the economy, but the fine scenery supports a healthy tourist trade. Area: 453 sq km; population: 37,000; capital: Andorra la Vella.

Antwerp is a commercial and industrial centre in BELGIUM. Situated on the River Scheldt, it is also an important port handling much of West Germany's trade. Population: 207,000.

Apennines are a mountain range which forms the rocky backbone of the Italian peninsula. The highest

peaks rise to 3,000 metres.

Athens is the capital of GREECE and the cradle of a former great civilization. It is

Acropolis temple, Athens

still dominated by the ruins of magnificent temples such as the Parthenon which crowns the rocky Acropolis that rises more than 60 metres above the city. Population (with suburbs): 4,667,000.

Austria, a country of mountains, meadows and beautiful old cities, is situated in central Europe. Its climate of warm summers and cold winters, but with plenty of snow, makes it popular with tourists all the year round. Mineral resources include magnesite, oil and iron ore. The chief river is the Danube

The maritime climate is basically temperate. Winters rarely become extremely cold and summers tend to be cool. Rainfall is fairly evenly distributed throughout the year with late autumn and winter usually wetter than the rest of the year.

The climate is the result of vast low-pressure areas or cyclones known as North Atlantic depressions, passing over the continent. These depressions generally bring warm and moist masses of air in the form of rain-bearing clouds. The rain falls mostly on those regions nearest to the Atlantic: northern SPAIN, western FRANCE, IRELAND, UNITED KINGDOM, ICELAND, western SCANDINAVIA, northern GERMANY, the NETHERLANDS and BELGIUM. Another factor in the maritime climate is the Gulf Stream and its offshoot, the North Atlantic Drift. These oceanic currents warm the air moving over the coasts, preventing inland temperatures from dropping too low in winter. They also keep ports in the far north of Europe ice-free during winter. Consequently, a city such as GLASGOW which is roughly on the same latitude as Moscow is considerably less cold in winter.

The Mediterranean climate is formed by a high-pressure area or anticyclone over the Azores, a group of islands situated off the north-west coast of Africa. The Azores anticyclone moves northwards in summer, bringing warm air to the Mediterranean area and sometimes to many regions which have a maritime climate. The Mediterranean climate has warm summers and mild winters. Rain tends to fall mostly in the late autumn and winter. Regions with this climate are southern and eastern Spain, southern France, most of ITALY, MALTA and southern GREECE.

The continental climate is formed in the heart of a landmass that is far from the sea. This climate produces very cold winters and hot summers. It is found in the *Meseta* or central plateau of Spain which is enclosed by the PYRENEES in the north and the Sierra Nevada in the south, and in eastern Scandinavia comprising FINLAND, SWEDEN and eastern NORWAY. In this part of Europe the climate originates in an area of high pressure over the northern part of the Eurasian landmass which incorporates the USSR. The effects of this air mass extend to central Germany and northern Italy.

various nations to co-exist peacefully. Even in the 1900s, two world wars broke out, within little more than 20 years of each other, resulting in the loss of tens of millions of lives. The second of these great conflicts ended in 1945 and left a devastated continent. However, the destructive force of the weapons being developed, particularly nuclear bombs, meant that something had to be done to prevent another catastrophic war. Western European nations realized that they had better try to work together for the common good and put away the rivalries of the past.

Therefore, during the second half of the 1900s a sense of common purpose was born in the shape of the European Economic Community, or the Common Market, as it came to be known. The aim of this movement was to try to realize an age-old dream of transforming a continent of different nations into one harmonious unit with no frontiers, sharing the same benefits and a single identity of being Europeans.

Above: East Berlin seen from across the wall erected in 1961 by the communist East German authorities to halt the flow of refugees to the West. With its slogan calling for freedom for political prisoners in East Germany, the wall typified the division of Europe into 2 politically opposed camps after World War II. Berlin, a divided city, became the focus of rivalry between the United States and the Soviet Union. Relations between East and West improved from the late 1960s, leading to more trade.

Climate
Western Europe has three basic types of climate: maritime, Mediterranean and continental. But the climatic regions do not have precise boundaries and they merge into one another.

which flows through VIENNA. Most of the population is Roman Catholic and German is the official language. Austria was once a great imperial power but became a small state after World War I. In 1938 it became part of Germany, but this union ended in 1945. Since then it has remained neutral. Area: 83,850 sq km; population: 7,574,000; capital: VIENNA.

B Barcelona is SPAIN's largest industrial and business centre. Situated in the north-east, it has one of the country's few good har-

bours. It is a major shipping centre and its industries pro-

Barcelona Cathedral

duce textiles, paper, glass, leather and metal products. Population: 1,745,000.
Basel is a major industrial and commercial centre in SWITZERLAND. It stands on the River RHINE. Population (with suburbs): 369,000.
Belfast is the capital of NORTHERN IRELAND, which forms part of the UNITED KINGDOM. It is situated on the River Lagan where it joins Belfast Lough and is the chief port and industrial centre of the province. Population: 362,000.
Belgium is a small and densely populated country

situated between FRANCE and the NETHERLANDS. It is mostly

Bomb explosion, Belfast

flat, rising to the Ardennes mountains in the south-east. The coastal climate is temperate, but conditions are more extreme inland. Most Belgians are Roman Catholic. The Flemings in the north speak Flemish, an old form of Dutch, and the Walloons in the south speak French. Belgium's many industries produce chemicals, iron and steel, motor vehicles and foodstuffs. The country achieved statehood in 1831 and still has a monarchy. Area: 30,513 sq km; population: 10,048,000; capital: BRUSSELS.

At times these three climates encroach on each other and weather conditions then differ from the normal pattern. At other times the weather of much of Western Europe is seriously disturbed by the invasion of large masses of cold air from the polar regions and unusually cold conditions and heavy snowfalls occur.

Key to colour range

- Tundra
- Coniferous forest
- Mountains and hills
- Forest
- Woodland
- Grassland and farmland
- Scrub
- Semi-desert
- Desert

Benelux is the customs union of 3 neighbouring countries in Western Europe: BELGIUM, the NETHERLANDS and LUXEMBOURG. The union was set up in 1948.

Berlin is the largest city in Germany and was that nation's capital until 1945. The western sector is separated from the east by a 41-km wall erected in 1961 by the East German authorities to prevent mass defections to the West. West Berlin, which is larger than the eastern sector, is surrounded by East Germany but forms part of the FEDERAL REPUBLIC OF GER-MANY. Population (West Berlin): 1,951,000.

Berne is the capital of SWIT-ZERLAND. It is situated in the heart of the country amid mountains and has many fine Gothic churches and buildings. Population (with suburbs): 283,000.

Birmingham is the 2nd-largest city of the UNITED KINGDOM and one of the world's biggest industrial centres. It is situated in the Midlands. Population: 1,059,000.

Black Forest is a major tourist area in West Germany. It is a beautiful region of wooded uplands in the south of the country.

Bonn is the capital of the FEDERAL REPUBLIC OF GERMANY. It stands on the River RHINE and is chiefly a government and educational centre. The composer Beethoven was born in the city. Population: 285,000.

Bordeaux has a worldwide reputation for the excellent quality of wines produced in the surrounding region. It is situated on the River Garonne in south-west FRANCE with access to the sea through the Gironde Estuary. It is an important indust-rial city and major port. Population (with suburbs): 591,000.

Brussels is the capital of BELGIUM and also of the 9-nation European Economic Community. It stands between the Flemish- and French-speaking parts of Belgium. Population (with suburbs): 1,042,000.

Grande Place, Brussels

C Channel Islands are dependencies of the UNITED KINGDOM. The 9 islands in order of size are: Jersey, Guernsey, Alderney, Herm, Brechou, Bouhou, Jethou, Lihou and Sark. The islands lie close to FRANCE and have a mild climate. English is the chief language but French is the official language of Guernsey. But many people

Plant and animal life

Climate and soil types largely determine the various kinds of vegetation.

In the tundra region of northern Europe plant life is restricted to mosses and lichens because of the cold weather. This simple form of vegetation is also found on the ALPS at altitudes above 2,000 metres.

South of the tundra region lies the boreal or northern forest. This consists mainly of conifers such as pine, fir and spruce which can resist the cold. The northern forest also has deciduous trees, such as the birch, which shed their leaves in autumn. The boreal forest zone is too cold for much agriculture. But barley and potatoes are major crops and grass is grown as winter food for dairy cattle.

Farther south is the region of mixed forest of

Cattle
Pigs
Sheep
Fishing
Reindeer
Grapes
Citrus fruit
Apples
Olives
Potatoes
Flowers
Flax

Sugar beet
Rice
Maize
Wheat
Barley
Oats
Rye
Tobacco
Cotton
Vegetable oil

Right: As a general rule the farther north in Western Europe, the higher the rainfall and the lower the average winter temperature. Conversely, winter temperatures in the south are usually higher while rainfall is less. Rainfall in Bergen, London and Lisbon is greater than in Athens mainly because these cities lie on the western fringes of Europe and are the first to receive the moist air masses from the Atlantic. Winter temperatures in northern Europe are also modified by the Gulf Stream's warm waters which prevent excessive freezing and result in relatively mild winters.

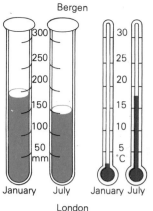

Bergen

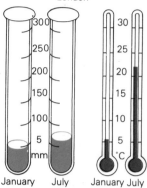

London

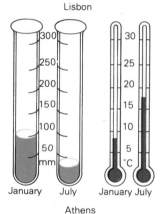

Lisbon

Left: Despite widespread use of modern methods and mechanization, Western Europe is not self-sufficient in food production, having to import much of its grain. Because of climatic conditions and terrain, Britain, France, the Netherlands and Denmark have the most highly developed agricultural industries.

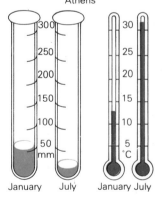

Athens

speak a dialect based on old French. The Channel Islands' economy is based on agriculture and tourism. And low taxes have attracted many new residents. The islands are self-governing but ruled by the British crown. Area: 194.6 sq km; population: 134,000.

Clyde is the chief commercial river of SCOTLAND. It flows through GLASGOW and past great shipyards before entering the Atlantic Ocean. It is 158 km long.

Copenhagen is the capital of DENMARK and is situated on the east coast of Sjaelland,

one of the islands forming Denmark. Its most famous landmark is the statue of the little mermaid at the harbour recalling Danish author Hans

Mermaid, Copenhagen

Andersen's fairy tale. Population (with suburbs): 1,380,000.

Corsica is an island province of FRANCE in the Mediterranean. Area: 8,681 sq km; population: 290,000.

D Denmark is a country in northern Europe consisting of a peninsula and a group of islands. It is mostly flat and its climate is mild and humid with fog and mist throughout the year. Winters tend to be cold and damp. The language is Danish and most of the people are Evangelical Lutheran. Den-

mark is a very important producer of food-stuffs such as pork, bacon, cheese, eggs and butter. Farmers also grow wheat, rye and barley, much of this to feed livestock. Machinery and transport equipment are the main industrial products. A monarchy since 1849, the country has overseas territories such as the 18 Faeroe Islands in the north Atlantic and Greenland, the world's largest island. Area: 43,069 sq km; population: 5,155,000; capital: COPENHAGEN.

Dublin is the capital of the

Irish Republic. It stands on the River Liffey on the east coast of Ireland and is an industrial centre and a busy port. Population: 568,000.

E Edinburgh is the capital of Scotland. Its centre is dominated by a huge rock with an ancient castle on the summit. The city is world-famous for its annual festival of the arts. Population: 467,000.

England is the largest of the 3 countries forming the island of Britain. It is mountainous in the north-west and the land generally

oak, ash, beech, hornbeam and other broad-leaved trees. This forest is the natural vegetation of the region, although little of the great primeval forest of central Europe survives today. The BLACK FOREST of southern Germany is an example of this type of vegetation. In the wetter and cooler parts of this region, the chief cereal crop is oats. However, in warmer, drier areas, wheat is the most important crop, while rye is grown on less fertile soils. Potatoes remain important and beet pulp is a leading cattle food. Dairy and beef cattle are reared on lush lowland pastures. The countries with the greatest number of cattle per square kilometre are the Netherlands, Belgium and DENMARK.

In the Mediterranean where rain is not so regular or abundant much of plant life is of the scrub or *maquis* type. This is found particularly in the south of France and in Italy, and consists of shrubs and gnarled plants such as the evergreen olive tree. The olive tree, like other plants indigenous to the Mediterranean lands, is adapted to conserving moisture during the summer drought. Fruits, including grapes for wine, and cereals, such as barley and wheat, flourish in this region, but much of the farmland has to be irrigated in summer. The region lacks large tracts of rich pasture, which are needed for cattle-rearing and dairy farming. Sheep and goats are the chief farm animals.

Wildlife has been considerably reduced with

Above: Iceland's economy is based almost totally on fishing, especially of cod. In 1975 Iceland extended its fishing limits from 80 to 320 km to preserve stocks.

Below: Hot, dry summers and limited mechanization make farming difficult in some Mediterranean countries. In Minorca farmers may still use animals to pull ploughs.

the spread of civilization. Before recorded history, mammoths and great oxen roamed the continent. Recently, governments have seen the danger in wiping out certain animals and have taken measures to protect them.

In the tundra, the reindeer is the most important animal. It provides meat, milk, clothing and even transport for the Lapps who live a semi-nomadic life in northern Scandinavia. Other animals of the tundra include the rat-like lemmings, Arctic foxes, bears and ermines.

The mixed forests are rich both in mammal and bird life. There are several varieties of deer and large beasts of prey such as the bear, wolf and wildcat. Gamebirds include grouse, pheasant, partridge and snipe, while the songbirds are represented by thrushes, blackbirds, larks and many varieties of finches. Many of these birds live in urban areas. Large birds of prey such as the eagle and the osprey live in remoter regions and because of their dwindling numbers are closely protected.

In the Mediterranean region there are still wild boars, goats and sheep. There is also considerably more reptile life such as snakes, including venomous ones, and lizards because of the warmer conditions.

Fish are an important source of food, especially in the countries of north-western Europe that face the Atlantic, and in some southern nations, such as PORTUGAL.

Land Features

Western Europe has much magnificent and varied scenery. There are high glaciated mountains, lofty plateaux and broad, fertile plains. Much of the scenery of north-western Europe was shaped during the Pleistocene Ice Age which ended only about 10,000 years ago. Glaciated mountain scenery is found in Scandinavia and upland Britain, while Finland is a land of lakes, which occupy ice-scoured basins. Other glacial scenery is found on the North European plain, where winding ridges of glacial moraine occur.

Southern Europe's main feature is the extensive Alpine mountain system, the world's youngest fold mountain range. The Alps were raised by continental drift as the plate bearing Africa moved northwards, pushing smaller plates in the Mediterranean region against Europe. Starting about 26 million years ago, the sediments between the plates have been raised up into gigantic and complex folds. The tensions created by these earth movements also cause faulting, and blocks of land were raised up into horsts, while other blocks sank between roughly parallel faults to form rift valleys, such as that occupied by the River RHINE. The plate movements are still continuing, as evidenced by earthquakes in southern Europe and the region's only active volcanoes, in south-west Italy.

Mountains

Western Europe has two main mountain systems: the north-west highlands and the Alpine system.

The north-west highlands are situated in north-west France (Brittany), Ireland, WALES, north-west ENGLAND, northern SCOTLAND, Ice-

Left: The growth of industry in Europe has helped to raise living standards in regions that were once poor and backward. At the same time, many of the processes involved, such as oil refining, the manufacturing and production of plastics and chemicals, have led to increased environmental pollution creating hazards for human, animal and plant life. To combat this, governments have passed national and international laws to control dangerous industrial processes.

Below: The Aletsch Glacier in Switzerland is a vast river of ice that advances in winter and retreats during the warmer months. Much of Europe was covered in glaciers during the ice ages of 30,000 years ago and more. The ice, often kilometres thick, carved out the broad valleys and the glittering peaks that form the fine scenery of today.

land and Scandinavia. In the north of Scotland and the Baltic Shield part of Scandinavia, the rocks date from the Pre-Cambrian era. These are some of the oldest known to man and were first formed several thousand million years ago. The north-west highlands rise to their highest peak, 2,468 metres above sea level, at Galdhøppigen in Norway. These mountains are not as high as the Alps because they are older and highly eroded.

The Alpine system includes the Sierra Nevada in southern Spain, the Pyrenees, the French, Swiss and Austrian Alps that curve around northern Italy, and other ranges that extend through Eastern Europe as far as the Caucasus Mountains. The highest peak in Western Europe is Mont Blanc, which rises 4,807 metres above sea level.

Other mountain regions include the central uplands such as the *Meseta* in Spain, the Massif Central in France, the Ardennes between Belgium and LUXEMBOURG and the uplands of Bavaria in southern Germany. These mountains are older than the Alps but younger than the north-west highlands.

Plains

The Central European Plain extends from the

language and most of the people are Roman Catholic with important Protestant and Jewish minorities. Agriculture and industry are equally important. French cheeses and wines are world-renowned and there are important iron ore deposits and coal in the north. Industry covers a vast range of products including aircraft and motor cars. France is also supreme in fashion and perfumery. The French have a republican government. Area: 547,026 sq km; population: 54,412,000; capital: PARIS.

Frankfurt is the business and financial centre of the FEDERAL REPUBLIC OF GERMANY. Frankfurt's international airport is Europe's largest. The

Goethe, born Frankfurt

city also produces chemicals, electrical equipment and precision instruments. It is the birthplace of the poet Goethe. Population: 626,000.

G **Geneva** is a French-speaking city in western SWITZERLAND. It is the headquarters of many leading international organizations such as agencies of the United Nations. Population (with suburbs): 323,000.
Genoa is ITALY's chief port. It dates from Roman times. During the 1200s it was a major sea power and the

rival of VENICE. Population: 801,000.
Germany, Federal Republic of, also known as West Germany, is Western Europe's most populated country. At the heart of the continent, it consists of plains in the north rising to the ALPS in the south. The climate is generally temperate, but the winters are cold with snow in the mountains. About half of the people are Roman Catholic and the language is German. The country is among the top 6 richest in the world. It has vast coal and iron ore deposits and

highly developed industries. Of the 26 million people in work, more than 35% are in industry. Chief products are chemicals, machinery, motor vehicles and electrical machinery. West Germany came into being after Germany was divided in 2 after World War II. It has a federal system of government comprising 10 states called länder. Area: 248,577 sq km; population: 61,991,000; capital: BONN.
Gibraltar is a British Crown Colony situated at the southern tip of SPAIN at the entrance to the Mediterranean

British Isles in the west across northern France, Belgium, the Netherlands and central Germany to the Asian border more than 3,000 kilometres to the east. The plain is the most heavily populated region of Western Europe and many of the region's great cities are situated on it. Most of Western Europe's industry and agriculture is also located there.

The peoples of Western Europe

Western Europe covers only about 2.5 per cent of the world's total land area. But it contains more than eight per cent of the world's people. As a result, Western Europe is thickly-populated, with an average of about 96 people to every square kilometre. This is nearly twice the population density of Eastern Europe, and it is also higher than the average population density for Asia which has, by far, the world's largest population.

Of the larger countries in Western Europe, Iceland, Norway, Finland and Sweden have the lowest population densities – 2, 13, 14 and 19 per square kilometre respectively. On the other hand, the Netherlands, Belgium, West Germany and the UNITED KINGDOM have population densities of 349, 329, 249 and 231 people per

Right: About 40% of the land in the Netherlands lies beneath sea level, and more than 140 bad floods have occurred in 700 years. The Dutch people have steadily won back more land from the waters to provide fertile soil for growing food and space for industries. Known as *polders*, these reclaimed areas are protected from the sea by dykes, or sea walls, which are constantly reinforced.

square kilometre respectively. The main reason for the high population density is that Western Europe is mostly industrialized and great urban agglomerations have been created, including PARIS, LONDON, MADRID, ROME, ATHENS and West BERLIN. In fact, more than 70 per cent of West Europeans live in cities and towns. In some countries, the rural population is extremely small. For example, less than three per cent of the people in the United Kingdom are engaged in agriculture and only seven per cent of West Germans work on the land.

The population of Western Europe, however,

Right: European prosperity has made it possible for millions to travel abroad. As a result the peace and beauty of many places have been marred by crowds of tourists. However, there are still unspoilt areas with no hotels, yachting marinas, discotheques, restaurants or petrol stations. This expanse of silvery sands and crystal-clear sea set amid deserted hills is by the Atlantic Ocean on the west coast of Ireland.

Sea. It is an important military base. The colony, only 6 sq km in area, has been British since 1704, but Spain has demanded its return.

Gibraltar, the Rock

Population: 33,000.

Glasgow is the 3rd-largest city of the UNITED KINGDOM and the largest city of SCOTLAND. Situated on the CLYDE, it is one of Britain's greatest ports and shipbuilding centres. Glasgow's industries include shipbuilding, engineering, iron and steel and the distilling of whisky. Population: 894,000.

Greece is a country in south-east Europe. Its territory includes hundreds of islands in the Mediterranean, the largest of which is Crete. It is mostly mountainous with plains in the east

where the famous old cities were built. The climate is mild in the north, but with cold winters. Summers are hot in the south and winters mild. The language is Greek and most of the people are of the Greek Orthodox faith. Of the 3.2 million work force 41% are in agriculture. Wine, olives and olive oil are the chief products. Greece operates one of the world's largest merchant fleets. The country was a monarchy until 1973 when it became a republic. Area: 131,944 sq km; population: 9,424,000; capital: ATHENS.

H **Hague, The,** is the seat of government of the NETHERLANDS and also houses the International Court of Justice. Population: 678,000.

Government buildings, The Hague

Hamburg is the largest port of the FEDERAL REPUBLIC OF GERMANY. Situated on the river Elbe, it is about 80 km from the North Sea. Popula-

is now increasing at a slower average rate than any other part of the world. The average rate of increase between 1970 and 1976 was only 0.6 per cent per year. Countries with rates of increase above average included Ireland and Spain, with annual increases of 1.3 and 1.1 per cent respectively. But the populations of AUSTRIA, West Germany and the United Kingdom were increasing at well below the Western European average, at yearly rates of only about 0.2 per cent. Such figures contrast with those of Africa, 2.7 per cent per year, and Latin America, 2.8 per cent. This contrast is reflected in the average age of the people. In Africa, the population is youthful, with 44 per cent of the people being under 15 and only 2.9 per cent above 65. By comparison, in Britain, only 16 per cent of the people are under 15 and about the same proportion are over 65.

The mostly prosperous people of Western Europe, with their highly-developed social services, also live, on average, far longer than the people in the developing world. For example, the average life expectation at birth in PORTUGAL is 65 for men and 72 for women, while in the Netherlands, it is 71 for men and 77 for women. In some developing countries, the average life expectation for both men and women is less than 40 years.

Until recently, scholars often divided the people of Western Europe into three main groups: the Nordic people of the north; the Alpine people of the centre; and the Mediterranean people of the south. However, such features as hair and eye colouring, nose shapes, blood groups, and so on vary so much that no one can say that the majority in one region have certain features. Thus, it is wrong to say that all north Europeans are tall and fair, while all south Europeans are short and dark.

Languages

Most of the languages of Western Europe developed from proto-Indo-European, which some linguists believe was once spoken in a region of Asia, somewhere between what is now Iran and northern India. European languages derived from proto-Indo-European belong mainly to four basic groups: the Germanic or Teutonic group, the Romance group, the Celtic

Below: Intricate lacework and colourful embroidery on the bodice and pinafore is a feature of the traditional costume of Norway.

Below: Efzones, members of the Greek state ceremonial guard, wear one of the most strikingly unusual uniforms in Europe.

Below: A tight bodice and a flared *dirndl* skirt are part of the national costume worn by women in Austria.

Below: The all-white costume of this English Morris dancer has bells on the legs.

Below: Bright colours, ribbons, sashes and frills are distinctive features of traditional costumes of southern Italy.

tion: 1,699,000.

Helsinki is the capital and largest city of FINLAND. It is also the country's main port exporting wood products. But ice-breakers are needed in winter to keep the seaways open. The city is situated on a peninsula surrounded by islands and dates mostly from the 1800s. Industries include shipbuilding, paper-making and sugar refining. Population: 492,000.

Iberian Peninsula is located in south-west Europe. It includes SPAIN, POR-TUGAL and GIBRALTAR.

Iceland is a rocky, volcanic island state in the north

Leif Ericsson, Reykjavik

Atlantic near the Arctic Circle. The Gulf Stream gives it a relatively temperate climate. Iceland has many hot springs (geysers) and about 200 volcanoes. Fishing, especially for cod, is the main source of wealth. Iceland became an independent republic in 1918 after being part of DENMARK. Area: 103,000 sq km; population: 232,000; capital: Reykjavik (population: 84,856).

Ireland is a republic that occupies most of the island of the same name. Its official title is Republic of Ireland. It consists mainly of rich farm-lands and pastures with a rocky and hilly region in the west and south-west. Ireland has a temperate climate with abundant rainfall during the year. Most of the people are Roman Catholic. The official languages are Irish, a form of Gaelic, and English. Ireland's traditional products are meat and dairy products. During the 1950s the government began developing industries with investment from abroad. Once ruled by Britain, it began a struggle for independence in 1916 and declared itself a republic in 1949. Area: 70,283 sq km; population: 3,316,000; capital: DUBLIN.

Ireland, Northern occupies over 15% of the area of Ireland and forms part of the UNITED KINGDOM of GREAT BRITAIN and NORTHERN IRELAND. It is often called Ulster because it forms part of the Irish province of that name. It is chiefly agricultural, but it also has textile, tobacco, food and shipbuilding industries. About 60% of the people are Protestant and the rest Roman Catholic. Area: 14,146 sq km; population: 1,536,000; capital: BELFAST.

group, and Greek. The Germanic languages include English, German, Dutch, Flemish, Danish, Norwegian, Swedish and Icelandic. These languages are spoken by the peoples of northern Europe.

The Romance languages are mainly spoken in southern Europe. They include Italian, Spanish, French, Portuguese and the Swiss dialect Romansh. These languages evolved from the Latin spoken by the Roman legions which conquered Europe 2,000 years ago.

The Celtic languages were spoken widely in Western Europe in early times. Now they are a dying breed. They are Welsh and Scottish Gaelic in Britain and Breton in north-west France. In the Irish Republic the government has declared Irish Gaelic a national language together with English in a bid to keep this ancient tongue alive. Other Celtic languages like Cornish and Manx became almost extinct, although attempts have been made to revive them.

Most of the languages now spoken in Europe are fundamentally related and share many basic words. For example, wine is *vino* in Italian and Spanish, *wein* in German and *vin* in French.

Above: Every year in the Basque city of Pamplona fighting bulls are turned loose for an ancient sport in which men test their courage. The Basques speak their own language and have always striven for independence from Spain, some of them using violence to achieve their aims.

Spanish is a Romance language but it has many Arabic words dating from the Moorish occupation of Spain. Though Teutonic, English has many Romance words.

There are two languages, however, which do not belong to the Indo-European family and have nothing in common with them. Finnish is a member of the Finno-Ugric group spoken in the

Below: Fine silken shawls with long fringes are an attractive part of women's traditional dress in Spain.

Below: The kilt's tartan or colour pattern denotes the wearer's clan or family and is the traditional dress of Scotland.

Below: A tall black hat worn over a lace cap, a shawl and silver-buckled shoes are features of Welsh traditional dress.

Below: Leather shorts known as *lederhosen* are often worn by men in the southern mountainous regions of Germany.

Below: Heavy wooden clogs and a dainty lace cap present a contrast in the national costume of the Netherlands.

Italy is a slender boot-shaped peninsula extending from southern Europe into the Mediterranean Sea. It also includes the large islands of SICILY and SARDINIA. The chief mountain ranges are the ALPS in the north and the APENNINES forming a rocky spine. There are also three active volcanoes: VESUVIUS, STROMBOLI and ETNA. Of the 20 million work force some 15% are in agriculture, wine being a major export. Italy has supplies of natural gas and mercury. It also has highly developed engineering, pharmaceutical and tex-

tile industries. Its motor cars are sold worldwide. The country did not become one nation until 1861, and in 1946 the people voted to end the monarchy and set up a republic. Area: 301,225 sq km; population: 58,009,000; capital: ROME.

L Liechtenstein, a small state ruled by a prince, is situated in mountains between SWITZERLAND and AUSTRIA. Most of the people are Roman Catholic and German is the official language. The economy is based mainly on agriculture, but major com-

panies, attracted by low taxes, have their headquarters here. Area: 157 sq km; population: 22,000; capital: Vaduz (population: 4,600).

Lisbon, capital of PORTUGAL, is the country's largest city and an important industrial centre. It lies on the River TAGUS and has one of the world's best harbours. Population (with suburbs): 1,034,000.

Liverpool is a major port and industrial city in north-west ENGLAND. It is situated at the mouth of the River Mersey. Population: 540,000.

Loire is FRANCE's longest river. It rises in the Cevennes mountains and flows 1,040 km into the Bay of Biscay.

Chambord Castle, Loire

London is the capital of the UNITED KINGDOM OF GREAT BRITAIN and NORTHERN IRELAND and the focal point of the Commonwealth, an association of states that once formed The British Empire. It is one of the world's largest cities and is an important financial, commercial, industrial and cultural centre. Situated on the River THAMES, the port of London, despite its decline in recent years, still handles much trade with other countries. Heathrow, to the west of the city, is a major international airport. London is also the centre of

Baltic regions. Many experts believe that it originated from migrant peoples who came from eastern Asia in the distant past. The other language is shrouded in mystery. It is Basque, which is spoken by the inhabitants of a region in the Pyrenees which includes northern Spain and south-western France. Some linguists claim that Basque belongs to a linguistic grouping that includes Chinese and Turkic and has members in Eastern Europe, the Indian sub-continent and aboriginal North America.

Attempts have been made to equate languages with nations and races. These have failed, because languages can be learned by anyone. Thus, nowadays, English is used as a first language by members of all the world's races. Similarly, all the nations of Europe have more than one language. This has led to discord in some countries, where minority language groups are seeking to preserve their own culture, even by establishing secessionist political parties.

Traditional and modern ways

Television, the motor car and the jet aircraft have effectively made the world smaller. Nevertheless, there are still some distinctive life styles left. To a certain extent, they are determined by

Left: Italian houses have flat roofs and small windows fitted with shutters in order to keep them cool during the hot summers. Pasta, such as spaghetti served with spicy sauces, is one of the many delicious foods. Wine and coffee are the most popular beverages and fresh fruit is an important part of the diet.

Below: The sloping roof and large windows of British houses are designed to attract as much sunlight as possible in a climate that is often rainy and dull. The British consume lots of milk, eggs and meat and are fond of chocolate and sweets. Beer and tea are the most popular beverages.

Left: Wooden shutters are common on French houses. French cooking shows enormous variety and is considered by many people to be the best in the world. Among famous food products are crusty bread and creamy cheeses such as brie and camembert. Wine and coffee are the most popular drinks.

climatic, geographical, political or economic factors. People in isolated places, such as islands, remote peninsulas and sparsely-populated regions, and people who wish to differentiate themselves from other peoples tend to maintain traditional ways of life. Thus, the Lapps of northern Scandinavia live very much the same semi-nomadic life with their reindeer herds as they have done for centuries. In the west of Ireland, strong traditions survive in story-telling,

Britain's road, rail and air networks, and has an extensive underground railway system. Every year it is visited by thousands of tourists. Population: 7,028,000.
Luxembourg is a small state between BELGIUM and West Germany. Its climate is mild and much of its territory is in the Ardennes mountains. The people speak French, German and the Luxembourgeois dialect and are mainly Roman Catholic. There are large deposits of iron ore and iron and steel are the chief industrial products. Farming is

also important. The country is ruled by a grand duke. Area: 2,586 sq km; population: 371,000; capital: Luxembourg-Ville (population: 78,000).

M **Madrid,** the capital and largest city of SPAIN, is situated at the centre of the Spanish plateau. It is also Europe's highest city, being 655 metres above sea level. It has hot summers and cold winters. Local industries make a range of products, including electrical goods and agricultural equipment. Population: 3,146,000.

Malta is an island state in the southern Mediterranean where a warm climate at-

National Palace, Madrid

tracts many tourists. Most of the people are Roman Catholics and the official languages are Maltese and English. Malta exports textiles, clothing and footwear, and is important in international shipping. Once a British colony, Malta became independent in 1964. Area: 316 sq km; population: 304,000 (1976); capital: Valletta (population: 14,000).
Man, Isle of, is situated in the Irish Sea midway between Britain and IRELAND. The climate is temperate. Tourism and agriculture are the 2 main sources of

income. It has its own parliament called the Tynwald but is ruled by the Lord of Man who is the British sovereign. Area: 546 sq km; population: 56,000; capital: Douglas (population: 20,000).
Manchester now forms part of the Greater Manchester Metropolitan county. It is the industrial centre at the heart of the old cotton industry in north-west ENGLAND. The Manchester Ship Canal (opened 1894) has made the city a major inland port. Population: 490,000.
Marseille is the biggest port of both FRANCE and the

folk music and dance, as they do in other Celtic areas, such as Wales and Northern Ireland. In Scotland, the kilt is worn by men quite often as a normal day-to-day garment rather than as ceremonial dress, just as the women of Brittany often wear their traditional national costumes.

In these places religion exerts quite a strong influence. Most Irish people are devout practising Roman Catholics. The Welsh are a religious

Below: Greek houses are usually sparkling white to reflect the hot rays of the Sun and to keep the interior cool. Small bits of grilled lamb served with rice as in kebabs, makes a popular dish with fresh vegetable salads. Grapes and figs are among the fresh fruits commonly eaten and wine is the national drink.

people. In Scotland, too, the Sabbath is still widely respected as a day of rest and devotion.

In economically developed communities, life styles have some similarities. Homes usually have some labour-saving devices, but the uses to which they are put vary. Eating habits are partly influenced by what grows in a local environment. Northern Europeans tend to prefer foods like butter, milk, cakes, potatoes, puddings and other substantial items. Beer is the most popular

alcoholic drink. In the south, food is generally more spiced and colourful, laced with garlic and brightened by vegetables, such as red and green peppers, purple aubergines and tomatoes. Wine is the main drink, whether red with meat or white with fish. The people of the south generally enjoy food for its own sake, particularly the French. Many Italian, French and Spanish families regularly treat themselves to a meal in a restaurant.

The environment also determines the type of dwelling people live in. In northern Europe people are probably more concerned with warmth and comfort and they will have carpets, curtains and wallpaper. In the south, where people spend much of their time out of doors in the sunshine, houses are designed for coolness with marble or tile floors and shutters on the windows to keep the sun out and let the air in.

Left: Houses in Spain are usually white to keep them cool and they have balconies where people can enjoy the evening air. Fish, especially crayfish and lobster, is a favourite dish and fresh fruit includes oranges, lemons, melons and grapes. Wine is the national drink.

Economy

Western Europe is one of the world's most prosperous regions. The gross domestic product, or GDP (the total value of all goods and services), is almost as large as that of the United States. But the per capita GDP (the GDP divided by the population) was about US$5,100 in 1976, compared with $7,890 in the United States. However, Western Europe's per capita GDP was three-quarters as large again as that of the USSR.

In Western Europe, countries with the highest GDPs were West Germany, the United Kingdom, Italy and France. But, in terms of per capita GDPs in 1976, the league table was headed by SWITZERLAND, Sweden, West Germany and Denmark, with per capita GDPs of $8,880, $8,670, $7,380 and $7,599 respectively. Of the larger nations, France ($6,550) came 9th, the

---

Mediterranean. It is also France's 2nd largest city and a major industrial centre. Population (with suburbs): 1,005,000.
Milan is ITALY's 2nd city and the country's business centre. Its industries include motor cars, textiles, chemicals and light and heavy engineering. Population: 1,705,000.
Monaco is a small state ruled by a prince. It lies on the south-east coast of FRANCE near ITALY. The people are mostly Roman Catholic and French is the language. It is best known for its

annual grand prix motor race and its gambling casino. Area: 1.89 sq km; population: 25,000; capital: Monaco-Ville.

Monaco Grand Prix 1966

Naples is ITALY's 3rd largest city and a major port of the Mediterranean. Dominated by the volcano VESUVIUS, it is one of Europe's most picturesque cities and dates back to 500 BC when it was a Greek colony. Its main industries are engineering, clothing and food processing. Population: 1,224,000.
Netherlands is a low-lying country bordering the NORTH SEA. Much of its coast has been reclaimed by the building of dykes. The climate is temperate. The language is Dutch and the main religions are Roman Catholicism and

Dutch Reformed. The Netherlands has few minerals but dairy and livestock farming and manufacturing are highly developed. It is a constitutional monarchy. Area: 40,844 sq km; population: 14,272,000; capital: AMSTERDAM.
North Sea is the stretch of water, north of the ENGLISH CHANNEL, between Britain and mainland Europe. It is an important shipping area. Fishing and the drilling for oil and natural gas are the main activities.
Norway is a mountainous country in the west of SCAN-

DINAVIA, and about 30% of it lies in the Arctic. The coastline has many deep inlets called fjords and there are some 150,000 islands of which only 2,000 are inhabited. The coastal climate is temperate but inland conditions are more extreme. Most of the people are Lutheran and the language is Norwegian. Traditionally the fishing and timber industries, and tourism and the merchant navy, have been the mainstay of the economy. Now vast offshore oil deposits are important. Hydro-electricity provides

Top: Wine is an important export of many southern European countries.

Middle: Concorde, the first commercial civil aircraft to fly faster than sound, was designed and built by British and French engineers.

Bottom: Large deposits of natural gas in the North Sea are adding greatly to the energy resources of countries like Britain, the Netherlands and Norway.

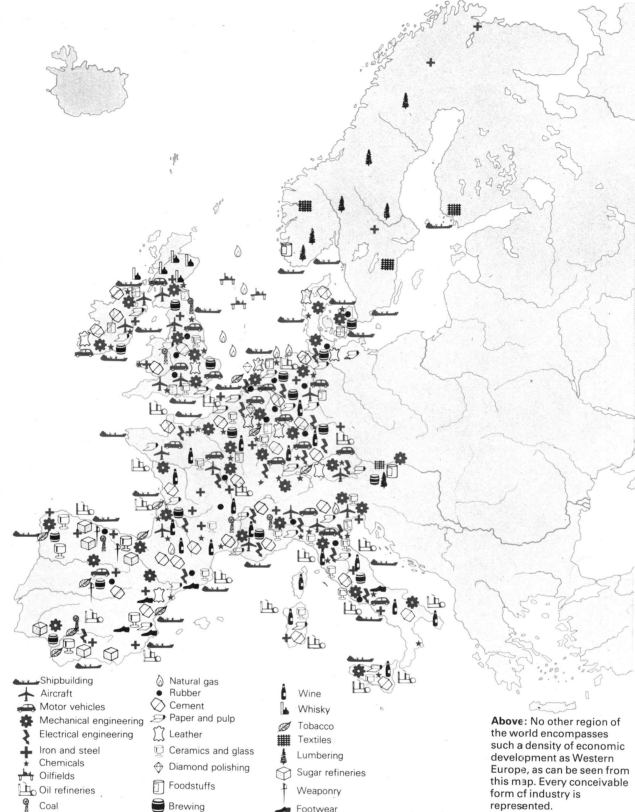

⚓ Shipbuilding
✈ Aircraft
🚗 Motor vehicles
⚙ Mechanical engineering
⚡ Electrical engineering
✚ Iron and steel
★ Chemicals
⊔ Oilfields
⬡ Oil refineries
⚱ Coal

◊ Natural gas
● Rubber
◇ Cement
⌇ Paper and pulp
⊔ Leather
⊡ Ceramics and glass
◈ Diamond polishing
▤ Foodstuffs
⛁ Brewing

🍾 Wine
🍶 Whisky
🍃 Tobacco
▦ Textiles
🌿 Lumbering
⬜ Sugar refineries
⚔ Weaponry
👢 Footwear

Above: No other region of the world encompasses such a density of economic development as Western Europe, as can be seen from this map. Every conceivable form of industry is represented.

much of the country's power. Norway is a monarchy which became independent in 1905. Area: 324,219 sq km; population: 4,123,000; capital: OSLO.

O **Oslo,** the capital of NORWAY, is the country's largest city and industrial centre, with a major ice-free port. Population: 462,000.

P **Paris** is the capital and largest city of FRANCE — an administrative, financial and cultural centre. It is situated on the River SEINE and is an important inland port.

Local industries are associated with the manufacture of cars, aircraft and chemicals. But the city is particularly famous for its fashion

Arc de Triomphe, Paris

houses, jewellery and perfumes. Paris is one of the world's most beautiful cities, and is visited by thousands of tourists every year. Population (with suburbs): 8,424,000.

Po is the longest river in ITALY. The river rises in the ALPS and flows eastward for 672 km into the Adriatic Sea. The main cities it passes include Turin and Cremona.

Portugal is a state in the IBERIAN PENINSULA in southwest Europe. The land is a broad coastal plain enclosed by mountains. The climate is temperate, but more ex-

treme inland. The language is Portuguese and most of the people are Roman Catholic. Almost 30% of the people work in agriculture and fishing. Cork, sardines and wine are important products. Industrial exports include textiles, footwear and clothing. There is also a good tourist trade. Portugal was a monarchy until it became a republic in 1910. Area: 92,082 sq km; population: 8,663,000 (1970); capital: LISBON.

Pyrenees are a range of mountains separating FRANCE from SPAIN. Some of the

peaks rise to more than 3,000 metres.

R **Rhine** is one of Europe's major international rivers, connecting many important industrial cities. It rises in SWITZERLAND and flows for 1,120 km through Germany and the NETHERLANDS into the NORTH SEA.

Rhône is a river rising in SWITZERLAND and flowing more than 800 km south through FRANCE into the Mediterranean Sea.

Rome is the capital of ITALY and a religious and cultural centre of worldwide import-

UK ($4,020) was 13th, and Italy ($3,050) was 14th.

In international trade, Western Europe plays a dominant role. In 1976, the countries of the EEC and EFTA *(see page 16)* accounted for 40 per cent of the world's total imports and 39 per cent of the total exports. Western Europe's economic strength arises from its highly efficient farming, its mineral resources and, above all, its great manufacturing industries.

Agriculture

Western Europe produces a wide variety of farm products, notably cereals, potatoes and other root crops, and meat and dairy products. The Mediterranean region produces fruits, such as oranges and lemons, and about 75 per cent of the world's olive oil. Western Europe also makes nearly two-thirds of the world's wine, especially in France, West Germany and the Mediterranean nations. Farming is largely intensive and, outside Scandinavia, between one-half and three-quarters of the land is farmed.

Mining

Western Europe possesses reserves of various minerals. Iron ore is especially important and leading producers are Sweden, France, Spain, Norway and the United Kingdom. Other minerals include antimony (Italy), bauxite (France), cobalt (Norway, France, Finland), lead (Sweden, Spain), mercury (Spain, Italy) and uranium (France). However, many metal ores are imported.

The chief fuel source was formerly coal and Western Europe still produces about 10 per cent of the world's output. The major coal producers are the United Kingdom, West Germany, France, Spain and Belgium. In recent times, oil and natural gas have become major fuels. In 1977 Western Europe produced only about two per cent of the world's crude oil. However, its share of world production was growing, largely as a result of the exploitation of North Sea deposits, notably by the United Kingdom and Norway.

The Netherlands, the United Kingdom, West Germany, Italy and France are leading producers of natural gas. An alternative source of power is hydro-electricity, especially in mountain regions.

Above: Strong industrial economies depend greatly on iron and steel production, which is particularly well developed in northern Europe. The famous Krupps works of West Germany has always been an important source of these vital materials both in time of peace and war.

Manufacturing

The Industrial Revolution of the late 1700s transformed the lives of millions of people. It first took place in the United Kingdom and from there it spread to Germany, France and other countries. Because of its initial lead, Western Europe is still far more industrialized than Africa, Asia and South America.

Western Europe accounts for more than one-fifth of the world's steel production, with West Germany, the United Kingdom, France and Italy in the lead. Also, Western Europe is a high energy consuming area, using more than ten times as much energy per person as in the African continent.

The chief manufactures are machinery and transport equipment, other metal products, textiles, chemicals and a great variety of consumer goods and processed foods. Western Europe produces more than one-third of the world's cars and the United Kingdom, France

---

...ance. It is built on the Seven Hills by the River TIBER, 27 km

Piazza Republica, Rome

from the Mediterranean Sea. The VATICAN CITY is the focal point of the Roman Catholic Church. There is a wide range of industries making products such as glass, cement and machinery. The city is also a communications centre for road, rail and air traffic. Population: 2,884,000.
Rotterdam is the 2nd-largest city of the NETHER-LANDS and a major European port. It is situated on the New Maas River, a branch of the Lower RHINE, and so is connected to the European waterway system. The New

Waterway canal gives large ships access to the port. And the building of Europort in the 1960s downstream of Rotterdam stimulated trade. It now handles much of West Germany's imports and exports. Important industries include oil refining, ship-building and engineering. Population: 1,023,000.
Ruhr is a river in the FEDERAL REPUBLIC OF GERMANY. It rises in Duisburg and flows 230 km to join the River RHINE. The Ruhr Valley is the industrial heart of Germany. It forms a huge conurbation based on high-quality coalfields.

S **San Marino**, located in north-east ITALY, claims to be the world's oldest republic, tracing its foundation to AD 301. It is ruled by 2 captains-regent who serve for 6 months. The language is Italian and the religion Roman Catholicism. Area: 60.5 sq km; population: 21,000; capital: San Marino on Mount Titano.
Sardinia is the 2nd-largest island in the Mediterranean. It is ruled by Italy. Tourism and mining for lead and zinc are the main forms of economic activity. Area: 24,090 sq km; population:

1,568,000; capital: Cagliari.
Scandinavia is a region in northern Europe comprising SWEDEN, NORWAY and DENMARK.
Scotland occupies about 30% of the UNITED KINGDOM OF GREAT BRITAIN AND NORTHERN IRE-LAND. It is mountainous in the north where Ben Nevis, the highest point in the British Isles, rises to 1,392 metres. The lowlands in the centre are the most heavily populated area and the south is mainly hills. Scotland also includes hundreds of islands, the largest of which are the Hebrides in

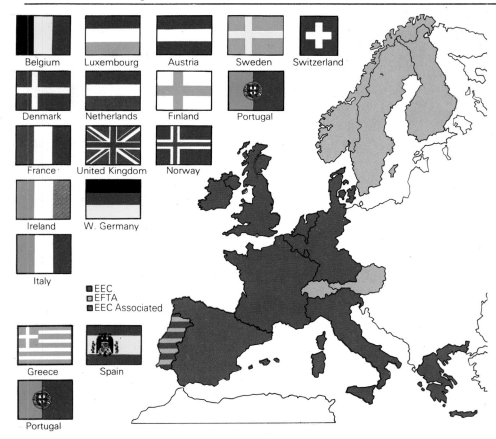

Belgium Luxembourg Austria Sweden Switzerland

Denmark Netherlands Finland Portugal

France United Kingdom Norway

Ireland W. Germany

Italy

■ EEC
□ EFTA
■ EEC Associated

Greece Spain

Portugal

Netherlands. EFTA was established in 1960 with seven members: Austria, Denmark, Norway, Portugal, Sweden, Switzerland and the United Kingdom. Both organizations set out to make trade easier by reducing tariffs – the taxes countries impose on each other's products. Through EFTA, Swedish cars became cheaper in Britain and British manufactures cost less in Sweden. EEC countries also reduced tariffs and set out to create an economic union, sharing currency and taxation systems. In 1973 the United Kingdom. Denmark and Ireland joined the EEC.

Trade was stimulated, the countries became richer and living standards rose, although economic problems in the second half of the 1970s caused setbacks. The less developed southern nations benefited by the economic growth in the north. For example, many northerners took their holidays in the south, bringing a new source of income. Also, as labour costs in the north rose, goods made in the south became more competitive in the north. As a result, the gap between the north and south has begun to close. In 1978 three countries, Greece, Portugal and Spain, applied to join the EEC.

Above: The European Economic Community (EEC) or Common Market and the European Free Trade Association (EFTA) were formed during the 1950s to promote trade between the member states by reducing or abolishing tariffs (the taxes imposed by governments on imported goods). The EEC began with 6 members as a closely-knit organization which aimed at uniting all its members into one economic and political unit. EFTA, which was established later, was a looser association with no central organs of control. In 1973 Denmark and Britain left EFTA to become members of the EEC. In the same year the remaining members of EFTA drew up an agreement with the EEC to enable free trade in industrial goods between the 2 blocs.

and West Germany are also major producers of commercial vehicles. The region also makes a quarter of the world's television sets and more than one-third of the world's tonnage of merchant vessels.

The main industrial regions extend from the UK across the north European plain. They first grew up around coalfields, but the development of hydro-electricity and the use of oil and natural gas has led to other industrial areas growing up in such places as northern Italy, the Netherlands, Scandinavia and Switzerland.

The age of co-operation
An important change in the economy of Western Europe has occurred in recent years. This was the movement towards greater co-operation among industrial nations. Co-operation is epitomized in the European Economic Community (EEC) and the European Free Trade Association (EFTA). The EEC came into being in 1958, with six members: Belgium, France, West Germany, Italy, Luxembourg and the

Above: The vast headquarters in Brussels of the European Economic Community, or Common Market, houses thousands of officials from the 9 member states forming this powerful economic bloc: Belgium, Britain, Denmark, France, West Germany, Ireland, Italy, Luxembourg and the Netherlands. The countries of the EEC aim at removing trade barriers to build prosperity, and to achieve closer political union to avoid the bitter conflicts which have troubled Europe in the past.

the north-west and the Orkneys and Shetlands in the north-east. Some communities in the Highlands of the north and in the islands speak Gaelic. Most of the people are Protestant. Scotland has coal and rich petroleum and natural gas resources in the NORTH SEA. It is mainly industrial but its agriculture is very productive, especially in dairy farming and livestock. Scotland was joined with ENGLAND by the Act of Union in 1707. Area: 77,176 sq km; population: 5,226,000; capital: EDINBURGH.

Seine is an important river in FRANCE. It rises near Dijon in the south-east and flows 760 km to the ENGLISH CHANNEL near Le Havre.
Severn is Britain's longest river. It rises in WALES and flows 355 km to the Bristol Channel.
Shannon is the longest river in IRELAND and the British Isles. It flows 400 km to the Atlantic.
Sicily is the largest island in the Mediterranean. Ruled by ITALY, it is separated from the mainland by the Strait of Messina. It is an important source of oil and sulphur.

Area: 25,708 sq km; population: 4,902,000; capital: Palermo.
Southampton is one of the main cargo and passenger ports of Britain. It occupies a fine site where the rivers Test and Itchen flow into Southampton Water. Many industries are associated with the port. Population: 214,000.
Spain is a country in south-west Europe occupying most of the IBERIAN PENINSULA. It is mostly a plateau with the PYRENEES mountains in the north and the Sierra Nevada in the south. North

General Franco

Spain has a temperate climate. Inland, the summers are hot and winters cold. The south is mild most of the year. Spanish is the main language. Catalan is spoken in the north-east and Basque in the Basque province in the north. Most of the people are Roman Catholics. About 25% of the 13 million people in work are in agriculture and another 25% are in industry. Wine is an important product as is olive oil, and ships, cars and machinery are also made. Tourism brings many millions of visitors. From the civil war

Contemporary Western Europe

The six years of World War II which ended in 1945 left Western Europe exhausted and almost ruined. Germany, defeated by the allied forces of Britain, France, the United States and the Soviet Union, was divided into four sectors, under foreign military rule. Its industry had been shattered and many of its great cities, such as Dresden and Cologne, were in ruins.

France, Italy and Belgium had also been major battlegrounds and were badly scarred. Even Britain, which had not been invaded, had been battered by attacks from aircraft and rockets and several cities were damaged.

At the end of the war, victors and vanquished alike realized they would have to work together to rebuild their nations. In this task, they were greatly helped by economic and financial aid from the United States. As a result, Germany once more became a powerful and prosperous nation and much of Western Europe went the same way.

The end of the Empires

The Western European nations also co-operated in mutual defence against attacks from outside.

Right: Once a great power and still a city of unique beauty after more than 700 years, Venice is threatened by the sea it once ruled. Built on more than 100 islands criss-crossed by canals and linked by bridges, the 'Queen of the Adriatic' is slowly sinking and each winter the floods rise higher. Because of its beauty, which millions of tourists go to see each year, many international efforts are being made to save the city. Meanwhile, the gondola, the symbol of Venice, is still very much used for transport.

Below: Coventry Cathedral symbolizes the rebirth of a city almost totally destroyed during World War II. The modern cathedral reflects the ruins of the former place of worship, built during the Middle Ages and engulfed in flames during the air raids.

The Cold War reached a dangerous crisis with the Soviet blockade of West Berlin from 1948 and so in 1949 the North Atlantic Treaty Organization (NATO) was established. This was an alliance comprising Belgium, Britain, Denmark, France, West Germany, Greece, Iceland, Italy, Luxembourg, the Netherlands, Norway, and Portugal. It was also joined by Canada, Turkey and the United States.

In 1947 Britain gave independence to India. This set off a process which accelerated from the end of the 1950s and a long list of British colonies in Africa, Asia and South America won their independence – some of them peacefully, others after armed struggle.

France followed Britain's example in its African territories and Belgium granted independence to its vast empire in the Congo (now Zaire). The Netherlands withdrew from its possessions in Indonesia and thus a new body of nations known as the third world came into existence.

France experienced turbulent times in the mid 1950s in Indo-China and was forced to withdraw from its colonies there. Following the war in Algeria, France was on the verge of civil war, but General Charles de Gaulle came to power in 1958 and restored stability.

Portugal and Spain gave up their colonies belatedly in the 1970s. Both countries had been dictatorships. Dr Antonio Salazar, absolute ruler of Portugal from 1932, died in 1970. Four years

---

ending in 1939, Spain was ruled by General Franco till his death in 1975. It then became a constitutional monarchy. Area: 504,782 sq km; population: 37,580,000; capital: MADRID.
Stockholm is the capital and largest city of SWEDEN. It is situated on a group of islands on the east coast. Industries include shipbuilding, iron and steel, textiles, and wood products. Population: 1,501,000.
Strasbourg is the commercial, industrial and trading centre of Alsace, FRANCE. Situated on the River RHINE

and the Marne-Rhine and Rhône-Rhine canals it is also a busy inland port. Population (with suburbs): 355,000.
Stromboli is an island off SICILY with an active volcano rising to 926 metres.
Sweden is a country in SCANDINAVIA and part of it lies within the Arctic Circle. In the north-west, mountains run along the border with NORWAY. These slope towards the Gulf of Bothnia where there is a small coastal plain. In contrast to the forest-clad uplands, the central and southern regions consist of rolling plains and

hills. The climate is cold in the north but milder in the south. The country has iron ore, silver, zinc and copper deposits, and large timber resources. There are also numerous sites in the mountains for hydro-electric power generation. Motor cars, aircraft and metal products are manufactured. Swedish is the main language but Finnish is also spoken. The Lapps of the north have their own language. Most of the people are Lutherans. Sweden has been a constitutional monarchy and neutral since 1809.

Swiss watch manufacturer

Area: 449,964 sq km; population: 8,354,000; capital: STOCKHOLM.
Switzerland is a small, mountainous country in central Europe. It has warm summers and cold winters with much snow, making it a favourite of tourists the year round. About 65% of the people speak German, 18% French and 12% Italian. There is also a Latin dialect called Romansh. Dairy farming is important and wine is also produced. The country is famous for its clocks and watches besides producing drugs, machine tools and

later, his successor's regime was overthrown in a bloodless revolution. One of the first actions of the new government was to give independence to Angola and Mozambique. General Francisco Franco, who had ruled Spain as a dictator from 1939, died in 1975. The totalitarian state died with him and Spain became a democratic nation with a constitutional monarchy.

The monarchy did not survive in Italy where a national referendum set up a republic in 1946. The Greek monarchy was also abolished by a referendum in 1973. In 1974 the military dictatorship which had ruled Greece since 1967 was overthrown and democratic government restored.

New dangers

By the 1970s most of Western Europe was rich, but a new and dangerous phenomenon appeared. This was guerrilla warfare conducted mainly in cities. The most persistent form began in the late 1960s in NORTHERN IRELAND. The Irish Republican Army launched a campaign of bombings and shootings to try to force the British government to unite the mainly Protestant province with the predominantly Roman Catholic Republic of Ireland in the south.

The violence spread to Britain on several occasions and scores of people were killed or injured in such cities as London and BIRMINGHAM.

The same type of violence broke out in Italy. By the 1970s the Italian communists had become the biggest single political group. However, the moderate policies of the communists had led to the emergence of left-wing fanatical groups, such

Above: Modern high-speed road systems have made it possible for millions of people to travel long distances quickly. However, motorways have often spoiled the appearance of natural surroundings by creating concrete jungles like this 'spaghetti junction' in France.

Below: Benidorm was a fishing village in the 1950s. In less than 10 years it became a major tourist resort visited by millions every year. It was typical of the rapid development of the tourist industry in Spain which brought prosperity to that country.

as the Red Brigades. These people carried out campaigns of terror which culminated with the assassination in 1978 of former prime minister Aldo Moro.

Urban guerrillas also operated in West German cities. The Baader-Meinhof group carried out bank raids, hi-jacked aircraft, held hostages for ransom and killed government and police officials as well as members of the business community.

Economic problems

By the late 1970s Western Europe and, indeed, the rest of the developed world, faced new problems for which there seemed to be no satisfactory answers. The enormous growth in productivity which had produced so much prosperity had also led to inflation and currency instability. In tackling this problem, governments cut down on production causing unemployment to rise sharply. As the 1980s dawned, Western European governments were seeking ways of preventing excessive inflation without causing too much unemployment.

Culture

There was no immediate radical change in the arts after 1945. Men and women who had made their marks earlier were still active. They included painters like Pablo Picasso, Georges Braque and Henri Matisse in France and the British sculptors Henry Moore and Barbara Hepworth. There was also no great change in symphonic music. Composers like Igor Stravinsky of the USSR, and Ralph Vaughan

---

foodstuffs. It is also a major international financial centre. The country is a federation of cantons and has been neutral since 1815. Area: 41,288 sq km; population: 6,448,000; capital: BERNE.

T Tagus is the longest river in the IBERIAN PENINSULA. It rises in central SPAIN and flows 905 km west across PORTUGAL into the Atlantic ocean.
Thames is the longest and most important river in ENGLAND. It rises in the Cotswold hills and flows 338 km east.

Tiber is the 2nd-longest river in ITALY. It rises in the APENNINES and flows 392 km west into the Mediterranean Sea, passing ROME.

U United Kingdom of Great Britain and Northern Ireland is a monarchy occupying most of the British Isles off the west coast of Europe. It consists, in order of size, of ENGLAND, SCOTLAND, WALES and NORTHERN IRELAND. The many hundreds of islands include the Hebrides and the Orkneys and Shetlands in the north and the, Isle of

Tower Bridge, London

Wight in the south. There are Crown dependencies with their own parliaments such as the CHANNEL ISLES and the ISLE OF MAN. The country is mountainous in the north and west and has a temperate climate. Oil, natural gas and coal are leading resources. The UK is one of the world's major economic powers. Its products include, aircraft, motor cars, ships, transport equipment, heavy and light machinery, textiles and foodstuffs. Its agriculture is highly efficient. The language is English. One in 4 in Wales speaks Welsh and

Williams of the United Kingdom continued a tradition that belonged to 50 years earlier.

The cinema was the first art form to be affected by the social changes produced by the war. Italian directors like Roberto Rossellini and Vittorio de Sica developed a style that became known as neo-realism. This depicted the daily struggle to make a living experienced by the poor and the unemployed. Realism also appeared in a new wave of drama that began in Britain with plays like *Look Back in Anger* by John Osborne. Cinema and theatre were no longer merely suppliers of escapist entertainment.

Television also had a major effect. Distant wars and all their horror were brought vividly to life in millions of homes. There was also the fear that modern weapons of mass destruction could set off a holocaust. These factors combined to produce a political awareness that often resulted in demonstrations that developed into violent street battles. The art forms of this sector of society produced the protest songs and some of the varieties of rock music which were aimed at the ruling 'establishment'.

The prosperity of the 1960s brought independence to young people and this led to a

Right: The French student rising of 1968 sparked off riots in Paris and indirectly led to the resignation of Charles de Gaulle as President of the Republic. The troubled events partly stemmed from government measures to modernize the economy which affected education. The students joined with workers who were on strike in the Paris region.

Below: Schemes to build a tunnel under the English Channel date from the early 1800s when Napoleon's armies were poised to invade Britain. Though technically feasible, the high costs have always proved a deterrent.

tremendous development of 'pop' music, much of it based on rock, itself evolved from the jazz of the American Blacks. The feeling of independence also affected women, resulting in the so-called women's liberation movement. A new feeling of emancipation was born. Literature, the cinema and drama became frank and outspoken. It became commonplace for words to be used and scenes to be shown that before 1939 would have been punished by imprisonment.

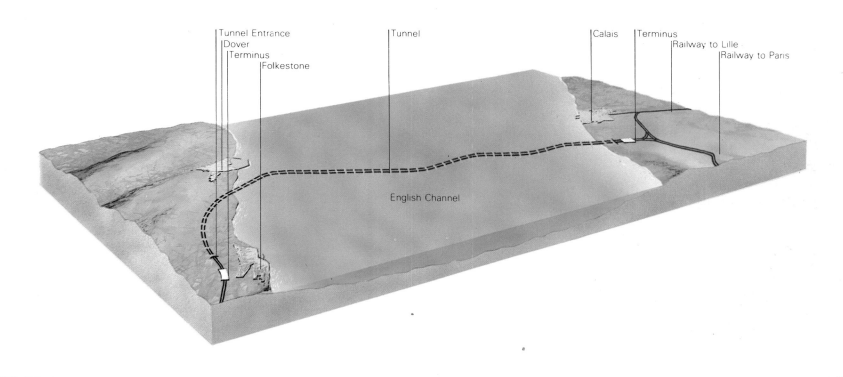

English Channel

Pope John Paul II

there are Gaelic-speaking groups in north Scotland. Area: 244,046 sq km; population: 56,377,000; capital: LONDON.

V **Vatican City State** is the world's smallest sovereign state. Situated in ROME, it is the seat of the Roman Catholic Church and is ruled by the Pope. The best known building is the Basilica of St Peter. The Vatican Museum contains some of the world's greatest art treasures. About 1,000 people live in the city most of them church officials. The Vatican is all that remains of the Papal States which once covered central ITALY. It is only 44 hectares in area.
Venice is one of world's most beautiful cities. It stands in north-east Italy on some 120 islands crisscrossed by canals and connected by graceful bridges. Population: 362,000.
Vesuvius is an active volcano about 12 km from NAPLES. It is 1,280 metres and its first recorded eruption in AD 79 destroyed Herculaneum, Pompeii and Stabiae.
Vienna is the capital of AUSTRIA and once the seat of a large European empire. It is an important port of the River Danube and a manufacturing centre. Population: 1,615,000.

W **Wales** occupies about a 10th of the area of the UNITED KINGDOM OF GREAT BRITAIN AND NORTHERN IRELAND. Situated in the west of the main island, Britain, Wales is mainly mountainous with its highest peak, Snowdon, rising to 1,085 metres in the north-west. Wales has regular rain especially along the western coast. Coal and steel are the most important industries and they are located in the south. About one person in four speaks Welsh and most of the people are Protestants. Wales formally became part of ENGLAND in 1536. Area: 20,761 sq km; population: 2,731,000; capital: Cardiff (population, 281,000).

Z **Zürich** is the largest city of SWITZERLAND and an international financial centre for the gold and money markets. It is in the German-speaking region. Population (with suburbs): 708,000.

Eastern Europe, including the world's largest nation, the Soviet Union, is united by its communist philosophy. But within this huge bloc, there is much human diversity based on long-standing cultural traditions.

Eastern Europe

Eastern Europe occupies some 6,306,000 square kilometres which is about 65 per cent of Europe's total area. However, if the vast Asian sector of the SOVIET UNION is included, the region has an area of more than 22,000,000 square kilometres and dwarfs Western Europe. It is a political entity rather than a distinct geographical area. Therefore, countries such as Finland and Greece, which are physically in Eastern Europe, are not included in its territory.

The nations of Eastern Europe are those with communist governments based on that of the Soviet Union, the largest and most powerful of the countries. These states are: ALBANIA, BUL-

Below and **right**: The maps show the nations of Eastern Europe. The Soviet Union (*right*) is a vast land-mass, while the other states occupy a very small area which is outlined only. The area is shown in detail *below*.

GARIA, CZECHOSLOVAKIA, the GERMAN DEMOCRATIC REPUBLIC (East Germany), HUNGARY, POLAND, ROMANIA, and YUGOSLAVIA.

Since the late 1940s when the Cold War between East and West was reaching its height, Western politicians have described Eastern Europe as being behind an 'iron curtain' and termed the countries surrounding the Soviet Union its 'satellites'. However, this is not completely accurate. Yugoslavia and Albania do not accept Soviet leadership and are fairly independent in their affairs. Even countries

Reference

A **Albania** is a small country on the eastern shore of the Adriatic Sea between YUGOSLAVIA and Greece. The country's mineral resources include chromium, coal and petroleum. About 66% of the people work in agriculture. Once part of the Turkish empire, Albania was a monarchy from 1928 until occupied by Italy from 1939 to 1943. It then became an independent communist

state but it later isolated itself from the SOVIET UNION and China. Area: 28,748 sq km; population: 2,868,000; capital: Tirana (169,300).

Archangel is the northernmost large city in the world. It lies just 180 km south of the Arctic Circle in the far north of the SOVIET UNION. An important port, it is kept clear by icebreakers when it freezes from November to May. The city's main industries include timber, furs and fish processing. Population: 383,000.

Armenia is the smallest of the 15 republics that form

the SOVIET UNION. Farming is the main occupation, but Armenians are also skilled in finance, trade and the arts. Armenia adopted Christianity as its official religion in AD 301, the first region to do so. Area: 29,800 sq km; population: 2,800,000; capital: Yerevan (928,000).

Azerbaidzhan is the 9th-largest of the SOVIET UNION's 15 republics. It is situated in south-east Europe between ARMENIA and the CASPIAN SEA. Most of the people are Muslims and the 2 chief languages are Iranian and Russian. Azerbaidzhan is rich in

oil, copper, cobalt and iron ore. The soil is fertile and there are excellent pastures for livestock. Tobacco is an

Old couple, Azerbaidzhar.

important crop. Area: 86,600 sq km; population: 5,600,000; capital: BAKU.

B **Baikal** is the 9th-largest lake in the world, occupying 31,500 sq km in the central highlands of SIBERIA. It is also the deepest lake in the world with a depth of 1,620 metres. The lake contains 20% of the world's surface fresh water and the surrounding region is rich in minerals and timber.

Baku is the capital of the Soviet republic of AZERBAIDZHAN. The city lies 12 metres below sea level on the

Severnaya
Zemlya

New Siberian
Islands

Wrangel Is.

Central Siberian
Plateau

Verkhoyansk Range

Cherskiy Range

Bering Sea

F   S   R

Tura

Magadan

Okhotsk

Kamchatka

Sea of Okhotsk

Ob

S   I   B   E   R   I   A

Lensk

Baikal

Sakhalin

SOVIET SOCIALIST REPUBLICS

Tomsk

Novosibirsk

Irkutsk

Vladivostok

erdlovsk

Omsk

Kazakhstan

L. Balkhash

Alma Ata

Frunze

Kirghizia

Tashkent

Tien Shan

Uzbekistan

Tadzhikistan

Dushanbe

Communism Peak

istan

bad

l Sea

Right: A great part of
Eastern Europe is subject to
the continental type of
climate which results in very
cold winters and hot
summers, as can be seen
from the average
temperatures shown in the
diagram. Rainfall also tends
to be relatively low and
droughts are not
uncommon. The chief cause
is the vast expanse of the
Eastern European land
mass, which reduces any
modifying effect of the sea.

Warsaw

Moscow

Novosibirsk

January July   January July

January July   January July

January July   January July

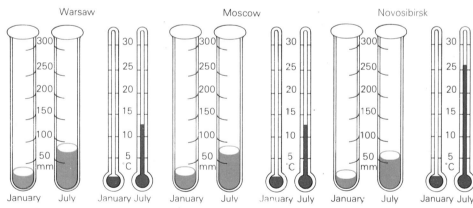

south-west shore of the CAS-
PIAN SEA. Baku is at the centre
of a vast oilfield and it has a
major petroleum industry. It
also has chemical works,
shipyards, and steelworks.
Population: 1,406,000.
Balkans are part of a mountainous region in south-east
Europe. Within this region
are located ALBANIA, BULGARIA,
Greece, YUGOSLAVIA and the
European part of Turkey.
Baltic Sea is found in northern Europe and is bounded
by Denmark, Sweden, Fin-
land, SOVIET UNION, POLAND
and Germany. Its area is
422,000 sq km.

Belgrade is the capital and
largest city of YUGOSLAVIA.
Belgrade was rebuilt after
1866 when it was liberated
from the Turks. It was also

National Museum, Belgrade

rebuilt in 1945 after being
seriously damaged in World
War II. Population: 746,103.
Berlin, East is the sector of
Germany's largest city
which is the capital of the
GERMAN DEMOCRATIC REPUBLIC.
A 41-km wall separates it
from the western sector
which forms part of the
Federal Republic of Ger-
many. The wall was built in
1961 by the East German
authorities to stop
thousands of refugees leaving for the West. East Berlin
occupies 404 sq km of Berlin's total area of 885 sq km.
Population: 1,101,123.

Black Sea is a large inland
sea bounded by the SOVIET
UNION, Turkey, BULGARIA and
ROMANIA. Its area is 425,000
sq km.
Bosnia-Herzegovina, one
of the 6 republics that make
up YUGOSLAVIA, was formerly
2 separate states which were
ruled by the Turks from the
1400s to the 1800s. They
then became part of the
Austrian empire and after its
defeat in 1918 they became
regions of Yugoslavia. Area:
51,129 sq km; population:
3,746,111; capital: Sarajevo
(249,980).
Bucharest is the capital and

largest city of ROMANIA. It lies
on a plain in the south of the
country and is crossed by
the River Dimbovita, a tributary of the DANUBE. Bucharest
is also Romania's largest
industrial centre. Clothing,
furniture, chemicals and
electrical goods are its chief
products. Population:
1,565,872.
Budapest is the capital and
largest city of HUNGARY. The
city consists of Buda, which
stands on a hill on the west
bank of the DANUBE, and Pest
which is on the plain. Budapest has many fine build-
ings. The parliament was the

inside the Soviet bloc such as Hungary and Romania operate their economies or conduct their affairs with foreign countries in a manner often different from that adopted by the Soviet Union.

Politicians in the West have also often accused Eastern European governments – especially the Soviet government – of being suspicious and allowing little freedom for the individual. This is true to a certain extent but there are reasons in history and geography for these attitudes.

Most of the people in Eastern Europe live in a vast plain which is open to the west and east. Throughout history these people have been repeatedly invaded and have undergone great suffering. Therefore they tended to feel insecure and exposed to attack from outside. This has helped to shape their outlook which, to some Western Europeans, can appear as suspicious and even hostile and which has led to authoritarian forms of government.

These factors have also resulted in Eastern Europe being less wealthy and developed than the West. However, with its great natural resources it is a part of the world that could become extremely prosperous.

Climate

Eastern Europe has an enormous range of climatic conditions because its territory includes the vast regions of the Asian part of the Soviet

Above: Tens of thousands of people crowd Red Square in Moscow for the anniversary of the 1917 revolution that brought communism to power. The huge square is the scene of many parades and is next to the Kremlin, the fortress which is the seat of the Soviet government.

Union. Some of the lowest temperatures ever recorded have been registered in the region around Verkhoyansk in northern SIBERIA.

These conditions contrast with the searing heat of the arid deserts along the southern Asian borders of the Soviet Union where even winter temperatures seldom go below 22°C.

Much of Eastern Europe has a continental climate – including inland Poland, East Germany, Czechoslovakia, Hungary, Romania, Bulgaria and the mountainous parts of Albania and Yugoslavia. The continental climate produces hot summers and cold winters, often with considerable snowfall.

In coastal areas along the BALTIC, the climate is more temperate, while along the Yugoslav coast it is of the Mediterranean type with warm summers and mild winters. The region around the BLACK SEA and the western shores of the CASPIAN have a generally mild climate while parts of the CAUCASUS such as GEORGIA and Soviet Central Asia are sub-tropical.

The land

Eastern Europe and the Asian part of the Soviet Union consist basically of vast plains edged by mountains in the north, east and south. The plains contained within the mountains are crossed by the URALS, traditionally regarded as the dividing line between Europe and Asia.

The lowland countries are the German Democratic Republic, Poland, Hungary and most of the Soviet territory outside Europe. The plains range in altitude from about 150 metres to 300 metres. In the Soviet Union the plains are known as the steppes, grasslands which are given over to agriculture, especially cereal crops, as in the UKRAINE and KAZAKHSTAN. The Alfold, the rolling lowland of Hungary, is another example of these plains.

Mountains

Along the south the main mountain ranges are the CARPATHIANS, the Dinaric Alps of Yugoslavia and the Caucasus which have some of the highest peaks in Europe. Further to the east and into Asia, major ranges extend for thousands of kilometres to the Chinese frontier. These are the Pamir, Tien Shan, Altai and Sayan systems which form a mighty barrier between the Soviet Union and Southern Asia.

---

largest building in the world when it was built in 1904. Population: 2,063,306.

Bulgaria is a small mountainous country in the east of the BALKANS. The landscape consists of 2 mountain ranges that run parallel from west to east. The plain in the north is crossed by the DANUBE. The climate is mild in the south and along the BLACK SEA coast in the east. The weather is more extreme in the north with much colder winters. Most of the people speak Bulgarian, a Slavonic language similar to Russian. There is

also a Turkish-speaking minority. The Eastern Orthodox Church and Islam are the 2 chief religions. About 50% of the 4,000,000 working people are engaged in agriculture while 1 in 3 works in industry. Bulgaria has coal, lead, uranium, zinc and copper. Machinery is an important export. In addition to cereals, Bulgaria produces cotton and tobacco. Another famous product is 'attar of roses', a fragrant oil used in perfumery. Formerly a monarchy, Bulgaria became a republic when the Communist Party came to

power in the country in 1944. Area: 110,912 sq km; population: 8,938,000; capital: SOFIA.

Byelorussia is the 6th-largest of the SOVIET UNION's 15 republics. It is situated in the west of the Soviet Union on the border of POLAND. The language is very similar to Russian but it had no written form until the 1800s. About 40% of the people work in agriculture in which livestock breeding is important. Motor vehicle manufacture, tanning, textiles and wood processing are Byelorussia's main industries. Area:

207,600 sq km; population: 9,350,000; capital: Minsk (1,189,000).

C Carpathians are a range of mountains extending for some 1,400 km in CZECHOSLOVAKIA and HUNGARY. The mountains form a broad semi-circle and their highest peak is Gerlachovka (2,664 metres) in Czechoslovakia. The mountains are heavily wooded and their wildlife includes bears, wolves and lynxes.

Caspian Sea is the world's largest inland body of water. A vast salt lake, it covers 371,800 sq km on the Soviet border with Iran in South-west Asia. But its area is gradually shrinking because

Wolf in Carpathians

Above: Prague, capital of Czechoslovakia, is a beautiful city dating from the AD 800s. It stands on the banks of the Vltava river at the heart of the picturesque region of Bohemia, and presents a fine view of ramparts, turrets, spires and bridges.

Mountain ranges also rise along the edges of the great plains of northern and central Siberia, but these are not as high as in the south. The Central Siberian Uplands are between 600 and 900 metres high. The East Siberian Highlands are higher with peaks of about 3,000 metres. This mountainous area includes many volcanoes in the region of the Pacific coast.

Plant and animal life

With the inclusion of the Asian zone the vegetation of Eastern Europe covers a large range from cold desert forms in the Arctic to hot desert plants in the equally barren south. Between these extremes there are dense forest and plains.

In the tundra, the narrow cold region along the northern edge of the Soviet Union, the soil a few centimetres under the surface is permanently frozen. Trees are few and stunted. Vegetation consists mainly of mosses and lichens which provide food for reindeer and caribou. These are kept as domestic animals for their meat, milk and hides, and also as pack animals. During the milder seasons the tundra is also inhabited by bears, wolves, foxes, lemmings and voles. There are also many birds such as swans, partridges and ducks, but they migrate during winter.

To the south of the tundra lies the boreal or northern forest. This consists chiefly of conifer trees which can resist the cold: spruce, fir and larch, with a sprinkling of deciduous trees such as birch. Most of the boreal forest is found in the Soviet Union. It occurs elsewhere in Eastern Europe in higher mountain reaches.

Elk, reindeer, moose, roe deer and bears

---

of heavy evaporation. The main rivers flowing into it are the VOLGA, Ural, Terek and Kura.

Caucasus is a range of high mountains in the south-west of the SOVIET UNION between the BLACK SEA and the CASPIAN SEA. Many of the peaks rise to more than 3,000 metres.

Communism Peak is the highest mountain in the SOVIET UNION, rising to 7,497 metres. It is situated in the lofty Pamir range on the border with Afghanistan and was first climbed in 1933.

Croatia is one of the 6 republics of YUGOSLAVIA. It is situated in the north of the country on the borders with Italy, Austria and HUNGARY. It is mountainous and wooded and has a 145-km coastline

Dubrovnik, Croatia

on the Adriatic Sea. Croatia became part of Yugoslavia in 1919 after being successively ruled by Hungary, Turkey and Austria. Area: 56,538 sq km; population: 4,426,221; capital: Zagreb (566,224).

Czechoslovakia is a country in the heart of Europe which emerged as one nation only in the 1900s. Its landscape is one of mountains, forests and rolling plains. Winters are cold and summers humid and warm. Some 64% of the people are Czech and 30% are Slovak, each a distinct ethnic group speaking its own language. Some 4% are Hungarian-speaking. About 16% of the 8,000,000 people in work are in agriculture and about 40% work in industry. Czechoslovakia produces motor cars, iron and steel and machinery. There are deposits of coal, copper, silver and uranium. The country came into existence after World War I. In 1939 it was occupied by Germany and after World War II it became a multi-party state until the communists took power in 1948. In 1968 Soviet troops invaded Czechoslovakia be- cause they feared that policies being carried out by the Dubcek government were contrary to the interests of the Soviet Union. Area: 127,876 sq km; population: 15,340,000; capital: PRAGUE.

D **Danube River,** is Europe's greatest international waterway. It rises in the Black Forest in southwest Germany and flows eastward for 2,850 km into the BLACK SEA. More than 300 rivers flow into the Danube and canals connect it to the rivers Rhine and Main in

inhabit this type of forest. The smaller animals include polecats, wolves, badgers, weasels, squirrels, hares and beavers. Bird life is plentiful including geese, lapwings, owls and many varieties of songbirds.

The central regions of Eastern Europe were once covered in great mixed forests of oak, ash, beech and elm. These have been cleared over many years to make way for agriculture and villages, and eventually the large cities. Today the mixed forests are located in the mountainous ranges of Czechoslovakia, southern Poland, parts of Romania and Bulgaria and in the Caucasus.

Grasslands extend along the south-eastern and south-western coasts of the Soviet Union in Hungary, Poland, Romania and in the basin of the River DANUBE. In these regions many small rodents such as field mice and hamsters make their homes. These small animals provide food for birds of prey such as eagles, falcons, and hawks.

In the warmer and drier Mediterranean regions much plant life is of the scrub type known as *maquis* which gives a green covering to the hillsides. Characteristic trees of this area are the olive and the cork oak and various varieties of pine and cedar. Palm trees grow in the sub-tropical areas. Animal life in this zone includes many reptiles such as the venomous adder.

Above: The Tatras, which reach over 2,000 metres, are the highest mountains in Czechoslovakia. They are in the eastern part of the country in Slovakia.

Below: The vast Bialaweska Forest in Poland is a natural preserve where herds of bison, wolves and bears roam as they did in ancient times.

Larger animals include wildcats, boars and antelopes. In the deserts of the Asian part of the Soviet Union there are also poisonous spiders and cobras.

People and ways of life

Language has always been extremely important as a major form of national identity in Eastern Europe. In this way it is more than just a form of communication, it is one of the living proofs of nationhood.

A bewildering number of languages are spoken in the region but most belong to either the Indo-European or Ural-Altaic families. The languages in each family are thought to come from a common source, which often accounts for the similarities among them.

The Indo-European family can be further sub-divided and one section, the Balto-Slavic group, forms the largest language group in Eastern Europe. As the name implies, these languages are spoken by the Slavs who are probably the descendants of Indo-European speakers who settled in the area as farmers and herdsmen several thousand years ago. Language is now the only common element among these people. Physically they vary considerably. Many of those who live near the Mediterranean tend to be shorter and darker while many of those to the north in BYELORUSSIA tend to be tall and fair.

The eastern Slavs are composed of Russians, Byelorussians and Ukrainians. Each group has its own language but they are all very similar.

Germany. An international commission controls all river traffic.

Don is an important river in the south of the European part of the SOVIET UNION. It rises from a small lake near Tula and flows south for 1,952 km into the Sea of Azov. A canal connects it to the VOLGA at its nearest point 60 km away.

Dresden is a beautiful city in East Germany famous for its fine porcelain. It also has many modern industries. Dresden was almost totally destroyed in air raids during World War II, but many of its fine buildings remain. They date from the days when Dresden was the capital of the kingdom of Saxony. Population: 508,298.

E **Estonia** is the 13th-largest of the SOVIET UNION's 15 republics. It is situated on the eastern shore of the BALTIC SEA in the north-west of the USSR. Much of Estonia is a high plateau scattered with lakes and marshes. Winters are cold and summers are rarely hot. The people speak Estonian, a Baltic language, but Russian is also used. Agri-culture is the most important activity, but textiles, machinery and wood products are also manufactured. Estonia became part of the Soviet Union in 1940. Area: 45,100 sq km; population: 1,400,000; capital: Tallinn (408,000).

G **Georgia** is the 10th-largest of the SOVIET UNION's 15 republics. It is situated in the CAUCASUS mountains, which have some of the highest peaks in Europe. In the west, where it borders on the BLACK SEA, Georgia has a dry climate while the east is warm and humid. Coal and petroleum are the chief mineral resources. Most of the people work in agriculture. Citrus fruits, tobacco and wine are

Georgian Orthodox Church

the main products. Georgia also has industries that produce motor cars, iron and steel, machinery and cement. About 66% of the population is Georgian and the remainder belong to minorities such as the Greeks, Ossetians and Azerbaidzhanis. Georgia became part of the Soviet Union in 1921 when the Red Army overthrew a moderate socialist government which had been set up in the wake of the Bolshevik Revolution of 1917. Area: 69,700 sq km; population: 4,963,000; capital: Tbilisi (1,028,000).

Left: Despite the growth of modern industry, handcrafts still survive in many parts of Europe, for example, the lace being sold by this woman in Yugoslavia.

Right: Shoppers crowd the great central hall with its ornamental fountain in the GUM department store in Moscow. Situated on Red Square, this huge emporium is entirely owned and run by the state.

Below: The Hungarian plains west of the Danube provide rich pastures for cattle, especially these white bulls. Traditional, colourful costumes like the one worn by the young cattlemen are still popular in Hungarian country districts.

The southern Slavs, found mainly in Yugoslavia, speak Serbo-Croat, while the Bulgarians also have a Slavic language, despite the fact that they were descended from Asian tribes who conquered local Slavs and were then absorbed by them. The western Slavs include the Poles, Czechs, Slovaks, Slovenes and Ruthenians.

Of all the languages, however, German, which is from the Teutonic branch of the Indo-European family, is the most important in international commerce and the mother tongue of the German Democratic Republic. The Lithuanians and Latvians also form a distinctive Indo-European linguistic group as do the Armenians. Romanian is a language partly Latin and partly Slavic in origin. This is because the country was once a Roman colony and many of its present day inhabitants are descended from Roman colonists. Albanian, too, is thought to be an Indo-European language and is the last survivor of the Thraco-Illyrian languages once spoken throughout the Balkans. Albanian consists of two dialects: Tosk, which is spoken south of the River Shkumbi, and Gheg, which is spoken north of the river. Greek, Latin and Turkish words are also found in the language.

The Ural-Altaic family, although smaller, still includes some important language groups. The Finno-Ugric sub-section, for example, includes

German Democratic Republic is the eastern part of Germany which emerged as a separate state after World War II. Also known as East Germany, it is the smaller of the 2 Germanies both in area and in population. East Germany is the world's leading producer of lignite (soft brown coal). Other minerals include potash, antimony, arsenic and uranium. Before World War II the region was mainly agricultural but today some 75% of the population works in industry. Chief products are chemicals, fertilizers, textiles, synthetic rubber, motor vehicles, transport equipment and footwear. About 60% of the population is Protestant and the official language is German. After being occupied by Soviet forces, the German Democratic Republic was set up in 1949 following the formation of the Federal Republic of Germany in the west. Area: 108,178 sq km; population: 16,786,000 (1976 est); capital: EAST BERLIN.

H **Hungary** is a landlocked country to the north of the Balkan peninsula. The chief river is the DANUBE. Hungary has some coal, petroleum, natural gas and iron ore. About 25% of the popu-

Vineyards, Hungary

lation works in agriculture and 46% in industry which includes food-processing, machinery and transport equipment. Most of the people are Roman Catholic but there are important Protestant, Orthodox and Jewish minorities. Magyar is the main language but German, Romanian and Serbo-Croat are also spoken. Hungary was under German occupation during World War II. The communists came to power in 1947. In 1956 a rising against the regime was crushed with the help of Soviet troops. Area: 93,032 sq km; population: 10,766,000; capital: BUDAPEST.

K **Kazakhstan** is the 2nd largest of the SOVIET UNION's 15 republics. Situated in central Asia, it extends from the CASPIAN SEA to China. Once largely a desert, much of Kazakhstan has been transformed into fertile land by major irrigation schemes. Most of the people work in agriculture, with cereals as the main crop. Kazakhstan also has rich deposits of coal, nickel, zinc, copper and lead. More than

Above left: The traditional woman's costume of Russia.

Above right: The national dress of Moldavia, one of the Soviet republics.

Above: The oriental style of the national dress of Uzbekistan indicates that this is one of the Asian republics of the Soviet Union.

Above: Traditional Czech costume has a gaiety and verve that seem perfectly suited for performing the energetic local Slavonic dances.

Above: The restrained elegance of the man contrasts with the patterned design of the woman's dress in the Hungarian national costume.

Above: Ukrainian national dress is equally flamboyant for male and female, as can be seen in the man's flowing blouse and the girl's lacy cap.

Magyar, from Hungary, Estonian and Finnish.

The Altai section includes Mongolian and Turkic languages found mainly in Soviet Asian republics such as Kazakhstan.

Besides these two major families there are other lesser families. For example, the Eskimo language comes under the Amerindian family while the Georgian is part of Caucasian. And various Asian languages are spoken in Asiatic Russia.

Nowhere is the diversity of languages and peoples more apparent than in the Soviet Union where there are more than 60 languages in a population of some 250 million. The principal ones are Russian, which is spoken by 53 per cent of the people, Ukrainian by 17 per cent, Uzbek by 4 per cent and Byelorussian by 4 per cent. The Soviet authorities have done much to preserve the range of languages and have encouraged the development of literature. Much of this is done to spread the word of the Communist Party throughout its vast territories. Some of the languages had no written forms so these were developed as one way of ensuring their survival.

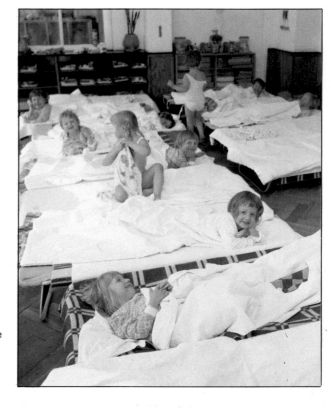

Right: Working mothers in Poland have no problems when it comes to looking after their children during the day. Factories provide creches free of charge where children can play, receive nursery school education and take a nap during the day.

50% of the people are Kazakhs and traditionally Islamic. Area: 2,717,300 sq km; population: 13,930,000; capital: Alma Ata (861,000).
Kharkov is an industrial city in the north-east of the UKRAINE. Its products include tractors, heavy vehicles, locomotives and turbines. It is also an important trading centre for farm products. Kharkov was the capital of the Ukraine until 1765 when it was succeeded by KIEV. Population: 1,385,000.
Kiev is the capital of the Soviet republic of UKRAINE. The city is very picturesque

being situated on a cliff overlooking the River Dnepr. It was the ancient capital of Russia and today it is one of the most important cultural centres of the SOVIET UNION. Kiev also has many major industries including machine tools and wood processing. Founded in AD 862, it has been attacked and ruled by Mongols, Lithuanians and Poles. Population: 2,013,000.
Kirghizia is the 7th-largest of the SOVIET UNION's 15 republics. It is situated in the south-Asian zone of the USSR and many of its in-

habitants are nomads who wander with their flocks of sheep, goats and camels in search of grazing grounds. The people of Kirghizia are

Sheep farmers, Khirgizia

mostly of Mongol descent and traditionally they are Muslim. Agriculture and livestock breeding are the chief economic activities. Kirghizia became part of the Russian Empire in 1855. Area: 198,500 sq km; population: 3,370,000; capital: Frunze (498,000).

L **Latvia** is the 12th-largest of the SOVIET UNION's 15 republics. Latvians are also known as Letts and their language is one of the oldest in Europe. Agriculture and industry play an equal part in the economy. Textiles,

chemicals and machinery are the chief industrial products. Riga is second only to LENINGRAD among the ports of the Baltic Sea. Latvia has been dominated by Germans, Poles, Lithuanians and Swedes. By the 1700s the country was part of the Russian Empire. Independent from 1920 to 1940, it then became part of the Soviet Union. Area: 63,700 sq km; population: 2,506,000; capital: Riga (816,000).
Lena River is in eastern SIBERIA and flows through some of the world's richest goldfields. The Lena rises in

Above: Colourful patterns on the woman's skirt are repeated in the jacket and gaiters of the man in Yugoslav national dress.

Above: Embroidered shirt-sleeves and trousers make the Bulgarian male's traditional dress even more colourful than the girl's.

Above: With light and bright materials and delicately made sandals, Romanian national dress has a delightfully summery look.

Above: Elegant knee-length boots for both man and woman, with lots of trimmings on the clothes, are features of Polish national costume.

Religion

The constitutions of the various governments guarantee the people freedom of worship. Nevertheless, the authorities are openly atheistic. They do not recognize any official religion and, apart from helping to maintain certain historical buildings such as cathedrals and monasteries, provide no financial help.

Despite this, the Roman Catholic Church has the overwhelming support of the people of Poland, where churches are usually full during services. In 1978, Cardinal Karol Wojtyla was elected Pope, the first to be appointed from a communist country. Hungary also has many devout Catholics while Czechoslovakia and the German Democratic Republic are predominantly Protestant. Religion in the Soviet Union has survived many attacks since the Bolshevik Revolution in 1917. The Orthodox Church continues to worship (as it does in Bulgaria and Romania, where the great religious feasts are Christmas and Easter) and there are nonconformist groups such as the Baptists. The Jewish religion still exists and in the Asian areas

Right: Many Polish young people volunteer to spend part of their holidays helping to bring in the harvest. Unlike other communist countries of Eastern Europe, where land belongs to the state or collectives, most Polish farms are privately owned.

the Baikal mountains and flows north-eastwards for 4,232 km into the Arctic Ocean. Lenin (1870-1924), who led the 1917 Russian Revolution and whose real name was Vladimir Ilich Ulyanov, took his political name from the Lena when he lived in exile in Siberia.
Leningrad is the SOVIET UNION's 2nd-largest city. It was founded in 1703 by Tsar Peter the Great as Russia's capital. Originally called St Petersburg, its name was changed to Petrograd in 1914 when Russia went to war against Germany. It was

Lenin in study, 1918

finally given its present name in 1924 when Lenin (Vladimir Ilich Ulyanov), one of the leaders of the Soviet Union, died. Leningrad is one of the world's great cultural centres and famous for its ballet, symphony orchestra and art galleries. The city also has many important industries. During World War II it heroically withstood a German siege for more than 2 years. Population: 4,372,000.
Lithuania is the 11th-largest of the SOVIET UNION's 15 republics. Lithuanian is the language of 80% of the people. The rest speak Russian. The majority of the population is Roman Catholic, the remainder being Protestant, Orthodox or Jewish. Agriculture and forestry are the chief economic activities, but Lithuania also has several light industries. It was a major power in Eastern Europe from the 1300s. In the 1800s it became part of Russia and remained so until 1918. In 1940 it was annexed by the Soviet Union. Area: 65,200 sq km; population: 3,323,000; capital: Vilnius (446,000).

M **Macedonia** is one of YUGOSLAVIA's 6 republics. A mountainous region, it borders with BULGARIA in the east and Greece in the south. Agriculture is the main economic activity, the chief crops being barley, maize, tobacco and wheat. Area: 25,713 sq km; population: 1,647,000; capital: Skopje (312,980).
Moldavia is the 2nd-smallest of the SOVIET UNION's 15 republics. It is situated in the south-west of the USSR and is known mainly for its extremely fertile black soil. Cereals and tobacco are the main crops. Moldavia became a Soviet republic after World War II. Area: 33,700 sq km; population:

Right: This diagram shows the main Soviet nationalities. The white areas denote regions which are virtually uninhabited.

- ◯ Russians
- ◉ Ukrainians
- ◉ White Russians
- ◉ Lithuanians
- ◯ Latvians
- ◉ Moldavians
- ◉ Armenians
- ● Iranians
- ● Georgians
- ● Finnish
- ◉ Chuvash
- ◉ Tartars and Bashkirs
- ● Kumuks and Balkans
- ◉ Kazakhs
- ◉ Kirgiz
- ● Uzbeks and Karakalpaks
- ● Turkmen
- ● Mongolians

of the USSR Islam is very strong. Buddhism, in Siberia, and Shamanism are also practised.

Sport and recreation

Eastern Europe excels in the Olympic Games. The various governments lavish help on promising sportsmen and women. As a result, countries such as the Soviet Union, the German Democratic Republic and Romania have produced outstanding competitors in international athletics, particularly in running, swimming and gymnastics.

Soccer is the most popular game, followed by ice hockey. Chess attracts many spectators in the Soviet Union especially when two grand masters are playing.

Fewer people own their own motor cars than in Western Europe. The vast majority, therefore, are not as independent when it comes to travel. Most take their holidays in their own country. Any foreign travel is almost completely restricted to other countries within Eastern Europe. Vacations are usually spent skiing in the mountains in winter in Czechoslovakia and southern Poland, or in rented cottages by lakes and forests in summer. The Black Sea coast of Bulgaria, Romania and the Crimean district of the Soviet Union are extremely popular resorts. Many of the holidaymakers who go there are

provided with free accommodation or given very cheap rates by their trade unions.

Family life

Most homes now possess the various amenities that make life easier, such as washing machines, refrigerators and television. Most of the city dwellers live in apartments. The bad overcrowd-

Below: The Soviet republic of Georgia is noted for the large number of people living to a great age. Some men are believed to have reached 140 and more while remaining active. Credit for this is given to the unpolluted atmosphere and to the healthy diet.

3,839,000; capital: Kishinev (472,000).
Montenegro is one of the 6 republics of Yugoslavia. A mountainous region, it is situated on the Adriatic coast. Most of the people work in agriculture or forestry. Livestock breeding, particularly sheep, goats and pigs, is also important. Montenegro was once a kingdom and became part of Yugoslavia in 1921. Area: 13,812 sq km; population: 529,604; capital: Titograd (98,437).
Moscow is the capital and largest city of the SOVIET UNION. It is also one of the

St Basil's, Moscow

most important political centres of the world because of the international communist movement. The city is also a centre famous for the arts and entertainment – a reputation given it by the Bolshoi Ballet, the Arts Theatre, the State Circus and the huge sports stadium. Moscow came close to being captured by the German armies during World War II but it was never taken. Population: 7,740,000.
Murmansk is the SOVIET UNION's chief port in the Arctic. Though far to the north, the harbour is kept ice-free all year round because of its closeness to the warm waters of the Gulf Stream. Founded in 1915, the port provided the Soviet

Union with a vital lifeline for supplies during World War II. Population: 369,000.

O **Ob** is a great river that rises in western SIBERIA and flows northwards for 4,000 km into the Arctic Ocean through an estuary 80 km wide. With its tributaries it makes 30,000 km of navigable waterways.
Odessa is a port in the SOVIET UNION on the north shore of the BLACK SEA near the Romanian border. It has 5 harbours and is an important industrial centre with oil refineries and factories pro-

ducing motor vehicles and aircraft. Population: 1,023,000.

P **Poland** is a country situated between East Germany and the SOVIET UNION. It is mainly flat with a temperate climate in the west which becomes more extreme in the east. Once mainly agricultural, Poland now has many developed industries including motor cars, shipbuilding and food processing. It has very large deposits of coal which are also exported. The German invasion in 1939 led to World

ing in MOSCOW, WARSAW and LENINGRAD, for example, which resulted from the devastation of World War II, has mostly been eliminated. High-rise blocks are now a prominent feature.

Women play an important part in the economy. In the Soviet Union and Poland, they drive buses, trains and even jet aircraft. Because women work so much, the government provides nurseries for young children free of charge.

Food

Eastern Europeans love substantial meals, so convenience foods are not common. Poland produces a fine variety of sausage and hams and dishes such as cabbage leaves stuffed with meat. A popular Hungarian dish is red spicy goulash stew served with rice, while in the Soviet Union delicacies include *pirozhki* (meat pasties), *shchi* (thick cabbage soup) and *borsch* (beetroot soup). Romania, Bulgaria, Hungary and the Soviet Union produce delicious wines. However, in the Soviet Union the most popular drink is tea served with lemon and no milk and taken with a spoonful of redcurrant jelly.

Natural resources

The Soviet Union has the major share of mineral wealth, which includes gold, uranium, petroleum, iron ore, titanium, molybdenum, coal, manganese and diamonds. Poland is an important source of coal, which is also found in Czechoslovakia and Hungary. Romania and Albania have important deposits of petroleum and natural gas.

Industry

All industry is owned by the state. Private ownership is practically non-existent except for a limited form in agriculture. Usually the economy is controlled by five or seven-year plans which set out how much coal, steel, textiles, motor cars, houses, shoes and various other goods are to be produced. This centralized socialist planning is designed to avoid the booms and slumps in the freer economies of Western Europe which often result in inflation or unemployment or sometimes both. Centralized planning, however, can create shortages in certain goods and overproduction of others because five-year plans cannot allow for unexpected demands for products such as light clothing during an unusually hot summer.

Until the late 1950s the state planning authorities gave priority to heavy industry which produced locomotives, power stations and heavy machinery. From the 1960s more consumer goods, including television sets, washing machines and motor cars, were produced, especially after the signs of popular unrest in Poland, Hungary and Czechoslovakia.

The Soviet Union, through its sheer size, is the major industrial country of Eastern Europe. However, industry is well developed in the German Democratic Republic, Czechoslovakia and Hungary.

The Eastern European countries collaborate through the Council for Mutual Economic Assistance (Comecon), which enables each country to make a specialized contribution to international economic development and prosperity.

Agriculture

Agriculture also comes under state control. The

Below: These enormous water ducts produced by Soviet heavy industry will form part of a gigantic power station in the Ust-Ilinsk region of the Soviet Union. The country has huge resources of hydro-electric power drawn from such long rivers as the Ob and Lena.

exception is Poland where private farmers own 80 per cent of the land. Otherwise farms are owned by the state or by collectives of farmers who share the profits derived from selling their produce to nearby towns and cities.

Farms come under the general system of centralized planning. However, in the Soviet Union collective farmers are allowed to have a small plot of land on which they grow fruit and vegetables and keep some livestock. The produce from these plots is sold at markets and this represents a rare form of permissible private enterprise.

The chief agricultural areas in the Soviet Union are in the west and south-west, and in Kazakhstan in central Asia. Agriculture also plays an important part in the economies of Romania, Bulgaria, Hungary and Albania. The large range of crops includes wheat, rye, barley, maize, oats, sunflower seeds, cotton, tea, wine (in Hungary, Romania, Bulgaria and the Caucasus) and fruit, ranging from apples to oranges, lemons and melons.

Eastern European agriculture is not as productive as its counterpart in the United States or Britain. One farmer in North America, for example, can produce as much as five Soviet

farmers. This situation is made worse if some natural disaster such as drought affects agriculture. Where this has occurred, Eastern European countries, particularly the Soviet Union, have had to buy large quantities of grain from Canada and the United States.

History

Eastern Europe suffered grievously during World

Left: Apart from Romania and Yugoslavia, which often follow independent foreign policies, the member states of the Comecon bloc conduct most of their trade with each other. However, trade with the West began to grow in the 1970s.

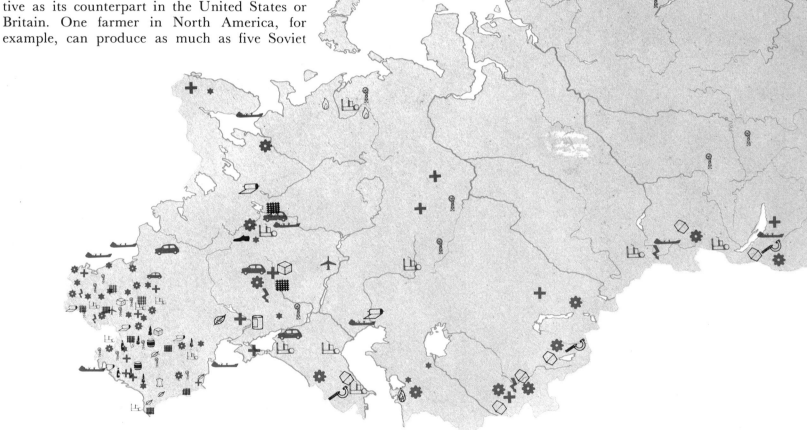

War II. There were 20 million dead from the Soviet Union alone. And millions died in Nazi prison camps either because of neglect or through deliberate policies of extermination. However, the war enabled the USSR to exert a strong influence over Eastern Europe and after the fighting had ceased many countries became communist states and accepted Soviet leadership. But in 1948 Yugoslavia broke away from

Right: Religious architecture in Eastern Europe varies from country to country, from the onion domes of Russia to this painted church in Romania.

Below: Eastern Europe has vast natural wealth, especially within the territory of the Soviet Union. Despite this, the region is less industrially advanced than other areas of the world such as the United States and Western Europe.

Shipbuilding
Aeroplanes
Motor vehicles
Mechanical engineering
Electrical engineering
Iron & Steel
Chemicals
Oil refining
Coal
Gas

Leather
Foodstuffs
Brewing
Wine
Tobacco
Textiles
Lumbering
Sugar refining
Footwear
Precision Instruments
Paper & pulp
Cement

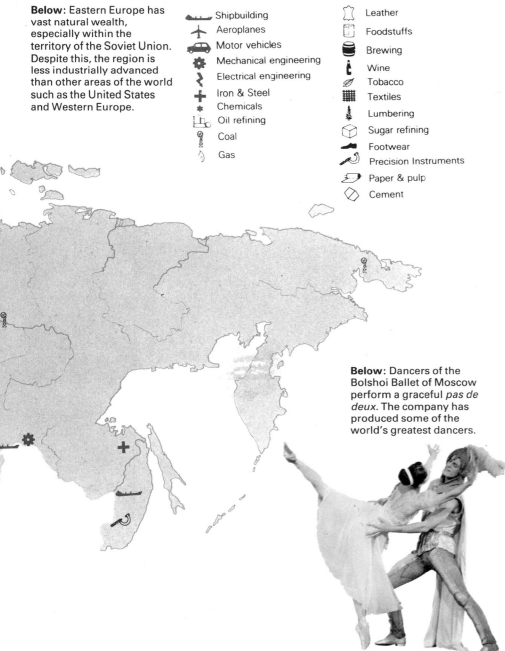

Below: Dancers of the Bolshoi Ballet of Moscow perform a graceful *pas de deux*. The company has produced some of the world's greatest dancers.

Soviet domination and adopted an independent foreign policy while maintaining a communist system. In 1949 the Council for Mutual Economic Assistance was set up to help rebuild the shattered economies, and in 1955 the Warsaw Pact military alliance was formed. This comprised Albania, Bulgaria, Czechoslovakia, the German Democratic Republic, Hungary, Poland, Romania and the Soviet Union. Albania left the alliance in the early 1960s after a bitter quarrel with the Soviet Union.

The Cold War

Relations between Eastern and Western Europe worsened after World War II. Berlin, the German capital, was under the control of the United States, Britain, France and the USSR. In an attempt to take over the city the Soviet Union blockaded the western sector, trying to force out the American, British and French forces. However, the plan was thwarted because for more than a year essential supplies were airlifted into the besieged city.

In 1953 the Soviet leader Stalin died and relations with the West showed signs of improvement. However, the Soviets were determined to maintain their authority in Eastern Europe. In 1956, for example, major riots broke out in Poznan, Poland, and a full scale revolt was unleashed against the communist government of

---

1870-1924). The tsarist government was swept away and replaced by a communist system. The Soviet Union suffered heavy losses during World War II but it emerged victorious to become, with the USA, one of the world's 2 superpowers. Area: 22,402,200 sq km; population: 266,036,000; Capital: MOSCOW.

T Tadzhikistan is the 8th-largest of the SOVIET UNION'S 15 republics. Cotton and textiles are important and there are deposits of uranium, oil, lead and zinc.

Area: 143,100 sq km; population: 3,488,000; capital: Dushanbe (450,000).
Turkmenistan is the 4th-largest of the 15 republics of the SOVIET UNION. The Kara Kum (Black Sands) desert covers most of the country. Many of the people are farmers who also breed horses and sheep. Islam is the chief religion. Area: 488,100 sq km; population: 2,562,000; capital: Ashkhabad (299,000).

U Ukraine is the 3rd-largest of the 15 republics of the SOVIET UNION. For

many years Ukraine was the main source of wheat and other vital crops for the

Ukrainian pipers

Soviet Union and it still supplies a large amount of foodstuffs. Now there are also many industries, some based on the coal, iron ore, manganese, mercury, petroleum and natural gas found in the region. Area: 603,700 sq km; population: 49,100,000; capital: KIEV.
Urals are a range of mountains that extend 2,400 km from north to south in the SOVIET UNION. They form the natural frontier between the continents of Europe on the west and Asia in the east. Their highest peaks reach 1,800 metres.

Uzbekistan is the 5th-largest of the SOVIET UNION'S 15 republics. It lies in Soviet central Asia at the foot of the lofty mountains of the Pamir Knot. Uzbekistan has natural gas and petroleum. It also produces delicious fruits which are sold fresh or dried. Cotton is also a very important product. Area: 447,400 sq km; population: 14,115,000; capital: Tashkent (1,640,000).

V Volga is the longest river in Europe. It rises in the Valdai Hills south-east of LENINGRAD and flows

Culture

The arts receive general support from the state in Eastern Europe. Opera, ballet, orchestral music and the theatre and cinema are of an extremely high standard. Other cultural activities such as folk music and dance also receive generous help.

However, creative artists, especially in the Soviet Union, are limited in the topics they can deal with and the manner in which these topics are treated. Writers, painters, sculptors and composers cannot too openly oppose the ideals of the Communist Party. People who do so, such as the Soviet dissidents, are either imprisoned or exiled. Their works are prohibited although they are often circulated secretly. The two most celebrated examples are the poet and novelist Boris Pasternak, awarded the Nobel Prize after the publication outside the Soviet Union of his novel *Doctor Zhivago*, and Alexander Solzhenitsyn, who also won the prize. Pasternak died in disgrace and never collected the prize. Solzhenitsyn was sent into exile in the West because of his criticism of the Soviet system.

Even composers have not escaped official scrutiny. Dmitri Shostakovich and Sergei Prokofiev, who both created some of their greatest works after 1945, were criticized for their alleged excessive individualism.

Hungary. In both instances Soviet troops crushed the uprisings. In 1961, a new crisis with the West arose when the communist authorities built a wall across East Berlin to stop the flow of refugees to the West. And in 1968 Soviet troops, with detachments from other Warsaw Pact countries, invaded Czechoslovakia. This followed policies adopted by the Dubcek government which were considered to be against the general security of the region.

Above: The British, American and Soviet leaders met at Yalta in 1945 to plan the final attack on Germany.

Below: In 1968 Soviet tanks invaded Prague to bring about the downfall of the government of Alexander Dubcek.

Detente

Despite these events, relations with Western Europe gradually improved. Trade increased and more tourists from the West began to spend their vacations in countries such as the Soviet Union, Romania and Bulgaria.

The process of detente, begun after the death of Stalin, was continued when Nikita Khrushchev was in power during the 1950s and the 1960s. During the 1970s the Soviet Union took part in important international discussions with Western nations, such as the Strategic Arms Limitation Talks (SALT), to limit the growth of nuclear weapons. Relations with the United States also improved sufficiently to allow the two countries to co-operate in a space programme. The Soviet Union had made the first major advances with the first space satellite launching in 1957 and the first manned space flight in 1961.

south-east in a great curve for 3,690 km to empty through a vast delta into the CASPIAN SEA. The Volga is joined by canal to the DON, a major river in European Russia.

Volgograd is an important industrial city of the SOVIET UNION situated on the west bank of the VOLGA. It was called Stalingrad until 1961 and before that, Tsarytsin. The city won the world's admiration during World War II when its heroic fight against the might of the German forces came to symbolize the resistance of the Soviet people.

River Volga

W **Warsaw** is the capital of POLAND. It is a city of magnificent buildings and churches and parks. Many of the old buildings damaged during World War II were restored to their former glory. Warsaw produces textiles, machinery and foodstuffs and is one of Eastern Europe's major cultural centres. Population: 1,436,100.

Y **Yenisei** is one of the world's longest rivers. It rises in Mongolia and flows northwards through SIBERIA for 5,680 km into the Arctic Ocean. The Yenisei passes through land rich in timber, gold and graphite.

Yugoslavia is a country situated on the eastern shore of the Adriatic Sea. It is mainly mountainous and prone to earthquakes. Serbo-Croat, Macedonian and Slovenian are the main languages and the chief religions are Eastern Orthodox, Roman Catholicism and Islam. About 50% of the people work in agriculture. Mineral resources include lead, aluminium, copper, mercury, zinc, chromium and iron ore. Chemicals, non-ferrous metals, machinery and transport equipment are the main exports. About 500,000 people work in Western Europe. Yugoslavia came into existence in 1929 through the amalgamation of previously independent states. After World War II a communist government came to power. Yugoslavia, however, soon adopted a policy independent of Soviet communist leadership and practised neutrality in international relations. Area: 255,804 sq km; population: 22,347,000; capital: BELGRADE.

North America contains Canada, Mexico and the United States, the greatest economic power the world has ever known. If the United States suffers a setback, the effects reverberate around the world.

North America

Although North America is sometimes taken to comprise all the mainland and island territories between the Arctic Ocean and Colombia in South America, this section deals only with Canada, the United States (including ALASKA and HAWAII), and Mexico.

Land regions of North America

North America can be divided into five main land regions: the Canadian Shield in the north-east; the APPALACHIAN MOUNTAINS in the east; the eastern Coastal Plain extending from Cape Cod southwards to Yucatan; the Western Cordillera covering the entire western coastland far inland to include the ROCKY MOUNTAINS and most of Mexico, and the large Central Lowland which is surrounded by the other four regions except in the extreme Arctic north.

The Canadian Shield is a rocky region covering the north-eastern half of Canada (including Baffin Island) and a small area of the United States west of the GREAT LAKES. The horseshoe-shaped Canadian Shield (also known as the Laurentian Plateau) consists of worn-down rocks formed between 500 and 3,000 million years ago. Much of the north-western and central parts of the 'horseshoe' have been eroded and are now low-lying land. The north-eastern part rises to 1,500-2,500 metres. A chain of lakes extends along the north-western arm of the 'horseshoe', from the Great Lakes to the Beaufort Sea in the Arctic. It includes Lake of the Woods, LAKE WINNIPEG, Reindeer Lake, Lake Athabasca, GREAT SLAVE LAKE, Dubawnt Lake and GREAT BEAR LAKE. The region is rich in minerals but has little good agricultural land.

The Appalachian Mountains are a group of low-lying ranges that extend from the ST LAWRENCE RIVER nearly 2,500 kilometres south-westwards into northern ALABAMA. The highest peak, Mount Mitchell in NORTH CAROLI-

NA, rises to 2,040 metres. The Piedmont Plateau, an area of hilly ground east of the Appalachians, lies between the HUDSON RIVER and central Alabama.

The Coastal Plain, east of the Appalachians and Piedmont Plateau, dips evenly towards the Atlantic to end in marshes and swamps for much of its length.

The Western Cordillera comprises three sub-regions: the Pacific Coastland, the Intermountain sub-region, and the Rocky Mountains. The Pacific Coastland consists of two chains of mountains running roughly parallel with the coast. One rises steeply from the coast and includes the Olympic Mountains of north-west WASHINGTON State, and is called the COAST RANGES. The inner chain includes the Alaska Mountains, the Coast Mountains of Canada, and the CASCADE RANGE and Sierra Nevada. The Western Sierra Madre and several of the other ranges of Lower California are extensions of the two mountain chains. Large islands off the

Above: Saskatchewan, Canada's foremost cereal-producing province, produces over 60% of the country's wheat. Although nearly 3 times the size of Britain, the province holds only a million people, and 25% of the workforce are farmers. Faced with the challenge of cultivating the vast prairies with only a sprinkling of labour, Canadian farmers were among the first to use complex labour-saving machines such as combine harvesters over 50 years ago. Most of Saskatchewan's fertile farmland and most of its population are found near to the border with the United States.

Reference

A **Alabama,** a southern state of the US, is known as the 'Heart of DIXIE'. Over 50% of the state is forested. Cotton no longer dominates the now diversified economy. From the north-east, the APPALACHIANS extend almost to Birmingham, the state capital. Area: 133,667 sq km; population: 3,444,165, 25% of whom are Black.

Alaska is the largest state of the US in area, but has the smallest population. Its southern tip is separated from the other states by 800 km of Canadian territory. Since becoming a state

Alaskan oil rig

in 1959, Alaska has prospered from petroleum. In 1976, income per head of the population topped $10,400 – 63% higher than the US average. Area: 1,518,807 sq km; population: 302,173, 18% of whom are Eskimos, Aleuts and Indians; capital: Juneau.

Alberta, a Canadian province to the east of the Rockies, has its capital at Edmonton. 50% of the province's 1,838,037 people live there. Alberta is a prairie province rich in wheat, cattle, timber products, petroleum and natural gas. The

people are mostly of British, German, Ukrainian or Scandinavian ancestry, with over 30,000 Indians and Eskimos. Area: 661,188 sq km.

Aleutian Islands, a chain of volcanic islands extending 1,500 km south-west from the mainland, are part of ALASKA. Only about 6,000 people live there, mainly ranchers and fishermen. Area: 17,552 sq km.

Alexander Archipelago, see COAST RANGES.

Allegheny Mountains, rising to 1,200 metres in WEST VIRGINIA, form part of the Appalachians.

Appalachian Mountains are the main mountain system of eastern North America. The chain extends 2,500 km south-west from Quebec to Alabama. The highest peak, Mount Mitchell, rises to 2,039 metres.

Arizona is a state of the south-western US. Of its many tourist attractions, the GRAND CANYON is perhaps the best known. Arizona is a livestock-rearing state and 65% of its 1,772,482 people live in PHOENIX (the capital) and Tucson. Area: 295,024 sq km.

Arkansas is a southern

from ALBERTA and SASKATCHEWAN to New Mexico and TEXAS. The Ozark Plateau rises to 750 metres in the south-eastern Central Lowland, near the Coastal Plain.

Climate of North America

North America has two main climate patterns: mid-latitude and tropical. The mid-latitude pattern is derived from the movement of air from polar and tropical regions, and from the oceans. The extreme result of the clash between these air currents is found in the cyclones (storms with a spiral wind pattern) that strike the continent, moving usually from west to east. In summer, the cyclonic path shifts northwards, but the Canadian Arctic is generally outside the area of these storms. Most cyclones come in winter, either from eastern Asia or the nearby Pacific, to enter North America north of SAN FRANCISCO. The tropical, southern half of Mexico is only slightly affected by the cyclones; it is hot throughout the year except on high ground. Generally, North America receives most of its precipitation in summer.

In temperature and precipitation, North America has seven main regions. The Alaskan Canadian Arctic has very cold winters and cool summers, with little precipitation. Most of Alaska and Canada south of the Arctic, and the north-eastern area of the United States, have a cool, moist climate. The south-east of the United States, a small area in north-central Mexico, and the Pacific coastland of Alaska and Canada are

western coast include ST LAWRENCE ISLAND, KODIAK ISLAND, QUEEN CHARLOTTE ISLANDS and VANCOUVER ISLAND.

East of the Pacific Coastland, the Intermountain sub-region contains several river basins and high plateaux. These include the Yukon River Basin, the interior plateau (of British Columbia), the Colorado Plateau, the GREAT BASIN and the Mexican Plateau. The GRAND CANYON lies within the region.

The Rocky Mountains, which form the eastern edge of the Western Cordillera, extend from ALASKA southwards to NEW MEXICO. Their southward extension, the Eastern Sierra Madre, traverses north-eastern Mexico. Many peaks of the Rockies are over 4,000 metres.

The Central Lowland extends from the northern coastland of Alaska south-eastwards to the Coastal Plain region, covering about 25 per cent of Canada and 50 per cent of the United States. It includes all the mid-western states (except a small corner of the Canadian Shield), and dips southwards just into Mexico. In the west, near the Rocky Mountains, the Central Lowland incorporates the Great Plains, which slope downwards from the Rockies eastwards, in a belt

Above: Manhattan, New York, contains the Empire State Building, Rockefeller Center, Wall Street, UN Building, Broadway, Harlem, and Greenwich Village.

Below: Semi-desert scrub covers much of Mexico. This hot, dry plateau is in the Southern Uplands.

---

state of the US and has a fertile soil and a mild climate, together with rich mineral resources. The capital, Little Rock, was the centre of resistance to educational integration of the state's 19% Black population in 1957. Area: 137,539 sq km; population 1,923,295.
Atlanta, capital and largest city of GEORGIA, had a 1970 population of 496,953, although its urban area contained 1,370,164.

B **Boston** is the capital of MASSACHUSETTS and a leading cultural city. It was

once the centre of American

Boston Tea Party

Puritanism and the site of the Boston Tea Party in 1773. Metropolitan area: 2,753,700 sq km; population: 641,071.
British Columbia is Canada's westernmost province, bordering the Pacific. It is the main timber and fishing state, and is also rich in minerals. Nearly 50% of the province's 2,406,212 people live in Greater VANCOUVER, the capital. Area: 948,600 sq km.
Buffalo, a city in New York State, lies on Lake Erie, one of the GREAT LAKES. Most of its electricity supply is generated by the nearby NIAGARA

FALLS. Urban area: 1,130,000 sq km; population: 438,620.

C **California** is the most populous and 3rd-largest state of the US. It often leads the world in trends. Of its 19,953,134 people, 57% live in the urban area of LOS ANGELES and SAN FRANCISCO, but the state capital is Sacramento. Area: 411,015 sq km.
Cascade Range extends 1,100 km from northern California into British Columbia and rises to 4,394 metres.
Chicago is the most impor-

tant city of America's agricultural mid-west. It lies at the southern tip of Lake Michigan and has 3,366,957 people, but 6,979,000 in its metropolitan area.
Churchill River rises in north-west SASKATCHEWAN and flows 1,600 km to empty into Hudson Bay.
Cincinnati is an industrial city of OHIO and has 451,455 people but 1,104,668 in its urban area.
Cleveland is a leading inland port in OHIO. It became in 1978-79 the first US city to go bankrupt since the great depression of the 1930s.

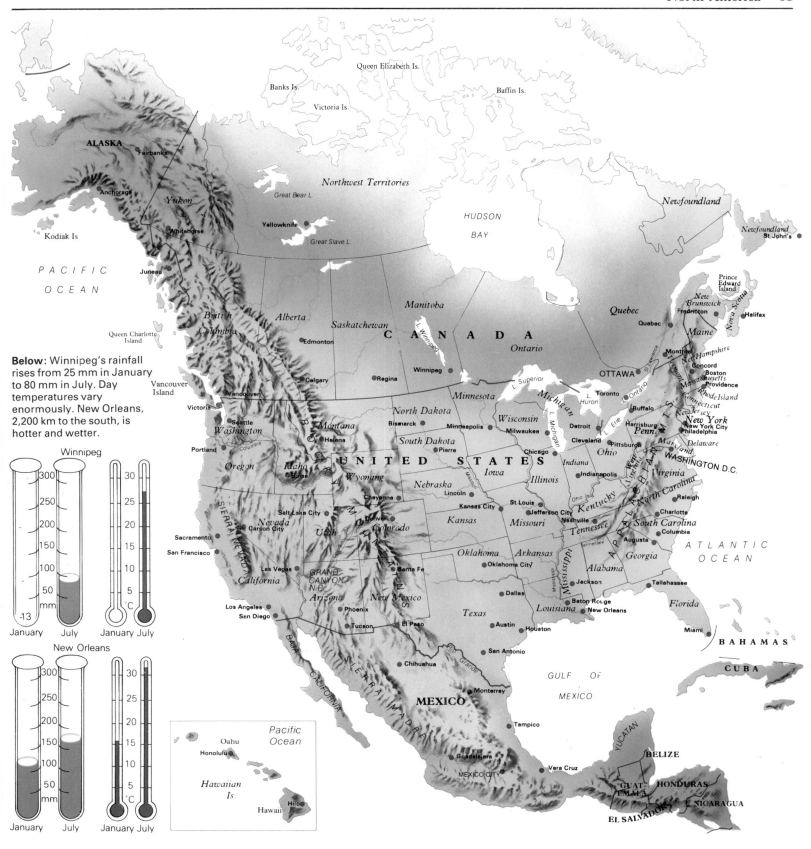

Below: Winnipeg's rainfall rises from 25 mm in January to 80 mm in July. Day temperatures vary enormously. New Orleans, 2,200 km to the south, is hotter and wetter.

Winnipeg

January   July   January   July

New Orleans

January   July   January   July

Pacific Ocean

Oahu
Honolulu

Hawaiian Is.

Hawaii   Hilo

Urban area: 2,064,194 sq km; population: 750,879.

Marine Towers, Chicago

Coast Ranges are a series of mountains along the west coast of North America, which extend 4,000 km from Alaska to southern California. They include the Alexander Archipelago (an island group formed by sunken mountains), and rise to over 6,000 metres.

Colorado, a scenic ROCKY MOUNTAIN state of the US, is mainly agricultural but mining has always been important. About 30% of its 1,581,739 people live in DENVER, the capital. Area: 270,000 sq km.

Colorado River flows 2,700 km from the Colorado Plateau into the Gulf of California. On the river, near the GRAND CANYON (which it formed by its own erosive power) stands the mighty Boulder Dam.

Columbia River rises in the mountain ranges of BRITISH COLUMBIA and flows nearly 2,000 km, forming part of the US – Canadian border, before emptying into the Pacific.

Columbus is the capital of OHIO and a leading manufacturing city. It has 540,025 people, but 916,228 in its urban area.

Connecticut is the southernmost of the NEW ENGLAND states, and is small but densely populated. Highly urbanized and non-agricultural, Connecticut's people are among the highest income earners in the US. Area: 12,973, sq km; population: 3,031,709; capital: Hartford.

Cordilleran Chain, see ROCKY MOUNTAINS.

D **Dallas**, Texas, gained notoriety as the city in which President Kennedy was assassinated in 1963. Population: 844,401, but

1,550,000 with its urban area.

Delaware, north-easternmost of the southern states, and the second smallest in the US, was the first to ratify the constitution. Area: 5,328 sq km; population: 548,104; capital Dover.

Denver, capital of Colorado, was founded on gold and boomed on silver. Urban area: 1,413,000 sq km; population: 487,000.

Detroit, Michigan, an inland port, is the world's biggest vehicle-producing centre. Urban area: 4,163,517 sq km; population: 1,492,507,

warm and rainy. Most of the western half of the United States (but well inland from the Pacific) is a semi-arid region that extends from Canada deep into Mexico. Most of the American Pacific coastland has warm, dry summers with cooler, wetter winters. To the south-east, a desert belt extends from near SALT LAKE CITY to the southern tip of Lower California. The tropical southern half of Mexico has wet summers and dry winters.

Natural vegetation

Tundra (a frozen, treeless plain with mosses, lichens and dwarfed vegetation) covers the Alaskan-Canadian Arctic. Taiga (marshy pine forest) covers most of the rest of Canada. It extends into the western United States as far south as the desert and semi-desert region, which runs into northern Mexico south of the Rio Grande. Grasslands cover the Central Lowland except for the northernmost 30 per cent. A small area of Canada to the north, and a large area of the United States to the east, of the Central Lowland, has a natural vegetation of broadleaf or coniferous forests. The natural vegetation of southern Mexico is tropical forest.

Hawaii

Hawaii is a group of 122 volcanic or coral mid-Pacific tropical islands extending 2,592 kilometres from south-east to north-west. The eight largest, including the only seven that are inhabited, lie in the south-east. Hawaii has a pleasant, mild climate cooled by the prevailing

Above: The decorated hide of a bison (American wild buffalo) illustrates the life of an Indian tribe. The bison, live or dead, played a vital part in Indian life, but the spread of the Europeans across North America doomed the animal — and consequently the Indian way of life — to near extinction.

south-westerly trade winds. Lowland January temperatures of 22°C rise to only 25° in July. Precipitation varies from 25 millimetres in the lowlands to several hundred millimetres on mountain peaks. Hawaii has a wide variety of natural vegetation.

North America: peoples and ways of life

North America has been peopled by immigrants. The first-known, the INDIANS (or Amerinds), arrived some 30,000 years ago from Asia (then joined to Alaska). The Aleuts and other ESKIMOS of the north probably began to settle in the country about 6,000 years ago. Europeans landed in strength on the continent from the 1600s, and brought slaves into the Americas from Africa to work for them. But the greatest immigration in history took place between 1820 and 1977, when 42 million people entered the United States from almost every country in the world. The Statue of Liberty in New York Harbour bears the words: 'Give me your tired, your poor, your huddled masses yearning to breathe free . . . . Send these, the homeless, tempest-tossed to me . . . .'

Peoples of Alaska

Alaska, the largest state of the United States, has the least people except for WYOMING. There are nearly four square kilometres of land for each

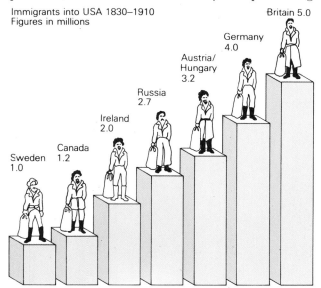

Immigrants into USA 1830–1910
Figures in millions

Sweden 1.0
Canada 1.2
Ireland 2.0
Russia 2.7
Austria/Hungary 3.2
Germany 4.0
Britain 5.0

Left: The first immigrant colony was founded in 1607 but the main influx to the United States started in about 1820, reaching its peak in 1907. The 7 countries shown in the diagram supplied the majority of the immigrants.

25% of whom are Black.
Dixie, or Dixieland, is a nickname for the southern states of the US. It has no agreed origin.

E Eskimos, a Mongoloid people, live along the northern coastlands of North America, and in nearby Greenland and Siberia. Over half of the world total of 65,000 Eskimos live in North America. The Europeanization of the continent has largely destroyed their traditional way of life. Many have found prosperity by working in the new technological in-

stallations of the north.

F Florida, the south-eastern-most state of the US, earns half of its total income

Eskimos eating

from tourism. Tallahassee is the capital. Area: 151,670 sq km; population: 6,789,443.
Fraser River rises in the Rocky Mountains of British

Columbia and flows 1,370 km to empty into the Strait of Georgia, South of Vancouver.

G Georgia, a south-eastern state of the US, is mainly forested. Its capital is ATLANTA. Area: 152,489 sq km; population: 4,589,575, 26% Black.
Grand Canyon, an awe-inspiring deep valley in north-western Arizona, has been eroded into beautifully coloured natural sculpture by the swift-flowing Colorado River.
Great Basin, an elevated

region between the Sierra Nevada and Wasatch Mountains, covers nearly 500,000 sq km. Having no outlet to the sea, the waters it receives either dry up or form lakes. The largest is Great Salt Lake.
Great Bear Lake covers 31,800 sq km in northern Canada, on the freezing Arctic circle.
Great Lakes, the largest group of freshwater lakes in the world, comprise lakes Superior, Huron, Michigan, Erie and Ontario. They are mainly in the US, on the Canadian border. Their com-

Alaskan. The state's population is 79 per cent White (mainly of German, English, Norwegian and Swedish descent), 18 per cent Eskimo, Aleut and Indian, and 3 per cent Black. Most Whites live in the towns of Anchorage, Fairbanks and Juneau. Few Alaskans were born in the state.

New England and Mid-Atlantic states

The New England states, which comprise MAINE, NEW HAMPSHIRE, VERMONT, MASSACHUSETTS, RHODE ISLAND and CONNECTICUT, were among the first to be settled by Europeans. Maine, New Hampshire and Vermont are over 99 per cent White in population, with people of British descent in the lead. Only 50 per cent of them live in towns and cities.

Massachusetts, Rhode Island and Connecticut have a White population of over 93 per cent, with Italians in the majority. The three states have a high population density and most people live in towns and cities. Massachusetts has an important fishing industry.

In the Mid-Atlantic states, which comprise NEW YORK, NEW JERSEY and PENNSYLVANIA, Italians are again the leading group. More than any other state, New York is the 'melting pot' of peoples and religions. It has 2,400,000 Blacks, 2,000,000 Jews, and some 700,000 Puerto Ricans.

NEW YORK CITY and BOSTON are leading financial centres, and Pennsylvania is probably the most important industrial state in the Union. But the nine states are not maintaining their former momentum, and there is a net loss of some 130,000 migrants each year.

The southern states

The southern states have a cultural unity that was cemented by the Civil War of 1861-65. They include 10 of the 11 rebel Confederate States (but not Texas): VIRGINIA, TENNESSEE, ARKANSAS,

Above: Roadside advertising is a prominent feature of the American countryside despite the emergence of a nationwide environmentalist movement. Food and drink vendors seek to tempt motorists on a Florida highway.

Left: Las Vegas, Nevada, famous as a leading gambling city, has been portrayed in many Hollywood films. Gamblers can try their luck at gaming tables or with slot machines such as these massed together at the Circus Casino.

Below: Tenement blocks rise 7 floors from the streets of Harlem, main centre of New York City's black community.

Right: Before World War II the relationship between income and class was fairly consistent. It could be represented by the pyramid model shown in figure 1. In the post-War era the incomes of manual workers — who make up 54 per cent of the working population — have risen substantially, which enables many of them to enjoy a middle class standard of living. Today's situation is more accurately represented by the diamond model shown in figure 2.

1

2

---

bined waters cover about 250,000 sq km, and drain land 3 times that area.
Great Salt Lake, see GREAT BASIN.
Great Slave Lake, fed chiefly by the Great Slave River, covers 28,500 sq km in northern Canada. It was not named after slaves, but after the Slave Indian tribe.
Guadalajara, the second city of Mexico, lies 470 km north-west of Mexico City in a rich farming and mining area. Its fine squares date from Spanish colonial times. Population of Greater Guadalajara: 1,856,879.

H **Hawaii**, 50th American state to join the US, lies

Honolulu, Hawaii

in the mid-Pacific, some 3,300 km from mainland America. It comprises 8 main and 14 minor islands. Hawaii is racially very diverse. Area: 16,706 sq km; population: 769,913; capital, HONOLULU.
Honolulu, capital of Hawaii, is the 'crossroads of the Pacific' for shipping. Population: 324,871, 50% of Hawaii's total.
Houston, largest city and industrial centre of Texas, is an inland port and transportation centre. Population: 844,401, but 1,980,000 in the urban area.

Hudson River rises in the Adirondack Mts. and flows some 500 km south to empty into New York Bay. Ocean-going ships carry freight north to Albany and barges then transport it via canals to the GREAT LAKES.

I **Idaho**, a mainly agricultural Rocky Mts. state is rich in gems and minerals. Area: 216,413 sq km; population: 713,008; capital, Boise.
Illinois, a mid-western prairie state, is heavily industrialized in the north-east. Capital: Springfield.

63% of the state's 11,113,976 people live in Greater CHICAGO. Area: 146,076 sq km.
Indiana, smallest of the mid-western states, has a diverse economy and a reputation for friendliness. Area: 93,994 sq km; population: 5,193,669; capital: IN-DIANAPOLIS.
Indianapolis, capital and largest city of Indiana, is an important industrial centre. Population: 744,624.
Indians (or Amerinds), a Mongoloid people, entered North America overland from Asia about 30,000

Left: Lacrosse, a fast ball game, uses nets on long sticks to drive the ball down the field and into the opponents' goal. It was devised by the Indians of North America and is now widely played throughout Canada. The Indians called it baggataway and as many as 200 could play. The Iroquois used it to train warriors. The game is now played by 2 teams of 12.

LOUISIANA, MISSISSIPPI, ALABAMA, GEORGIA, FLORIDA, SOUTH CAROLINA and North Carolina; and the four border states of DELAWARE, MARYLAND, WEST VIRGINIA and KENTUCKY. Although these four were slave states in 1861, they remained with the Union. The 'Deep South' prospered on cotton and the slave labour that picked it. In the 'Deep South' states the Black population now varies between 15 per cent in Florida and 37 per cent in Mississippi. Racial troubles continued into recent times. Many Blacks left the southern states to find work in the industrial north, but WASHINGTON D.C., the federal capital, still has a Black majority. The largest White ethnic group in the southern states is composed of people of German descent. In most southern states, less than 60 per cent of the people live in towns. The region has the lowest per capita income, and has never closed the prosperity gap with the north-east. Cotton is now less important, but industrial towns have sprung up at road, rail or river transport junctions, and the region attracts some 375,000 new immigrants a year. Sixty per cent of these go to Florida (the 'sunshine state') which is a popular haven for retired people. One in three workers in Virginia, one in six in Kentucky, and one in twelve in Arkansas is a farmer, but elsewhere agriculture is not now so important.

The mid-west
The vast mid-western region extends between the Mid-Atlantic and Rocky Mountain states. It comprises the wheat belt states of NORTH DAKOTA, SOUTH DAKOTA, NEBRASKA and KANSAS in the west; the predominantly maize growing states of MINNESOTA, IOWA, MISSOURI, ILLINOIS, INDIANA and OHIO to the east; and the Great Lakes states of WISCONSIN and MICHIGAN. Although the mid-west is the American 'bread and meat basket', it contains some of the Union's most important manufacturing centres, especially in Michigan, Wisconsin, Minnesota, Iowa, Illinois, Ohio and Missouri. Mid-western farmers also rear some 100 million cattle, swine and sheep. The great stockyards of CHICAGO have become world famous. That great city boomed as the transportation centre for grain, meat and industrial production.

People of German descent are the largest group in every state except North Dakota (where Norwegians lead) and Michigan (where Poles predominate). Despite prosperity, the region has a net loss through migration in every state except Wisconsin, Nebraska and Minnesota. Few Blacks live outside the industrial areas.

The Rockies and south-western states
The core of the 'wild west' portrayed in so many Hollywood films, lies between the mid-west and southern states, and the Pacific coast states. The northern Rocky Mountain states comprise MONTANA, WYOMING, COLORADO, UTAH, NEVADA and IDAHO. The south-western states are ARIZONA, New Mexico, OKLAHOMA and Texas. Only the last two have more than 12 people to the square kilometre. People of Mexican descent form major groups in all the south-western states, reflecting

Left: Canada's bleak Atlantic coastline is typified by Halls Harbor in the peninsular maritime province of Nova Scotia. Small coastal settlements like this form the bases of Nova Scotia's fishermen, who catch over 30% of all the fish landed in Canada.

Right: An icy mountain lake near Banff, Alberta, Canada, receives the waters of surrounding glaciers in the high peaks of the Rocky Mountains — Canada's western 'backbone'. Much of Canada is too bleak for normal habitation, and most of the population is concentrated close to the United States border.

---

years ago and spread throughout the Americas. Europeans destroyed the basis of their civilization environmentally and by war. About 2,000,000 Indians

Crow Indian woman

lived north of Mexico when the Europeans arrived. Some 500,000 now live in the US, mostly in reservations; and about 300,000 in Canada. Unemployment rates, usually above 30%, suggest that the Indian population have still not been able to adapt to the Europeanized culture. In the 1970s, US Indians demonstrated often against their plight.
Iowa, a mid-west state, lies between the Mississippi and Missouri rivers. It has 103 lakes, 91 state parks, and few immigrants. Area: 145,791

sq km; population: 2,825,041; capital: Des Moines.

J **Juarez** (Ciudad Juarez), a Mexican city founded as an early transportation centre, is connected by bridge over the Rio Grande with El Paso in Texas. Population: 436,054.

K **Kansas,** a mid-western state, lies at the centre of the US. Its diverse economy produces 20% of the country's wheat. Area: 213,064 sq km; population: 2,240,071; capital: Topeka.

Kentucky, among the northernmost of the southern states, has a varied economy. Mountains in the east give way to plains in the west. Area: 104,623 sq km; population: 3,219,311; capital: Frankfort.
Kodiak Island, habitat of the Kodiak bear, lies off southern Alaska. The first Russian colony was founded there in 1784. Area: 13,890 sq km.

L **Lake Erie,** see GREAT LAKES.
Lake Huron, see GREAT LAKES.

Lake Michigan, see GREAT LAKES.
Lake Ontario, see GREAT LAKES.
Lake Superior, see GREAT LAKES.
Lake Winnipeg, in southern Manitoba, receives the Red, Winnipeg and Saskatchewan rivers. Area: 24,514 sq km.
Laurentian Plateau (or Canadian Shield) extends like a huge rocky horseshoe around Hudson Bay, taking in the northern islands. It covers half the country's land area. Few people inhabit it. The north-eastern

Hawaii's population includes 39 per cent European inhabitants, 28 per cent Japanese, 12 per cent Filipino and seven per cent Chinese. The population increases by about one per cent each year through migration. The state is known for its natural scenic beauty and pleasant climate. Tourist attractions such as *hula* (dance), flower garlands and traditional welcomes stem from the Polynesian cultural past of the islands. All Hawaii's people live on only seven of the 122 islands.

Peoples of Canada

Canada, the world's second biggest country after the USSR, has only eight per cent of the population of North America. Its population of 24,000,000 occupies 9,976,185 square kilometres. Although the country extends more than 4,600 kilometres south to north, over 90 per cent of the people live within 320 kilometres of the border with the United States. By descent, 45 per cent of Canada's people are British or Irish; 29 per cent French; 6 per cent German; and 1·5 per cent Indian or Eskimo. Most of the rest are also European, with some of Chinese, Japanese or Negro descent. About 85 per cent of all people are Canadian born.

The largest religious group are the Protestants,

the area's past history. The Rocky Mountain states are predominantly European, with people of German descent in the lead. All 10 states are increasing their populations by migration.

Texas is more important in stockraising than any other state except Iowa. Oilmen are prominent in the life of Texas and also, to a lesser degree, of neighbouring Oklahoma. One of the many colourful groups that grew up in the United States are the Mormons, who trekked westwards to find a haven near the Great Salt Lake. There, the founders of the religion established SALT LAKE CITY in 1848.

The Pacific states

The two northernmost Pacific coast states of Washington and OREGON are over 95 per cent White in population, with people of German descent predominating. Crop and livestock raising are much less important than manufacturing. In CALIFORNIA, the third largest but most populous state of the Union, the 12 per cent of people who are non-White include Blacks and migrants from across the Pacific. About 91 per cent of Californians live in towns and cities – more than 50 per cent of them in the urban areas of San Francisco and LOS ANGELES (which includes the world's film 'capital' of Hollywood). The two cities have gained a reputation as trendsetters for Western cultural patterns. After Alaska, California has the highest per capita income of any state in the Union.

Right: The Royal Canadian Mounted Police once enforced the law throughout Canada on horseback. The 'Mounties' are now motorized and wear a less colourful uniform.

mountains rise to 2,600 metres.
Leon de los Aldamas (or Leon), an industrial, commercial and mining city, lies 325 km north-west of MEXICO CITY. Population: 496,598.
Long Island, the southeastern part of New York City at its western end, has more people than most of the states.
Los Angeles, the largest city in California and third largest in the US, contains the district of Hollywood, centre of the US film industry. Urban area of Los Angeles-Long Beach:

8,351,266 sq km; population: 2,816,061.
Louisiana, a southern state on the Gulf of Mexico, has rich resources including timber, petroleum and natural gas. Area: 125,675 sq km; capital: Baton Rouge. Nearly 33% of Louisiana's total population of 3,641,306 are Black.

M MacKenzie River, Canada's longest river, flows 1,600 km from the Great Slave Lake to the Beaufort Sea (part of the Arctic Ocean).
Maine, largest and north-

ernmost of the New England states, has a varied economy in which tourism is important. Area: 86,027 sq km; population: 993,663, over 99% of whom are White. Capital: Augusta.
Manitoba, Canada's most central state, has few people in the north. This prairie province now gains most of its income from manufacturing. The capital, WINNIPEG, contains over 50% of the province's 1,018,000 people. Area: 650,090 sq km.
Maryland, among the northernmost of the southern states of the US, is

important in manufacturing, agriculture and mining. Area: 27,394 sq km; population: 3,922,399, 77% of whom live in towns; capital: Annapolis.

Pilgrim Fathers reach land

Massachusetts, one of the smallest of the US states, in New England, is where the Pilgrims landed from the *Mayflower* in 1620. It is a leading historical and cultural centre of the US. Area: 21,389 sq km; population: 5,689,170; capital: BOSTON.
Mexico City, capital of Mexico, has expanded rapidly to become one of the world's most populous urban areas. Situated 2,241 metres above sea level, it was originally planned as a Spanish colonial city, but is now heavily industrialized. Population:

split into various denominations, including some 4,000,000 of the United Church of Canada and 2,500,000 Anglicans. There are some 9,000,000 Roman Catholics and over 250,000 Jews. About 14,500,000 speak English as their first language and 6,000,000, French. Some 3,500,000 Canadians have another language as their mother tongue. Over 65 per cent of Canada's 115,000 immigrants in 1977 came from (in descending order of numbers) Asia, Britain and Ireland, the United States, and the West Indies. Fifty per cent of them went to ONTARIO.

The agricultural heartland of Canada is Saskatchewan, the greatest wheat-producing area in North America. Twenty-five per cent of the people of the province are farmers, and they

Below: Aztec traditions are kept alive in Mexico by frequent festivals. They are celebrated with music and dance as well as the acrobatic feats shown here.

Right: Peasants walk homeward to their village of San Juan de Chamuca in Chiapas, Mexico's south-easternmost state. Forty per cent of Mexico's fast-growing population are from low-income farming families.

produce 60 per cent of Canada's wheat. MANITO-BA, Ontario and QUEBEC (close to the United States border) comprise the industrial centre of Canada, with over 25 per cent of their workers in manufacturing.

On average, the people of Ontario and BRITISH COLUMBIA are the richest Canadians. The comparatively tiny Atlantic provinces of NEW BRUNSWICK, NEWFOUNDLAND, NOVA SCOTIA and PRINCE EDWARD ISLAND are the poorest, yet (apart from Newfoundland) the most densely populated. However, these provinces provide most of the nation's fish catch.

Canada, a democratic, federal monarchy, has its capital at OTTAWA. Each of its 10 provinces has its own prime minister (or premier), but generally, Canadian provincial governments have more limited powers than American states. The YUKON TERRITORY and the NORTH-WEST TERRITORIES are largely controlled by the central government. Seventy-five per cent of all Canadians live in cities or small towns and live a European way of life adapted to a colder climate. Farmers, lumberjacks, miners, and the few remaining hunters and trappers of the northern 80 per cent of the country, have a lonely life.

The Mexican way of life
Culturally, Mexico is part of Latin America.

8,591,750, Greater Mexico City: 13,000,000.
Miami, Florida, is one of the most visited and fastest growing cities of the US. Urban area: 1,340,700; population: 334,859.
Michigan, a mid-western US state on the Canadian border, comprises 2 low-lying peninsulas divided by Lake Michigan. A prosperous state, it is mainly agricultural but contains in the DETROIT area the world's largest vehicle manufacturing centre. Area: 150,779 sq km; population: 8,875,083; capital: Lansing.

Milwaukee, largest city in Wisconsin, is an important manufacturing state. Urban area: 1,403,688 sq km; population: 717,372.
Minneapolis, largest city of Minnesota, is the twin city of St Paul. It is a trading and industrial port on the Mississippi. Twin city met. area: 1,813,647; population: 434,400.
Minnesota, a mid-western state on the Canadian border, has many rivers and lakes. It produces most of the US iron ore. Area: 217,736 sq km; population: 3,805,069; capital: St Paul.

Mississippi, a southern state of the US, has a thriving cotton and agricultural industry based on its warm, moist climate and rich soil – largely silt deposited by the Mississippi River. But the river also causes disastrous floods. Timber and minerals are also important resources. Area: 123,584 sq km; population: 2,216,912; capital: Jackson.
Mississippi River, longest river in the US, forms, with the Missouri River, one of the world's longest river systems. It rises in the north-central US near the Cana-

dian border and flows over 3,700 km to empty into the Gulf of Mexico. On the way it is fed by more than 250 tributaries.

St Louis, Missouri

Missouri, the southernmost mid-western state of the US, is crossed by the wide Missouri River and bounded in the east by the Mississippi River. The state is important both agriculturally and industrially. Area: 180,487 sq km; population: 4,677,399; capital: Jefferson City.
Missouri River is formed by the Gallatin, Jefferson and Madison rivers in Montana and flows about 4,000 km to join the Mississippi River near St Louis, Missouri.
Montana is the northernmost Rocky Mountain

Mexicans speak Spanish and Indian languages and 96 per cent are Roman Catholic in religion. (But in practice their religion often incorporates much of the pre-Christian cults.) Mexico's population of 72,000,000 is growing at the rate of over four per cent a year – faster than almost anywhere else in the world. Fifty per cent of all Mexicans are under the age of 16. The capital, MEXICO CITY, with a metropolitan population of 14,000,000, seems likely to become the world's most populous urban area. Other large cities include GUADALAJARA, MONTERREY, JUÁREZ, LEÓN DE LOS ALDAMAS and PUEBLA.

Mexico is a poor country, with less than 20 per cent of the per capita income of its rich northern neighbours. Forty per cent of all workers are farmers – a proportion four times as great as in the highly mechanized wheat and maize-belts of the American mid-west. However, Mexico is industrializing rapidly.

Mexico is sometimes called 'the land of the three cultures': Indian, Spanish and Mexican (a combination of the other two). A fourth culture, that of the United States, overshadows the modern way of life in the cities. City dwellers may live, work and shop in American-style buildings, but on Sundays they attend church for mass, socialize in the plazas, and watch bullfights in Spanish style. Many customs and rituals date from pre-European times.

Farmers generally live near to the land they till, in small villages with a church as the focus. Buying, selling or bartering at local markets is an important part of life. Village houses comprising one or two rooms may be built of *adobe* (dried mud and straw), brick or stone. Kitchens, usually outside the house walls, are covered by a lean-to roof. The style of village houses varies from region to region, reflecting Indian traditions. In the remoter parts of Mexico, such as Yucatan, the life style remains close to pre-Spanish, Indian patterns. Dress is a compromise between Indian, old Spanish, and modern Western styles.

Economy

The United States has the most powerful economy that the world has ever known. Its gross domestic product is about three times greater than that of either the USSR or Japan, and considerably greater than that of the whole of

Legend:
Cattle | Sugar cane
Pigs | Sugar beet
Sheep | Soya beans
Fishing | Rice
Fur trapping | Maize
Grapes | Wheat
Citrus fruit | Barley
Apples | Oats
Bananas | Tobacco
Potatoes | Cotton
Nuts | Sisal
Coffee
Cocoa
Flax

Above: The map of natural products in North America shows that fur farming and trapping remain important in the Canadian north. Rich fishing grounds lie off the coasts. Livestock abounds in Mexico, Texas, California and the Mid-western states — which also form the corn belt.

Asia (excluding the USSR). Although Americans are no longer the world's richest people (per capita), they are still among the world leaders. Except for natural rubber, the United States produces almost every commodity consumed throughout the world.

Canada has about 10 per cent of the population of the United States and 10 per cent of the American gross domestic product. Economically, Canada ranks among the world's top 15 nations, with a gross domestic product that tops China's and is double that of India. Mexico, with 30 per cent of the population of the United States, has less than 4 per cent of its gross domestic product.

Agriculture in the USA

The United States is the leading world producer

state of the US. Much of the state is rugged and mountainous. Agriculture and minerals form the basis of Montana's economy. Area: 381,087 sq km; population: 694,409; capital: Helena.
Monterrey, Mexico's third largest city, lies near the border with Texas. A 400-year-old Spanish city, it now has many industries. Population: 1,049,957.
Montreal, the largest city of Canada's Quebec province, is a leading cultural, commercial and industrial centre at the confluence of the St Lawrence and Ottawa rivers.

Its harbour is the entrance to the ST LAWRENCE SEAWAY. Population: 1,060,033; Greater Montreal: 2,720,413.
Mount McKinley, Alaska, is the highest peak in North America, rising to 6,198 metres.
Mount Rushmore, see SOUTH DAKOTA.

N **Nebraska,** a midwestern state in the central US, is a fertile farming region, originally part of the Louisiana Purchase (from France in 1803). Area: 200,018 sq km; population: 1,483,791; capital: Lincoln.

Nelson River flows from the north of Lake Winnipeg 650 km north-east into Hudson Bay. It also carries the waters of several other waterways.
Nevada, westernmost of the Rocky Mountain states of the US, is large in area but small in population, reflecting its mountainous and arid land. It is known for its gambling resorts such as Las Vegas and Reno. Area: 286,299 sq km; population: 488,738; capital: Carson City.
Newfoundland, once an independent dominion,

became Canada's 10th province in 1949. It includes Newfoundland island and the coastal region of Labrador (which has only 2% of the province's population). The province is known for cod fishing. Area: 404,519 sq km; population: 557,725; capital: St John's.

Barr'd Islands, Newfoundland

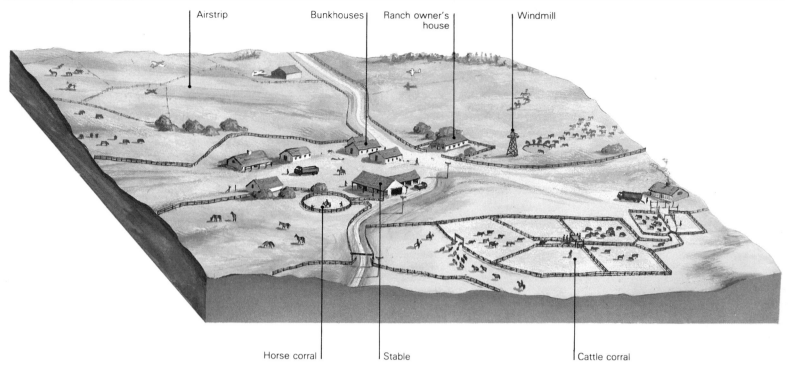

Airstrip   Bunkhouses   Ranch owner's house   Windmill

Horse corral   Stable   Cattle corral

of maize, its crop being grown almost entirely in the mid-western states. The country is second to the USSR in wheat production, grown mainly in a belt that extends from Illinois through Missouri, Kansas, Nebraska, North Dakota and Montana to Washington. The United States is also second to the USSR in world oats production, most of the American oats being grown in the mid-western states of Wisconsin, Iowa, Minnesota and South Dakota. The United States leads the world in the production of oranges

Above: Some Texas ranches exceed 400 sq km. Even the more modest ranch shown here has its own airstrip. Near the middle lie the ranch-owner's house, bunkhouses and the cook shack for the 'cowboys'. Other features include the corals for cattle and horses, stables, and the windmill that pumps well water to the surface. Many ranches have bulldozers and flamethrowers to help with the work.

Left: Hollywood, part of Los Angeles, California, is world-famed as the home of the American film industry. The picture shows a set for a 'western' cowboy film, typical of several thousands produced over the years. Although Hollywood is still an important film producing centre, it has long passed its prime.

(mainly Florida and California); apples (especially Washington, New York and Michigan); and tomatoes (mainly California). American production ranks fourth in sugar (especially Hawaii, Louisiana, Florida and California); and in potatoes (especially Idaho, Maine and California). The United States also leads in cotton, the most important states being Texas, California, Mississippi and other southern states. In tobacco, the United States ranks second to China, with North Carolina and other southern states growing almost the entire crop. In oilseeds, the United States leads in soya beans (mid-western and southern states); comes second in sunflower seed (especially Kansas); and is third in groundnuts (Georgia and other southern states). The United States figures in the top three cattle and pig raising nations, but is barely in the top 10 for sheep farming.

Mining and manufacturing in the USA

The United States leads the world in the production of copper (found mostly in Arizona, Utah, Montana and New Mexico); lead (especially in Missouri, Idaho and Utah); aluminium (especially in Washington and Texas); and magnesium (found mainly in Texas). In crude steel production, the United States ranks second

---

New Brunswick, a small Atlantic province of Canada, borders the north-east US. Many of its people are descended from immigrants who settled there from the US after the end of the Revolutionary War in 1783. Timber and mining are important industries. Area: 28,354 sq km; population: 677,250; capital: Fredericton.
New Hampshire, a small New England state of the US, has a thriving manufacturing industry. Area: 24,097 sq km; population: 737,681; capital: Concord.

New Jersey, a mid-Atlantic state, is the most densely populated state in the US. Over 50% of this busy industrial state is a low plain extending inland from the Atlantic. It lies between 2 major urban areas – New York and Philadelphia – and is a key transportation centre. North-eastern New Jersey is part of the New York urban area. Area: 20,295 sq km; population: 7,168,164; capital: Trenton.
New Mexico, a southwestern state of the US, is one of the largest but least populated. Deserts, canyons

and mountains cover most of its land, which is rich in minerals, petroleum and natural gas. Area: 315,115

Pueblo, New Mexico

sq km; population: 1,016,000; capital: Santa Fe.
New Orleans, famed as the birthplace of jazz, is the largest city of Louisiana and the chief US commercial centre on the Gulf of Mexico. Urban area: 1,045,809 sq km; population: 593,471.
New York, small in area, is the second most populous state in the US. Over 50% of its people live in Greater New York City, but the capital is Albany. The state is the main centre of American business and industry. Area: 128,402 sq km; population: 18,236,967.

New York City is one of the world's most populated urban areas. It incorporates 5 boroughs: Bronx and Manhattan on the mainland, Richmond on Staten Island, and Brooklyn and Queens on the west of Long Island. The North, Hudson, East and Harlem rivers that intersect the city are crossed by several bridges, tunnels and ferries. New York – northeastern New Jersey urbanized area: 11,571,899 sq km; population: 7,895,563.
Niagara Falls are 2 waterfalls on the Niagara River on

to the USSR; in pig iron, third to the USSR and Japan; and in iron ore, third to the USSR and Australia. Most of the American iron ore comes from the Lake Superior area. Pennsylvania, Ohio and Indiana are the leading steel-making states. The United States is also among the top four nations in the production of zinc (found especially in Tennessee); cadmium and silver (especially in Idaho); and gold (especially in South Dakota, Utah and Nevada).

The United States is also the world's chief producer of coal (mined mostly in West Virginia, Kentucky and Pennsylvania); and of natural gas, which along with petroleum is found mainly in Texas, Louisiana and Oklahoma. In 1977, the United States dropped behind Saudi Arabia to become the third largest petroleum producer. The United States leads in the world production of synthetic rubber and nylon, and is third to the USSR and Japan in rayon. It produces more electricity than the USSR, Japan and West Germany combined.

Despite its impressive list of natural resources, it is above all in manufacturing that the United States is unrivalled. It is the land of the machine and the gadget. It manufactures nearly as many vehicles as Japan, West Germany, Britain and the USSR combined. It has nearly double the number of vehicles in service on the roads of these four countries. Americans also possess more television sets than the peoples of those four countries.

In commerce and finance too, the United States leads the world. The three leading banks of international importance are all American: Bank of America, Citibank, and Chase Manhattan. The United States is the world's largest importer, and shares first place as an exporting

Above and **below**: The cold, vast, empty territory of Alaska became a boom region with the achievement of statehood in 1959, when commercial production of crude petroleum began. Oil is now piped across Alaska for export to other states.

Left and **right**: North America is a prime world source of good timber. Five important trees (not to scale) are shown. **1** The fine-grained White Oak is ideal for flooring and ships' timbers. **2** The Sugar Maple provides maple syrup and timber for furniture. **3** The Douglas Fir. **4** The White Pine, with soft straight grain, is ideal for house construction. **5** The Western Hemlock.

nation with West Germany. Its main trading partners are Canada, Japan and West Germany.

About 338,000 kilometres of railways link the towns and cities of the United States — more than the total rail extent of the next four leading countries: USSR, Canada, India and West Germany. However, the United States is now a road, rather than a rail, country. Only 50 per cent of the total number of the USA's passengers, and 30 per cent of its total freight tonnage, are carried on its rail network.

Despite its great wealth and economic power, the United States is declining in relation to the rest of the world. To a large extent this is because it neared its economic potential earlier than most other countries. About 22 per cent of the workforce are in manufacturing and some 3.7 per cent in agriculture.

Canadian agriculture and mining
In spite of its comparatively small population,

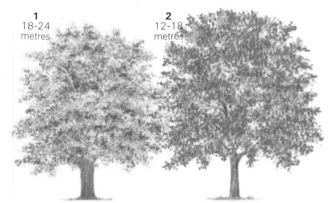

1 18-24 metres   **2** 12-18 metres

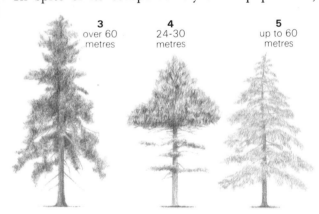

3 over 60 metres   **4** 24-30 metres   **5** up to 60 metres

---

the US-Canadian border. Horseshoe Falls lie on the Canadian side and American Falls are in the US. The falls, a tourist draw, are used to generate electricity.
North Carolina, a southern state of the US, was named after King Charles of England. It produces nearly 50% of the US tobacco crop and is important in food crops. Area: 136,198 sq km; population: 5,082,059; capital: Raleigh.
North Dakota, a mid-western prairie state, borders Canada. Most of the people live outside cities and

towns. Farming, mining and the production of petroleum and natural gas are important. Area: 183,022 sq km; population: 617,761; capital: Bismarck.

Eskimos of the NW Territories

North-west Territories cover over 33% of Canada's land surface, yet they contain only 46,386 people, over 65% of whom are Eskimos or Indians. Fishing and hunting are the main occupations. Area: 3,379,700 sq km; capital: Yellowknife.
Nova Scotia, a Canadian province, comprises a peninsula at the extreme southeast tip of the Canadian main land, together with Cape Breton Island. Its name is Latin for New Scotland. Most of the province's perimeter is Atlantic coastline. The province's

economy is based on farming, fishing, forestry, mining and industry. Area: 55,491 sq km; population: 828,571; capital: Halifax.

O **Ohio,** easternmost of the US mid-western states, is among the most industrialized. The state's mild climate and favoured position bordering Lake Erie give it advantages in agriculture and communications. Minerals and petroleum are important. Area: 106,765 sq km; population: 10,652,017; capital: Columbus.
Ohio River, eastern tribut-

and the fact that most of the country is unsuitable for cultivation, Canada ranks among the five leading cereal-producing countries in the world. The prairie provinces of Saskatchewan and Alberta form the main cereal-producing region. In the eastern provinces, the pattern of crop and livestock raising is more varied. Fruit is grown around the NIAGARA FALLS area. Fruit-growing, dairying and poultry raising are important in British Columbia. Agriculture and mining each account for about 16 per cent of Canada's income.

Canada is the world's chief nickel producer, and ranks third in zinc, platinum, silver and gold. Other minerals in which Canada is among leading producers include asbestos, cadmium, cobalt, copper, iron, lead, magnesium and potash. The country also mines coal, gypsum, titanium and uranium. Important mining provinces include Ontario, Manitoba, Quebec and British Columbia. The leading natural gas and petroleum province is Alberta which is linked by pipeline to the rest of the country. Canada is also among the chief timber, fishing and fur supplying nations. Most timber is felled in British Columbia. Canada's fishing grounds lie off the Atlantic and Pacific coasts and in the inland lakes. Fur trappers still operate in the north, but most furs now come from fur farms, especially mink.

Canadian manufacturing

Despite the importance of the farming, forestry, fishing and mining industries, over 60 per cent of Canada's income now comes from manufactur-

Above: 'Lakers' — big ocean-going ships — can carry Canadian grain from the Great Lakes through a network of waterways to the Atlantic Ocean for export throughout the world. Agricultural exports, once dominant, now account for only 12% of the value of Canada's exports.

Below: Acapulco, Mexico's leading tourist centre, on the tropical Pacific coast, is a regular port of call for luxury cruise liners. Tourists contribute an essential $3 billion annually to Mexico's foreign exchange earnings.

ing. The chief manufactures include food and beverages; vehicles; shipbuilding and transportation equipment; wood, paper and allied industries; metalworking; petroleum, natural gas and coal; chemicals; electrical products; machinery; printing and publishing; and textiles and clothing.

Over 85 per cent of all manufacturing wealth is produced in Ontario and Quebec provinces, and another nine per cent in British Columbia and Alberta. (The figures include petroleum refining.) Food and beverage processing is important in every province, but especially in Quebec. Ontario is highly important in vehicle production, Manitoba has an important rail centre at Winnipeg, Nova Scotia has shipbuilding and repair yards, and Prince Edward Island specializes in building small ships and fishing boats. The wood and paper industries are widespread, but especially important in Quebec, Ontario and British Columbia. Ontario's main industries are steel and metalworking. The latter is also the chief industry of Nova Scotia. Manitoba, Saskatchewan, Alberta and British Columbia lead in petroleum refining, and Alberta in petrochemicals. Over 65 per cent of all Canada's trade is with the United States.

Mexican agriculture

Mexico is a developing country with a per capita income of only 16 per cent that of the United States. Even so, it is eight times as great as the

ary of the Mississippi, is formed by the confluence of the Allegheny and Monongahela rivers at Pittsburg, where it flows 1,580 km to join the Mississippi.

Oklahoma is the north-easternmost of the southwestern states of the US. A prairie state with hills and mountains, Oklahoma is rich in minerals, petroleum and natural gas. In Oklahoma City (the capital with a 1970 population of 368,856) oil derricks stand in the city area. Area: 181,090 sq km; population: 2,559,253.

Ontario, a central province of Canada, ranks first in population and second in area. The province is important in agriculture, forestry, mining and manufacturing. Most of Ontario's people and cities (including TORONTO, the capital) are southeast on the Great Lakes. Area: 1,067,810 sq km; population: 8,264,465.

Oregon, a Pacific Coast state of the US, has a varied economy with important timber-based industries, hydro-electric plants and metal mines. Area: 251,181 sq km; population: 2,091,385; capital: Salem.

Ottawa, Federal capital of Canada, lies in Ontario on the Ottawa River, upon which timber is floated downstream. It is a well laid out city with impressive public buildings. Area: 521,341 sq km; population 304,462.

P **Pennsylvania,** a mid-Atlantic state of the US, is rich in iron ore, petroleum and natural gas, mines much of the country's coal and produces 25% of the US pig iron and steel output. Dutch territory seized by the British in 1664, the state was named after the English Quaker William Penn, who founded it. Area: 117,412 sq km; population: 11,793,909; capital: Harrisburg.

Philadelphia, in southeastern Pennsylvania, is a port on the Delaware River. It is a leading cultural, transportation and industrial centre. Urban area: 3,802,100 sq km; population: 1,950,098.

Phoenix, capital of Arizona, is the business and shipping centre for the agricultural and industrial produce of the Salt River Valley. Urban area: 863,357; population: 581,562.

William Penn

per capita income of India. Forty per cent of the Mexican workforce (about 6,650,000) are farmers. Despite land reforms since 1915, most peasants own no land or hold only tiny plots.

Eighty per cent of Mexico's total land is arid, or semi-arid needing irrigation to work it. About 68 per cent of cultivated land is sown with grain (including 53 per cent maize and nine per cent wheat). Leading crops on the rest of the farmland include beans, sugar cane, fruits, rice, vegetables, cotton and tobacco. Mexico ranks among the four leading nations in the production of coffee and oranges.

Mexico has some 28,000,000 cattle. Beef cattle graze in the drier pastures of the north. Dairy cattle are kept mainly in the central region. The country also has nearly 6,000,000 sheep, 11,000,000 pigs, and 10,000,000 goats. For work and transport, Mexico keeps nearly 12,000,000 horses, 3,000,000 mules, and 3,000,000 donkeys. This reflects the low proportion of one motorized vehicle to every 20 people. Nearly 25 per cent of Mexico is commercial forestland. The once reckless exploitation of forests for timber has been controlled since 1951. Important forest products include resins, pitch, fibres and turpentine. Agriculture, forestry and fishing provide about 20 per cent of Mexico's total income.

Mexican mining and manufacturing
Mexico, one of the earlier petroleum-producing countries and still among the world's top 15

producers, possesses vast untapped petroleum reserves. The country is also rich in a variety of minerals. With the USSR, it is the world's leading silver producer.

Thirty per cent of Mexico's workforce is employed in manufacturing and construction. The country's manufacturing industries have expanded rapidly since the 1940s, stimulating the economy generally. Important products include iron and steel, chemicals, electric wares, textiles and clothes, rubber, wood pulp and paper, cement, glass and handicrafts. Over 3,000,000 tourists contribute nearly $US 3,000 million annually to the country's income.

North America: history and culture
North America had well-established Indian and Eskimo cultures well over a thousand years ago. The Spaniards dramatically crushed cultures such as the Maya and Aztecs in war over 400 years ago. Further north, the Indians fought and lost several wars against the settlers from northern Europe. However, the northern Indian and Eskimo cultures were destroyed not so much by war, but by the mere presence of the Europeans, which undermined their traditional ways of life. One crucial factor, for example, was the destruction of the bison (American wild buffalo) by the European settlers. Once the Indian threat had diminished, settlers in many areas saw little advantage in remaining subject to the British, French or Spaniards. The American

Above: During the 1960s, the struggle of Black Americans against racial discrimination was led by Martin Luther King. King faced powerful opponents but won the support of President Kennedy. After winning the Nobel Peace Prize in 1964, King was assassinated in Memphis, Tennessee, in 1968.

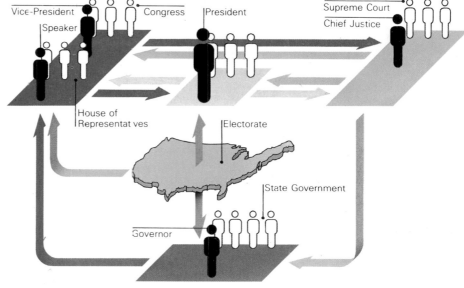

Judicial power
Executive power
Legislative power
State power
Electoral power

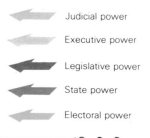
Above: Democratic Party offices in the Watergate Hotel complex were illegally broken into by some of President Nixon's supporters in 1972. The resultant scandal brought about Nixon's downfall.

Right: Aiming to prevent the rise of autocratic power such as they believed King George III possessed, the American founding fathers divided power under the American constitution between the President, Congress and the Supreme Court. Further complications were added to the system of 'checks and balances' by giving each state certain powers in its own right. Intent on democracy, the framers of the constitution decreed that there should be various elections every second year. Because elections are prepared long in advance, the United States is seldom without 'election fever'.

Vice-President • Congress • President • Supreme Court • Chief Justice • Speaker • House of Representatives • Electorate • State Government • Governor

---

Pittsburg, in south-west Pennsylvania, is the world's largest steel centre and has thriving metalworking industries. It is also a major world producer of aluminium. It is surrounded by coalfields which produce half the coke used in the US. Urban area: 2,500,300 sq km; population: 520,117.
Portland, largest city of Oregon, is an inland port near to the Pacific and accessible to ocean-going ships. Urban area: 821,897 sq km; population: 372,000.
Prince Edward Island is the smallest but most dense-

ly populated of the Canadian provinces. Located in the Gulf of St Lawrence, it is sheltered by Nova Scotia. Its mild climate and rich soil make it ideal for farming and fishing. Area: 5,657 sq km; population: 118,229; capital: Charlottetown – the only city.
Puebla (or Puebla de Zaragoza), an industrial city of Mexico, produces especially cotton goods and ceramic wares. Population: 482,155.

Q **Quebec,** largest and second most populous

province of Canada, has a population which is 82% French in origin and 88% Roman Catholic. Most of the people live in the south, the

Wood worker, Quebec

north being too bleak. 'Freedom for Quebec' has become the rallying cry of several political leaders who want to take Quebec out of the Canadian federal state and make it an independent country. Quebec is rich in resources and important industrially. It has most forestland but little farmland. Area: 1,540,668 sq km; population: 6,234,445; capital: QUEBEC CITY.
Quebec City, capital of Quebec province, has the character of an old European city, and is the only walled city in North America. Urban

area: 542,158 sq km; population: 177,082.
Queen Charlotte Islands in the north Pacific lie 100 km off British Columbia. Sparsely populated, they have about 4,000 people in their area of 9,596 sq km.

R **Rhode Island,** smallest state of the US, is largely on the mainland, but takes in several islands including Rhode Island itself. Densely populated, the state makes its income mainly from manufacturing. Area: 3,144 sq km; population: 949,723; capital: Providence.

Left: America's pop culture has found countless admirers throughout the world. Elvis Presley, rock and roll king of the 1950s and 60s, became the dream hero of millions of girls of every nationality. His death in 1977, at the age of 42, failed to diminish his cult status.

Below: Elections, frequent and fervent, take on the character and excitement of festivals in the United States. After each state has decided which presidential candidate to support, state delegations converge on Washington. The picture shows the Carter versus Ford presidential elections of 1976.

of the American fleet at Pearl Harbor, Hawaii. By 1945, the victorious United States had become the first superpower. The 'Cold War' against the USSR and its allies dominated the post-war years. This was based on the supposed Soviet threat to Europe. In 1950-53 the United States provided the bulk of the UN force that came to the aid of South Korea against North Korea and China. While the United States countered communism abroad in the name of freedom, its own oppressed minorities demanded equal rights at home. Black resistance to the banning of Black children from better, Whites-only, schools led to violent clashes in Little Rock, Arkansas, in 1957. The use of federal troops to impose desegregation (mixing) revived bitter memories of the Civil War. Massive civil rights marches to demand equality for Blacks followed, and drew sympathy from President Kennedy. His assassination in 1963 was followed by the

colonists freed themselves from the British by 1783 and Canada became quasi-independent as a British dominion by 1867. Mexico, having gained independence from Spain by war in 1821, was conquered by France in 1863 and had to fight to regain its independence in 1867.

An eventful century (1865-1968)
In the 50 years between the Civil War and World War I, the United States grew to a nation of 100 million. It slowly recovered from the economic Great Depression of 1929-33, and was propelled into World War II in 1941 when Japan sank part

murder of the Black leader Martin Luther King early in 1968, and the killing of Robert Kennedy (brother of the president) later in the year. The gun-law of the wild west still bedevilled the United States, whose private citizens kept 100 million guns as a cherished right.

Comparative decline
During the 1960s, military rivalry between the superpowers gave way to the costly but far less dangerous competition in space. In 1969, the United States achieved its target of 'putting a man on the moon by 1970'. In the 1970s, civil

---

Rocky Mountains (or The Rockies) are the main mountain system of North America. They extend over 3,500 km and are up to 560 km wide. The highest peak, Mt Logan, rises to 6,054 metres.

S St Lawrence Island, between Alaska and Siberia, has been a site of Eskimo culture for 2,000 years. Area: 4,434 sq km.
St Lawrence River, Canada, flows 4,000 km north-east to link the Great Lakes with the Atlantic.
St Lawrence Seaway, the largest artificial seaway in

the world, was completed in 1954 and extends 293 km from Montreal to Lake Ontario. It enabled shipping from the Atlantic to proceed to ports on the GREAT LAKES.
St Louis, a cultural, commercial and industrial centre, is the largest city in Missouri, US. Urban area: 1,826,907; population: 622,236.
Salt Lake City, capital of Utah, was founded in 1847 by the Christian Mormon sect. It is now a mining and manufacturing centre. Urban area: 557,635 sq km; population: 175,885.

San Antonio, an industrial city in Texas, contains the Alamo, a fortress famed for its part in the Texan-Mexican

Great Salt Lake

War 1835–36. Urban area: 864,014 sq km; population: 654,153.
San Diego, a leading defence centre of the US, lies on the coast of California, near the Mexican border. Urban area: 1,198,323 sq km; population: 696,769.
San Francisco, known for its Golden Gate bridge which spans the bay, was founded due to the gold rush of 1849. It is a highly international and colourful city and a financial and cultural centre. Urban area (with Oakland): 2,987,850 sq km; population: 715,674.

Saskatchewan, Canada's leading agricultural province, abounds in minerals in its sparsely populated forested north. The province produces 25% of Canada's petroleum and has large refineries. Area: 651,903 sq km; population: 945,000; capital: Regina.
Seattle, largest city of Washington state, is an international port. Urban area: 1,238,107 sq km; population: 500,000.
South Carolina, one of the smaller southern states of the US, is important for its timber, cotton, tobacco and

Left: 'Habitat' housing was a prominent feature of the 'Expo 67' international exhibition sited in Montreal in 1967 to commemorate 100 years of Canadian independence. The exhibition stood on land reclaimed to enlarge Ile Sainte-Helene and to create a new island, Ile Notre Dame. The soil for the reclaimed land came mostly from excavations carried out simultaneously to construct a Metro (underground railway) for the city. The stations incorporate modern shopping centres.

rights marches became associated with demonstrations against American participation in the Vietnamese civil war. Millions of Americans protested against the use of terror weapons in the attempt to defeat the communists in Vietnam. The war, which eventually engulfed Laos and Kampuchea (Cambodia), ended with a humiliating defeat for the United States in 1975 that dented American morale.

Meanwhile, the biggest political scandal for over a century developed. 'The Watergate caper' began with an illegal break-in at Democratic Party offices in the Watergate building, Washington D.C. The scandal soon assumed immense proportions in the media and had very far-reaching effects. Most of President Nixon's

Left: Language is a burning issue in Canada, with Quebec's politicians spearheading the demand for full equality of the French and English languages. The picture shows a dual-language road sign in English-dominated Ontario.

top aides were dismissed and some imprisoned for improper use of power. The president himself escaped impeachment (public examination of his role in the affair) only by resigning in 1974. His successor, the unelected President Ford, was in office during the final tragedy in Vietnam.

The Americans faced the 1980s in the knowledge that, although their country remained unsurpassed economically and militarily, its comparative power had waned internationally. Under President Carter in the late 1970s, the United States championed human rights throughout the world. Carter also deepened the friendship with China, a process begun, ironically, by Nixon at the height of the Vietnam War.

Canadian unity

The unification of Canada began in 1759, born out of the British defeat of the French and the capture of Quebec, Ontario, New Brunswick and Nova Scotia. Another 80 years passed before Newfoundland joined the federation as the tenth province. By the time that the Canadian Pacific Railway was completed in 1885, the federation stretched from the Atlantic (east coast) to the Pacific (west coast). Its full independence was recognized by the Statute of Westminster in 1931. From World War II onwards, Canada developed into a nation of world importance and ties with Britain weakened.

Above: Each of Canada's 10 provinces and 2 territories has its own coat of arms; *top to bottom and left to right:* Newfoundland, Ontario, Nova Scotia, Prince Edward Island, Saskatchewan, Alberta, British Columbia, Manitoba, New Brunswick, Quebec, Yukon, Northwest Territories.

---

agriculture. Its leading city and port, Charleston, suffered in the Civil War which began in the state. Area: 80,432 sq km; population: 2,590,516; capital: Columbia.

South Dakota, a mainly agricultural mid-western state, has extremes of climate. Mount Rushmore National Memorial (having the carved faces of 4 presidents) is in the south-west. Area: 199,552 sq km; population: 666,257; capital: Pierre.

T **Tennessee,** a southern state of the US, is 50%

rural, 50% urban. Agriculture, timber, mining and manufacturing are important. Area: 109,412 sq km;

Mt Rushmore, S. Dakota

population: 3,923,687; capital: Nashville.

Texas, the largest US state after Alaska, has gained a reputation for 'bigness'. Its biggest ranch is about 440 sq km, and it was an independent country in 1836–45. Known for its petroleum, Texas is also important in crop and animal farming, manufacturing and the aerospace industry (based at Houston, the largest city). Area: 692,408 sq km; population: 11,196,730; capital: Austin.

Toronto, capital of Ontario province, is Canada's

second largest city. It is Canada's leading financial, transportation and commercial centre. Met. area: 2,124,291 sq km; population: 633,318.

U **Utah** (named after the Ute Indians), is a Rocky Mountains state. It was nicknamed the Beehive state because its early settlers, the Mormons, worked 'like bees' to scratch a living from the salt beds and deserts. Mining is the chief industry. Area: 219,932 sq km; population: 1,059,273; capital: SALT LAKE CITY.

V **Vancouver,** the largest city in British Columbia, is Canada's main port on the Pacific, linked to the Panama Canal traffic. Population of urban area: 1,056,894.

Vancouver Island, largest island on North America's Pacific coast, covers 32,137 sq km.

Vermont, a small landlocked New England state of the US, was an independent country in 1777–91. Its name is French for Green Mountain, and timber is important. Area: 24,887 sq km; population: 444,732; capital: Montpelier.

Above: The Plaza of the Three Cultures in Mexico City, which comprises modern housing blocks alongside the ruins of Aztec and Spanish buildings, symbolizes the cultural history of Mexico. Most of the country's frequent festivals are Indian in origin, while popular spectacles such as bullfights came to Mexico with the Spaniards. Mexico's modern culture is overshadowed by that of its powerful northern neighbour, the United States, and future prosperity is likely to stem from the Western world's need of Mexico's vast petroleum reserves.
Below right: Despite its comparative poverty, Mexico played host to the Olympic Games in 1968, lavishing much money on fine buildings such as the Olympic Stadium (*shown*). Although liberal by Latin American standards, Mexico's government was challenged from 1968 onwards by left-wing students who demonstrated during the Olympics.

were agreed amicably between the two countries in 1963, 1967 and 1970. Internal unrest worsened from 1968 onwards, when students rioted and urban guerillas increased their activities. President Echeverria's father-in-law was among several Mexicans and foreigners kidnapped by guerillas in 1974, and some of the victims were killed. Two new Mexican states, created in 1974, brought the total number to 31, in addition to the federal district of Mexico City. The government nationalized major sectors of Mexican industry in 1975. Peasant action against delays in promised land redistribution were crushed by the police in 1975. Despite its poverty, Mexico has vast untapped petroleum reserves. During the Iranian oil crisis of 1979, the United States stepped up negotiations with its southern neighbour for the development of these reserves and the increase of oil exports to the Americans.

Cultural patterns
The culture of the United States and Canada generally reflects that of the Western world, Indian and Eskimo cultures having long gone into decline. Jazz music and abstract impressionism in visual art are among American contributions to Western culture. Mexico's colourful customs and ceremonies, often religious, stem from the blending of its three cultures. Original Indian dishes such as *tortillas* (thin pancakes filled, cooked and served in various ways) add variety to the national cuisine.

Although the British had been careful to integrate French Canadians after the defeat of France, their resentment of the anglicization of Canada did not disappear. In the 1970s, some French Canadians demanded complete independence as a separate nation of Quebec. The possible division of Canada into two nations is an important issue for the 1980s.

Events in Mexico
After the expulsion of the French in 1867, several revolutions occurred in Mexico. The country was under the rule of army generals for most of the period up to 1946. Civilian presidents ruled from then onwards. The Mexico-United States frontier posed problems because of the perpetual shifting of the course of the Rio Grande, which forms half the border. Territorial adjustments

Virginia, a southern state and one of the most historic places in the US, was named after Elizabeth I, the 'Virgin Queen'. Tobacco has long been the leading crop. Area: 105,716 sq km; population: 4,648,485; capital: Richmond.

W Washington, northwesternmost Pacific coast state of the US, is international in character. Forests cover 50% of the state, which is a centre of the aircraft industry. Area: 176,617 sq km; population: 3,469,167; capital: Olympia.

Washington D.C. (District of Columbia) is the federal capital of the US. Its Capitol and the presidential White House are among the world's best-known buildings. Its 174 sq km form an enclave between Maryland and Virginia. Population: 756,668.

West Virginia, one of the northernmost southern states of the US, separated from Virginia during the Civil War. Nicknamed the Mountain State, it has little good farmland but many minerals. It is the leading coal-producing state. Area: 62,629 sq km; population: 1,744,237; capital: Charleston.

Winnipeg, capital of Manitoba, lies 96 km north of the US border and is the main city for business between east and west Canada. Population: 553,000.

Wisconsin, a mid-western state of the US bordering the Great Lakes, is a dairyland region with many lakes and swamps. However, it is also important industrially. Area: 145,439 sq km; population: 4,417,933; capital: Madison.

Wyoming, a Rocky Mountain state of the US, is mainly a ranching region. Mountainous and dry, it has petroleum and natural gas, but no major urban areas and little manufacturing industry. Area: 253,597 sq km; population: 332,416; capital: Cheyenne.

Bonanza Creek, Klondike

Y Yukon Territory of Canada borders Alaska. It was formed in 1898 when the Klondike gold rush began near the Alaskan border. Its population, 18,388 in 1971, is rising fast and reached 22,392 in 1976. It is expected to double by 1985, following economic development. Area (recomputed in 1976): 299,600 sq km; capital: Whitehorse.

The restless volcanoes of Central America reflect the disturbed political conditions in this tropical, under-developed region, where most of the people are farmers and where living standards are low.

Central America

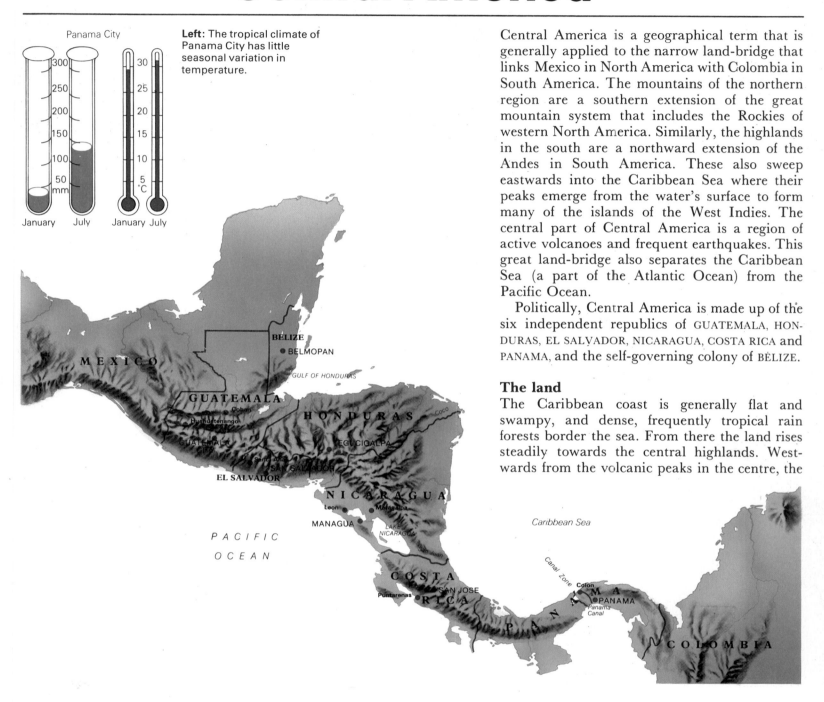

Panama City

January — July — January — July

Left: The tropical climate of Panama City has little seasonal variation in temperature.

Central America is a geographical term that is generally applied to the narrow land-bridge that links Mexico in North America with Colombia in South America. The mountains of the northern region are a southern extension of the great mountain system that includes the Rockies of western North America. Similarly, the highlands in the south are a northward extension of the Andes in South America. These also sweep eastwards into the Caribbean Sea where their peaks emerge from the water's surface to form many of the islands of the West Indies. The central part of Central America is a region of active volcanoes and frequent earthquakes. This great land-bridge also separates the Caribbean Sea (a part of the Atlantic Ocean) from the Pacific Ocean.

Politically, Central America is made up of the six independent republics of GUATEMALA, HONDURAS, EL SALVADOR, NICARAGUA, COSTA RICA and PANAMA, and the self-governing colony of BELIZE.

The land

The Caribbean coast is generally flat and swampy, and dense, frequently tropical rain forests border the sea. From there the land rises steadily towards the central highlands. Westwards from the volcanic peaks in the centre, the

Reference

B **Belize** (formerly British Honduras) is a self-governing British Crown Colony on the east coast, bordered by Mexico, Guatemala and the Atlantic Ocean. The old capital city on the coast, also called Belize, was destroyed by a hurricane in 1961. As a result, a new town called Belmopan was built some 80 km inland and became the capital in 1970. Belize has hot, low coastal plains and low mountains in the centre of the country. There are many dense forests, the trees of which provide valuable timber. Much of this is

Preparing chicle, Belize

exported, as are oranges and grapefruit. In terms of population, Belize is one of the emptiest countries in Latin America. Most of the people are farmers or fishermen, and are of African or MAYA descent, or a mixture of both. Many speak Spanish, although the official language is English. Area: 22,965 sq km; population: 161,900; capital: Belmopan (5,500).

C **Central American Common Market** is an organization formed by 5 states following the signing of a treaty of Central American Economic Integration in 1960. The original members were EL SALVADOR, GUATEMALA, HONDURAS, and NICARAGUA. COSTA RICA joined in 1962.

Costa Rica is a small, independent, Spanish-speaking republic sandwiched between Nicaragua and Panama. It has steamy, swampy and heavily forested coastlines on both the Pacific and Atlantic oceans. Most people live on the temperate central plateau. Costa Rica is unique in LATIN AMERICA in that it has no standing army. Almost all the people are white. The literacy rate and standard of living are also among the highest in Latin America, and there is a history of fairly stable, democratic government. The chief products are coffee, cocoa and sugar. Area: 50,898 sq km; population: 2,210,000; capital: San José (500,000).

E **El Salvador** is the smallest independent republic in Central America. It is also the most densely populated. The country extends along the Pacific coast between Honduras and

land slopes down to dry, narrow plains that fringe the Pacific seaboard.

Of the many rivers in the region, the shorter ones usually empty into the Caribbean and the longer ones wend their way into the Pacific. Several of these rivers have been dammed and their power harnessed for hydro-electric projects. Two huge bodies of inland water – the two largest lakes in Central America – lie within 24 kilometres of each other. They are Lake Nicaragua (7,800 square kilometres), with its unique freshwater sharks, and to the north Lake Managua (1,000 square kilometres). Both lakes lie within the boundaries of Nicaragua.

Climate and vegetation

As in most tropical regions, climate and temperature vary more with altitude than with the seasons. On the Caribbean coast the climate is generally hot, humid and unhealthy. As the land rises towards the high central plateau the climate becomes almost temperate. Most of the people live on the plateau or close to the Pacific coast, where conditions are bearable. The rainy season usually lasts from May to November, but the Caribbean coast is generally drenched with heavy rains all the year round.

The dense forests that clothe the Caribbean coasts and slopes yield valuable timber products such as cedar, mahogany, balsa, palm, pine and rubber. Orchids and other wild flowers grow in profusion in deep green stretches of jungle. The few plantations that have been established in the

Above: Guatemala's Peten region lies to the south of Mexico's Yucatan Peninsula and is a virtually unpopulated area of tropical forest. It yields mahogany and Spanish cedar.

Below: Lake Nicaragua, the largest lake in Central America, lies in western Nicaragua about 19 km from the Pacific Ocean and 113 km from the Caribbean Sea. It is 154 km long, 63 km wide and has a maximum depth of 70 metres. The lake is linked to Lake Managua in the north by the River Tipitapa.

region usually grow cacao or bananas. Higher up in the mountain valleys, where the soil is enriched with volcanic ash, there are thriving coffee plantations. The artificially irrigated Pacific coastal plains produce pasture for cattle and have banana plantations.

People and languages

Although the various countries that make up Central America have similar climates and land regions, and also produce similar products, their peoples vary widely. Of the 20 million or so inhabitants of the region, most are of Spanish or Indian ancestry, or a mixture of both. The people of Costa Rica are almost wholly White, whereas nearly all Guatemalans are of mixed ancestry. Panama, Nicaragua and Belize have the largest Black element – up to 40 per cent of the population in some cases.

Central America as a whole has one of the fastest growing populations in the world, but it is unevenly distributed. As in many other parts of the Third World, there is a strong drift to the towns where the standard of living, although often deplorable, is still much higher than in the country areas. Contrasts in living conditions are most plainly seen between densely packed El Salvador and Guatemala, for example, where only 50 per cent of the country is populated. Another stark contrast can be seen between Costa Rica – prosperous, literate and elegant – and Honduras, one of the most poverty-stricken nations in the whole of LATIN AMERICA.

Guatemala. The landscape is extremely mountainous, many of the peaks being extinct volcanoes. Coffee, cotton and sugar cane are the principal cash crops. The people are of mixed European and Amerindian ancestry. Successive military coups since 1945, followed by oppressive governments, resulted in the growth of militant dissident groups whose members kidnapped and ransomed company executives from Europe and the USA to bolster their funds and political objectives. Area: 21,393 sq km;

population: 4,600,000; capital: San Salvador (700,000).

G **Guatemala** is the most northerly of the independent Central American republics. It is bordered by Mexico, Honduras, El Salvador and the Pacific and Atlantic oceans. A high mountain range crosses the country from west to east and includes a number of active volcanoes. Earthquakes are common, and a particularly violent one in 1976 killed 25,000 people and severely damaged the capital, Guatemala City.

About 50% of the people are descended from MAYA IN-DIANS, the remainder being of mixed Spanish and Indian ancestry. The official lan-

Earthquake damage, Guatemala

guage is Spanish. Coffee is the principal export, with sugar, bananas, cotton, beef, and manufactured goods also sold abroad. Guatemala has claimed the self-governing colony of BELIZE since 1821 and broke off diplomatic relations with Britain in 1963 over this issue. Area: 108,889 sq km; population: 7,000,000; capital: Guatemala City (1,300,000).

H **Honduras** is an independent Spanish-speaking republic bordered by Nicaragua, Guatemala, El Salvador and the Atlantic

and Pacific oceans. The land rises from unhealthy tropical coastal swamps to temperate highlands in the interior. Much of the country is traversed by rugged mountains and 75% of the land is covered with valuable pine forests. Honduras is the poorest and least developed nation in Central America, and its capital, Tegucigalpa, is one of the few capital cities in the world without a railway. Most of the people are MESTIZO farmers, growing bananas, coffee, sugar and rice. Bananas are the main export crop, but timber and

The official language spoken throughout the region is Spanish, with the exception of Belize, where it is English. But even there 25 per cent of the people speak Spanish. In Panama many of the people are bilingual, speaking Spanish and English. There are also many thousands of pure-bred Indians who speak their own tribal tongues.

Ways of life

In the rural areas most homes are one- or two-roomed houses made of wood and covered with dried clay, with a thatched roof and earthen floor. Homes in the forested areas may be on stilts with one side left open to provide maximum air circulation. The homes of plantation owners are imposing mansions with acres of ground. Their workers are usually housed in neat, functional huts. Indian communities often own and farm their land communally.

The towns are trading centres where farmers bring their produce and display it in colourful, open-air markets. In addition to food, the Indians sell various handcrafted goods such as pottery, basketware and jewellery. The staple diet is maize and beans, an Indian legacy from the pre-Christian era. This is supplemented with home-grown rice, vegetables and fruit. Meat, when obtainable, is mainly chicken, beef and pork, and is served highly seasoned.

Clothing is simple, functional and suited to the climate. Cotton blouses and long cotton skirts are favoured by the women, who often display a splash of colour with their vivid headscarves and

Below left: There are large areas of poverty in Nicaragua, as this glimpse of a shanty town shows. Most Nicaraguans are descended from white and Indian ancestors. They work on the land growing crops and rearing beef cattle. But their income is pitifully low, and they usually live in primitive shacks.

Below: A colourful religious procession of Toltec Indians in Central America attracts curious sightseers. Today's Indians are the descendants of the pre-Aztec rulers of Mexico. Their faith is based on a fervent blend of serpent and other worship, and Roman Catholicism.

shawls. Men wear cotton shirts and trousers, often with a straw hat as a concession to the fierce sun.

Ninety per cent of the population of Central America is Roman Catholic, but there is complete freedom of worship throughout the region. Many Indians still follow tribal religions or a mixture of Catholic and ancestral practices.

Economy

Most people in the region are farmers. The main export products are bananas, coffee, cacao, rubber, coconuts, and chicle (the main ingredient of chewing gum). For home consumption beef cattle are reared and beans, manioc, coffee, bananas, citrus fruits, rice and wheat are grown.

There is little manufacturing and processing,

frozen meat are also important. Revolutions and warlike gestures against neighbouring El Salvador have marked political developments since 1945. Area: 112,088 sq km; population: 3,500,000; capital: Tegucigalpa (382,900).

L Latin America is a term that covers all the countries of Central and South America, including Mexico. Most of the people are descended from Spanish, Portuguese or French immigrants and, as a result, share a 'Latin' culture. Mexico is

Mayan Temple, Tikal

often regarded as part of North America for geographical purposes.

M Maya Indians at one time inhabited much of eastern Mexico, Belize, Guatemala, El Salvador and Honduras. Their civilization reached its peak between the AD 200s and 800s. They were overcome by the Spaniards in the 1500s and 1600s. They left a rich archaeological heritage, and the ruins of their cities are being excavated from the forests. About 1,500,000 of their descendants survive and still speak the Maya tongue.

Mestizo is a Spanish word to describe somebody of

mixed ancestry, usually of white and American Indian parentage.

Mulatto is a term used to describe a person of mixed white and Black parentage. The child of a mulatto is known as a *quadroon.*

N Nicaragua is the largest country in Central America. It is an independent Spanish-speaking republic lying between Honduras and Costa Rica, with coasts on both the Atlantic and Pacific oceans. About 75% of the people are MES-TIZOS, the remainder being

Indians, Blacks and whites. The *mosquitos,* who are the mixed descendants of Indians and Blacks, live on the Atlantic coast and offshore islands, which were formerly under British protection. They still speak English. Agriculture is the main occupation with coffee, tobacco, sugar and cotton the main crops. The Somoza family ruled the nation, often harshly, almost continuously from the 1930s, but a violent revolution in 1979 succeeded in toppling the regime from power. Area: 130,000 sq km; population:

the few goods that are made being articles of clothing, food, and basic necessities for everyday living. Gold, lead, silver, antimony and copper are mined in small quantities, and some of the forests yield timber of various kinds.

History and culture

Before the Spanish conquest in the 1500s, the west of the region had been ruled by MAYA INDIANS and later by the Toltecs. After some 300 years of Spanish rule, individual states established their independence. The period up to World War II was one of revolution and despotic government for most of these nations, in spite of attempts at Central American unity.

In 1948 all the independent republics joined other Latin American nations and the United States to form the ORGANIZATION OF AMERICAN STATES (OAS) for mutual aid and collaboration. All the states except Belize and Panama formed the CENTRAL AMERICAN COMMON MARKET, joined the Alliance for Progress *(see page 60)* and established a Central American Monetary Union. These steps were taken in the 1960s.

In 1963 the governments of both Guatemala and Honduras were toppled by military takeovers. Honduras returned to constitutional government in 1965, but in 1972 and 1975 there were two more successful takeovers. Guatemala returned to constitutional government in 1966. Guatemala has long claimed sovereignty over what is now Belize.

Above: Bananas make up about 50% of the exports of Honduras and provide the nation's main source of income. The banana industry was developed by United States fruit companies at the end of the 1800s. By the 1930s, Honduras was the world's leading exporter, but crop diseases in the 1940s cut production back to its present level.

In 1964 rioting broke out in Panama over demands for a new PANAMA CANAL ZONE treaty, and Panama broke off diplomatic relations with the United States. The constitution was suspended in Panama in 1968 when military leaders overthrew the government.

In 1969 El Salvador invaded Honduras over the plight of various Salvadoreans living in Honduras. A year later, Salvadorean troops were withdrawn. There was political unrest and violent opposition to the government of El Salvador in the late 1970s.

In 1979 civil war flared in Nicaragua. President Somoza's lengthy dictatorship was toppled by a revolutionary group, the Sandinistas.

Left: The Panama Canal was built by damming a river to form Lake Gatun. A 15-kilometre navigable channel was then cut to Lake Miraflores and Miraflores locks, leading eventually to the Pacific Ocean.

2,500,000; capital: Managua (412,500).

O **Organization of American States (OAS)** is an organization that developed from the International Union of American Republics originally convened in the late 1800s. It provides for collective self-defence and regional co-operation between members. It is made up of 32 Latin American nations plus the USA. All the Central American nations, with the exception of Belize, are members.

Ex-president Somoza

P **Panama** is an independent Spanish-speaking republic occupying the narrowest part of the isthmus (narrow stretch of land) that links North and South America. It is the southernmost of Central American republics and is bordered by Costa Rica and the South American nation of Colombia. Low mountain ranges cross the country and there are fertile green plains between the ranges. More than 50% of the land remains undeveloped because of dense jungle. Most of the people are of mixed white and Black ancestry with a few scattered tribes of Indians living in remote regions. Agriculture is the main occupation, with rice the chief crop. But most of the nation's revenue comes from the rent paid by the USA for the lease of the PANAMA CANAL ZONE. Area: 75,651 sq km; population: 1,932,000; capital: Panama City (467,300).

Panama Canal is a strategic canal that runs through Panama and links the Atlantic with the Pacific Ocean. It is enclosed by a narrow strip of land called the PANAMA CANAL ZONE and was built by the USA in the early 1900s. It is nearly 82 km long and has 12 locks.

Panama Canal Zone is a strip of land, 16 km wide, enclosing the PANAMA CANAL. It was established in 1903 by a pact signed by the USA and Panama which gave the former nation the right to build and operate the canal and govern the zone. It was originally leased in perpetuity, but by a new treaty negotiated in 1978, the USA will hand over control of the canal zone to Panama in the year 2000.

Colourful carnivals and the ostentatious life styles of the rich minority are belied by the miserable poverty in which many South Americans live. The current population explosion is creating problems for the future.

South America

South America is a land of contradictions. It is the fourth largest continent in the world, and although it is about twice the size of the United States it has only about the same number of people. Some of its citizens are among the richest in the world but millions of others are living near to starvation. Physically, the continent possesses some of the driest, wettest, hottest and coldest regions on Earth. There are also barren landscapes that contrast vividly with areas that are among the most fertile in the world. But throughout the continent, South America is a place on the move.

The land
South America is shaped roughly like a vast triangle, with its broad base facing the Caribbean and its apex pointing straight to the

Above: Forest clearance in Amazonia and other parts of Brazil goes on at the rate of about 13,000 sq km a year. This means that within 100 years there will be no forest left. The Brazilian government has launched a number of ambitious communications schemes to open up the heartland of the country, which until now has been clothed with virtually impenetrable rain forest. The Trans-Amazonian Highway is just one of these projects.

Antarctic, less than 1,000 kilometres south of TIERRA DEL FUEGO. The equator bisects the continent almost at its widest point, where Brazil bulges into the South Atlantic Ocean towards Africa. South America is linked to North America by the narrow isthmus of Panama in the north-west.

The land regions of the continent can be conveniently divided into four: the eastern highlands, the central plains, the ANDES and the Pacific coast.

The rivers of the continent are many and varied and include some of the world's greatest waterways. Most of them flow into the Atlantic. The AMAZON, the mightiest river on Earth, drains an area of 6,220,000 square kilometres. It rises in the Peruvian Andes and flows for 6,280 kilometres before reaching the Atlantic. The ORINOCO, with more than 400 tributaries, also flows into the Atlantic after draining a vast area along the borders of COLOMBIA and VENEZUELA and later through the middle of Venezuela. Economically, the RIO DE LA PLATA river system dominates the continent. The estuary, formed by the rivers Uruguay and Parana, cuts into the south-eastern coast of South America. It gives access to the landlocked republic of PARAGUAY, provides excellent harbours for Montevideo and BUENOS AIRES, and unlocks the wealth of the PAMPAS for trading partners in Europe and elsewhere.

South America has few large lakes, but two of these are world famous. Lake TITICACA, on the Bolivian-Peruvian border, is the highest large body of fresh water in the world. It lies in the Andes, nearly 4,000 metres above sea level and covers an area of 8,446 square kilometres. A regular steamship service plies its waters. An even larger body of fresh water is Lake Maracaibo, which covers 16,300 square kilometres in Venezuela. Oil wells on the lake

Reference

A Aconcagua, rising to 6,959 metres, is the highest peak in the western hemisphere. It is situated in the ANDES on the borders of Argentina and Chile.
Amazon, River is the greatest river in the world. Together with its tributaries it drains an area of 6,220,000 sq km that includes much of Brazil and large parts of Colombia, Ecuador, Guyana, Peru and Venezuela. The Amazon rises in the Peru-

vian Andes and flows 6,280 km due east to empty into the Atlantic through a vast delta.

Cocal village, Amazon

Andes is the longest chain of mountains in the world. It runs down the west coast of South America for 8,900 km.

It contains more than 50 peaks that rise to over 6,700 metres and includes many active volcanoes.
Araucanian Indians are a proud tribe of Indians numbering about 300,000 who live in southern Chile and Argentina. Their ancestors were never completely conquered by the Spaniards.
Argentina is an independent Spanish-speaking republic that occupies almost all of the southern part of South America. The ANDES rise majestically in the west forming the frontier with Chile. Argentina also has

borders with Bolivia, Paraguay, Brazil and Uruguay. The hot, humid, sparsely-covered CHACO in the north gives way to the PAMPAS — vast fertile grassy plains in the centre of the country. The sheep-rearing region of PATAGONIA in the south is cold and mountainous. The important estuary of the RIO DE LA PLATA in the north-east separates Argentina from Uruguay. BUENOS AIRES, the capital, stands on its shores. Argentina is the second largest producer of petroleum in South America, after Venezuela. The main

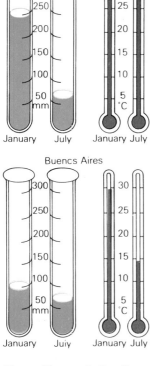

Manaus

January   July   January July

Buenos Aires

January   July   January July

Above: Manaus, in Brazil's Amazon basin, has a rainfall of 240 mm in January compared with only 60 mm in July, but the temperature hardly varies. Buenos Aires, on the other hand, has a rainfall that remains about the same, but a temperature variation of 15°C.

Galapagos Is.

and by the shore exploit the petroleum resources of this area.

Waterfalls are plentiful in South America. Angel Falls, on the River Caroni in south-eastern Venezuela, is the highest in the world. Its swirling waters drop 979 metres. The Kukenaam Falls, also in Venezuela, has a drop of 610 metres. The Iguacu Falls, on the borders of BRAZIL and ARGENTINA, provides a staggering volume of water, the potential of which for hydro-electric power has yet to be fully used.

Among the major groups of islands are the GALAPAGOS ISLANDS. They belong to Ecuador and lie 960 kilometres off the Ecuadorean coast. Because of their comparative isolation, they are a naturalist's paradise, with unique specimens of animal and plant life. Tierra del Fuego, the

exports are agricultural products including huge amounts of beef. The people are mainly of European descent. Area 2,776,889 sq km; population: 27,100,000; capital: Buenos Aires.

Atacama Desert, situated in northern Chile, is believed to be the driest desert in the world. Among its many minerals are large deposits of sodium nitrate and copper.

Aymara Indians are a significant tribe of Indians who live in the highlands of Peru and Bolivia. Nearly 1.5 million of them survive, eking out an existence under harsh conditions.

B Bolivia is a landlocked, independent Spanish-speaking republic in the west central part of the continent. It is bordered by Brazil, Paraguay, Argentina, Chile and Peru. In the west, two wide ranges of the ANDES enclose a high plateau, the *altiplano,* where most of the people live. In spite of rich deposits of gold, silver and tin, Bolivia is one of the poorest nations in South America, and the peasant farmers barely make a living.

Most of the people are Indians, and 50% of them can neither read nor write. There are two capitals – Sucre, the

Aymara child, Bolivia

official capital (126,700), and La Paz (725,400), the highest capital city in the world and where the seat of government is housed. Area: 1,089,581 sq km; population: 6,645,800.

Brasilia became the new capital of BRAZIL in 1960, replacing RIO DE JANEIRO 970 km to the south-east. Built on a plateau, the Brazilian architects Lucio Costa and Oscar Niemeyer were chiefly responsible for the brilliant design of the city. Population: 600,000.

Brazil is the largest country in South America and the fifth largest in the world. It occupies the north-eastern half of the continent and shares a frontier with every South American nation except Chile and Ecuador. The northern and western parts are heavily forested and are almost wholly drained by the River AMAZON and its tributaries. The north-eastern region, formerly prosperous, is arid and depressed. The temperate southern region, where most of the people live, boasts about 75% of the nation's agriculture and industry. In spite of Brazil's

nearest South America approaches to Antarctica, is a group of islands owned partly by CHILE and partly by Argentina. Despite their bleakness they are valuable for sheep rearing. The FALKLAND ISLANDS (*Las Islas Malvinas* to Argentina) are a British Crown Colony 480 kilometres off the Argentine coast in the south-eastern Atlantic. For a long time Argentina has disputed British sovereignty of the islands and claims ownership of them.

Climate and vegetation

South America's climate is as varied as its peoples and its geography. But although the weather can be stiflingly hot or bitterly cold, the unbearable extremes that are sometimes found in the United States and Canada, or in parts of Asia, for example, are unknown. The general climate for the whole continent is warm, with the exception of the Andes, where it is always cold. In the lowlands around the equator it is always hot and humid. The continent is drenched by rain-bearing winds from both the Atlantic and the Pacific oceans. The northern areas to the east of the Andes are watered by the Atlantic trade winds, while to the west of the mountains moist westerlies keep central and southern Chile well supplied with rain.

Above: This is one of the few oases in the barren Atacama Desert, said to be the world's driest region. No rain has fallen there for many years. It lies in northern Chile and extends southwards from the Peruvian border for about 1,000 km. Its large deposits of sulphur, copper, nitrates and borax make up most of Chile's wealth.

Left: The high Andes are bleak and windswept. Many regions are covered with glaciers that cut deep valleys in the rocky slopes on their way down to the Pacific Ocean. Volcanoes and earthquakes are common. A few hardy Indians defy the elements and have established small communities there.

The extremely arid coastal lands of PERU and northern Chile result from the action of the icy Humboldt Current. This sweeps up the Pacific Ocean from the Antarctic and cools the lower atmosphere, thus preventing rain from forming.

A huge amount of South America is covered in virgin rain forest. This includes northern and western parts of Brazil, parts of the Guianas, ECUADOR, Colombia, Venezuela, northern Peru, BOLIVIA, Paraguay and northern Argentina. Practically the whole of the Andean region is ice-covered rock or bleak, featureless desert. Scrubland and swamp dominate the central plains of Paraguay and northern Argentina. And windswept, rocky plateaux, covered with coarse grass and stunted trees, are features of PATAGONIA, in the lee of the Andes in the south-western part of the continent. In the bulge of Brazil there is a vast, cruel region of scrub and thorn where periodic droughts have left their mark on vegetation and population alike. The lowland plains of southern Brazil, URUGUAY and much of Argentina are mostly fertile and temperate, and form the agricultural heart of the continent.

Peoples and languages

The people of South America are made up of Indians, Blacks, Whites and mixtures of these. Indian influence is strongest in Paraguay and Bolivia and in parts of Colombia, Ecuador, Peru,

vast potential wealth from its natural resources, development has been hampered by poor communications. As a result, many people live in miserable conditions. Brazil is the only Portuguese-speaking nation in South America and most of the people are descended from the original Portuguese colonists, but there are also large numbers of Negroes and MESTIZOS *(see page 51)*. Area: 8,511,695 sq km; population: 121,409,000; capital: BRASILIA.

Buenos Aires is the capital of ARGENTINA. It is the second largest city in the southern hemisphere. It lies 274 km inland from the Atlantic on the west bank of the RIO DE LA PLATA estuary. Population: 8,966,800.

C **Chaco** (or Gran Chaco) is the name given to a wild, sparsely-inhabited plateau in the centre of the continent. It extends across parts of Paraguay, Bolivia and northern and western Argentina. Oil, timber and cotton are the main products. Bolivia and Paraguay fought over the area between 1932 and 1935.

Chile is an independent Spanish-speaking republic that runs like a narrow

Ex-president Allende, Chile

ribbon down the west coast of the continent between the ANDES and the Pacific. It shares frontiers with Argentina, Bolivia and Peru. In the north is the mineral-rich ATACAMA DESERT; in the centre, a highly populated fertile region; and farther south a wild, often beautiful land of lakes and mountains that includes the bleak plateau of PATAGONIA and the cold islands of TIERRA DEL FUEGO, both of which are shared with Argentina. Most Chileans are MESTIZOS *(see page 51)*, but there are also many European immigrants.

ARAUCANIAN INDIANS, in the centre and the south, make up about 2% of the population. Minerals, especially copper, constitute the main exports. Just over 30% of the people work on the land, and there are a number of important vineyards producing excellent wines. Area: 756,945 sq km; population: 11,207,000; capital: Santiago (4,500,000).

Colombia is an independent Spanish-speaking republic in the north-west of the continent. It is bordered by Venezuela, Brazil, Peru, Ecuador, Panama and the

Chile and Brazil. It is negligible in Uruguay and Argentina. The old taunt that the Spanish *conquistadores* 'first fell on their knees and then on the Indian' is sadly true in respect of the latter two countries, where the local inhabitants were virtually wiped out, often victims also of European diseases.

On the *altiplano* (a harsh, bleak, upland plateau) of Bolivia and Peru, some 500,000 sad-faced AYMARA INDIANS subsist on a sparse diet of potatoes, wheat and barley. They also eat the meat of alpacas and llamas, herds of which they keep, and fish which they catch from Lake Titicaca. About 300,000 ARAUCANIAN INDIANS farm parts of southern Chile. Their ancestors resisted Spanish occupation forces so successfully that these Indians remained independent as late as the 1800s when Chilean armies in the west and an Argentine force from the east finally subdued them.

The many Andean groups to be seen today are all that remain of an earlier INCA Empire that may have totalled 7,000,000 people. The Spaniards reduced them to about 2,000,000, but their culture revived to the extent that today

Above: Peruvian Indians have traditionally been skilled weavers. They work with wool and wear it often because of the sub-zero temperatures that are common in the mountainous regions where they live. The men wear *ponchos*, blankets with a hole in the middle, worn over the shoulders. The women often have gaily coloured blankets slung over their backs.

Left: The rapidly dwindling number of Indians who live in the densely forested areas of South America are hunters. Some use their skills to spear fish; others go hunting and fishing with bow and arrow. The tips of the spears and arrows are often tipped with *curare,* a deadly vegetable poison, or with the even more potent venom of the tiny arrow-poison frog.

about 6,000,000 of their descendants speak their language — Quechuan.

The last major group of indigenous peoples is made up of tribes in the rain forests of Brazil, the Guianas, eastern Bolivia and Peru, and southern Venezuela and Colombia. Sadly, they seem to be doomed by advancing civilization with its forest clearance schemes, the introduction of hitherto unknown 'western' diseases and a general indifference to the fate of 'non-productive' peoples.

Negroes were imported into parts of South America to work originally in the sugar cane fields because local Indian labour had become scarce through illness and harsh treatment. Slave ships ferried able-bodied workers from Africa in their millions. In spite of their inhuman circumstances, the Negroes brought a gaiety and a sense of rhythm and music that contrasted with those reflecting the melancholy of the Indian tribes. This attitude is characteristic of much of the Brazilian's outlook today where many of the Negroes originally settled.

The southern and south-eastern parts of the continent became the preserve of the white

---

Pacific and Atlantic oceans. Much of the land is mountainous. Almost 70% of the people are MESTIZOS *(see page 51)*, the remainder being whites of European descent, Negroes and Amerindians. Most of them depend on agriculture with coffee as the main export crop. However, Colombia is also rich in precious metals, emeralds and oil. Area: 1,138,914 sq km; population: 27,296,000; capital: Bogota (4,200,000).

D Devil's Island is an island in the Caribbean

Sea off the coast of French Guiana. It was once a notorious French penal colony (1852-1938).

Devil's Island

E Ecuador is an independent Spanish-speaking republic in the north-west corner of the continent. It is bordered by Colombia, Peru and the Pacific Ocean. The ANDES run north–south through the country, almost cutting it in half. Most of the people live in the sheltered valleys. One of the poorest nations in South America, Ecuador relies mainly on the export of bananas for its income, although the economy is expected to benefit from newly discovered oilfields. Only about 10% of the people are white; about

the same proportion are Negroes and the remainder are almost equally divided between pure-blooded Indians and MESTIZOS *(see page 51)*. Area: 270,670 sq km; population: 8,000,000; capital: Quito (800,800).

F Falkland Islands are a group of islands in the south Atlantic, lying 600 km off the coast of Argentina. They are a British Crown Colony made up of 2 large and about 200 smaller islands. They have long been claimed by Argentina, where they are known as *Las Islas*

Malvinas. The islands are rocky and wind-swept, their inhabitants relying mostly on sheep rearing for a living. Area: 11,961 sq km; population: 2,000; capital: Port Stanley (1,200).

French Guiana is a French overseas department on the north-east coast of the continent. It is bordered by Brazil, Surinam and the Atlantic. The densely forested interior gives way to a flat, treeless, narrow coastal strip where almost all the population lives. Most of the people speak French and have full French citizenship. The main

immigrants, almost all from Europe. Argentina, Uruguay and southern Brazil were always dominated by Whites, but since the mid-1900s they have become increasingly so. The temperate Mediterranean climate and almost unlimited opportunities for comparatively quick wealth in agriculture and industry have tempted millions from war-torn Europe and the Middle East.

The prevailing language throughout South America, with the exception of Brazil, is Spanish. Portuguese is the official language in Brazil. English is widely spoken and is a compulsory subject as a second language in most schools. In GUYANA (formerly British Guiana), SURINAM, and the French overseas department of FRENCH GUIANA, the official languages are English, Dutch and French, respectively. In addition millions of Indians speak their own tribal languages. This is particularly true of the GUARANI Indians in Paraguay, where Guarani shares the status of official language with Spanish.

Ways of life

Most people who have never been to South America have a mistaken, glamorized idea of life

Left: Sheep farming is a major occupation in Patagonia — a dry, windswept plateau in the south of the continent. Most of Patagonia lies in Argentina but the western fringe belongs to Chile. A legacy from the large numbers of Welsh settlers who arrived in Patagonia in the late 1800s is that Welsh is still spoken in some of the towns scattered along the length of the 1,600-km plateau.

Above: The *gaucho,* or South American cowboy, is one of the national symbols of Argentina and Uruguay. Today largely a traditional figure paraded for the tourists, he at one time made up the main workforce of the huge *estancias* (cattle ranches) of the pampas. A hard-bitten character and superb rider, he dressed in a flamboyant shirt and scarf and baggy trousers supported by a wide silver belt.

in the continent. Many have heard of its exciting, colourful carnivals, and they also know the unique rhythms of its dances, such as the samba. But this, of course, is not a complete picture. Most South Americans live in miserable poverty. Food, clothing and housing are still extremely limited. A few rich white people live in great luxury, own vast lands and have virtually the power of life and death over most of their servants. Many children cannot read or write. Almost every government is a military dictatorship.

---

export is bauxite, of which there are large deposits. Area: 91,000 sq km; population: 66,700; capital: Cayenne (35,700).

G **Galapagos Islands** are a group of volcanic islands in the Pacific, lying 970 km west of Ecuador, to which they belong. They are noted for their unique animals and plants, including a species of giant tortoise. The naturalist Charles Darwin (1809-82) made a special study of the islands in 1835. Area: 7,431 sq km; population: 3,800.

Guarani are a tribe of Indians, most of whom live in Paraguay. Although decreasing in numbers, about 200,000 survive. Guarani and Spanish are the official languages in Paraguay.
Guyana, formerly British Guiana, is an independent republic within the Commonwealth, lying between Venezuela, with a disputed frontier, and Surinam in the north-east corner of the continent. A densely populated, flat, coastal region gives way to tropical rain forest and savanna, which hamper communications. About

50% of the population are of East Indian origin while the remainder are of African descent, pure-blooded Indians and MESTIZOS *(see page 51).*

Rice harvest, Guyana

Sugar, rice and coconuts are the main products, but there are also rich deposits of bauxite. English is the official language. Area: 214,970 sq km; population: 839,400; capital: Georgetown (193,600)

I **Inca Indians** were an important group of Amerindians who came out of the Peruvian highlands in the AD 1200s to found an empire that included present day Peru and parts of Ecuador, Chile, Bolivia and Argentina. The Incas were excellent organizers and reached a high

standard in architecture and in crafts such as jewellery-making and pottery. They were defeated and destroyed in the 1500s by the Spanish *conquistador* Francisco Pizarro (c. 1478-1541).

L **Latin American Free Trade Association** (LAFTA) is an economic organization founded in 1960 for the purpose of ending trade restrictions among member states. These are: Argentina, Bolivia, Brazil, Chile, Colombia, Ecuador, Mexico, Paraguay, Peru, Uruguay and Venezuela.

Most of South America is under-populated in spite of having the swiftest population growth in the world. One of its greatest problems is the increasingly fast drift from the country areas to the towns. Peasants apparently prefer to share their wretchedness in overcrowded hovels than to face starvation in the bleak emptiness of the countryside. This aggravates the housing and food crises facing the cities.

It is true that fiestas and colourful carnivals abound. But those taking part may go into debt for years to pay for their entertainment, and there may be other hazards. In the famous Rio four-day carnival of 1979, for example, at least 100 people were murdered and 27 killed in traffic accidents.

City life is similar to that of any modern North American or European city. Life in the country is often brutish and short. Shelter is usually a primitive hut, lacking most amenities, including sanitation. Food consists mainly of vegetables (often rice and beans) with meat thrown in when it can be obtained. But the *gauchos* (cowboys) and *peones* (labourers) of the pampas are better off in this respect — they are among the greatest meat-eaters in the world. Coffee is the favourite drink, with *yerba mate* (Paraguayan tea) and hot chocolate also popular.

Clothing is adapted to the climate. Thin but colourful cotton garments are worn in the tropics, and heavier sheepskin or llama-skin wraps by those living in the colder, more mountainous areas.

Above: Carnival in Rio de Janeiro is a unique opportunity for the poorer people of the city to show off their fancy dress in 14 days and nights of music, dancing, feasting, drinking, fun and frolic in the streets.

Right: In the processing of coffee from berries to beans, the ripe coffee berries are first placed in a receiving tank. They are then pulped and later fermented. After being washed to get rid of waste matter, they are dried and hulled and finally packed in sacks ready for export.

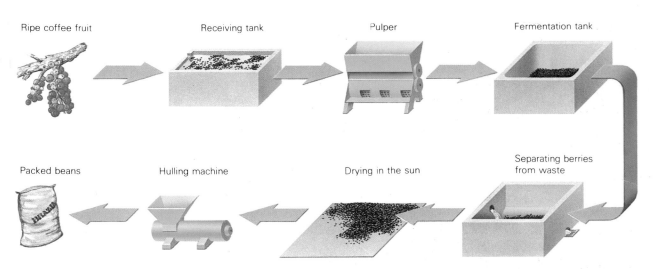

Ripe coffee fruit   Receiving tank   Pulper   Fermentation tank

Packed beans   Hulling machine   Drying in the sun   Separating berries from waste

M Mato Grosso is a densely forested, still largely unexplored state of western Brazil. The name means 'great forest'.

O Orinoco, River is one of the great river systems of the continent. It rises in Venezuela near the Brazilian border, flowing north-westwards and later east-wards for 2,062 km before emptying into the Atlantic through a wide delta on the Venezuelan coast close to Trinidad. Part of its course forms the border between Venezuela and Colombia.

P Pampas is a huge, grassy plain in central Argentina. It provides excellent pasture for sheep and

Indian of the Mato Grosso

cattle and forms the basis of Argentina's agricultural economy.

Pan American Highway is a system of highways 47,516 km long that runs from the USA-Mexico border to southern Chile. Offshoots connect the east and west coasts of South America and also link the capitals of 17 Latin American nations.

Paraguay is one of two landlocked, independent Spanish-speaking nations, the other being Bolivia. Paraguay has borders with Argentina, Bolivia and Brazil, and its outlet to the Atlantic is via the Parana and Paraguay rivers, flowing partly through Argentina into the RIO DE LA PLATA estuary. Most of the people are extremely poor and rely on exports of timber, meat, cotton, coffee and tobacco for their income. There is a large GUARANI INDIAN population, with two official languages, Spanish and Guarani. Area: 406,752 sq km; population: 3,029,000; capital: Asuncion (660,300).

Patagonia is a mainly desert region in the south of the continent. It is shared between Chile and Argenti-

na but usually refers to the Argentine portion. Many Welsh settlers arrived in the 1800s and their descendants are still numerous. Sheep-rearing is the main occupation but the region also has substantial deposits of coal, iron and oil.

Peru is the third largest nation of the continent, after Brazil and Argentina. An independent Spanish-speaking republic, situated on the north-west coast, it is bordered by Ecuador, Colombia, Brazil, Bolivia and Chile. Peru was for centuries the ancient home of the

Economy

South America is basically an agricultural continent. Coffee from such countries as Colombia and Brazil, and cereal and livestock products from the pampas are exported to North America and Europe in exchange for manufactured articles. But the potential mineral and forest wealth of the continent, and even its agriculture, have as yet hardly been developed. Lack of capital, enormous distances and hostile terrain, and the uneven distribution of wealth are contributory factors. However, there were signs at the end of the 1970s that Brazil, at least, was fully awake to its vast potential and was beginning to make giant strides towards becoming an economic superpower.

History and culture

South America consists of 12 independent nations and two European possessions. The independent nations are Argentina, Bolivia, Brazil, Chile, Colombia, Ecuador, Guyana, Paraguay, Peru, Surinam, Uruguay and Venezuela. The others are French Guiana (an overseas department of France) and the Falkland Islands (a British colony). Most of the nations were originally colonized by Spain, but Brazil was colonized by the Portuguese, Guyana by Britain and Surinam by the Netherlands. All except Guyana and Surinam achieved their independence in the 1800s, for the most part modelling their written constitutions on that of the United States.

After a depressingly familiar pattern of revolutions and dictatorships, military regimes clamped down in most parts of the continent in

Above: Caracas, the capital and largest city of Venezuela, is a product of that nation's booming oil industry.

Below: The Chuquicamata copper mine in northern Chile is believed to be the world's largest single copper-mining property.

the years following World War II. In Argentina President Juan Peron, with the help of his wife Eva, spent a flamboyant 10-year dictatorship alienating the Church, the army and the press, and was finally forced into inglorious exile. Later military governments trod an uneasy path fighting extremists from the left and the right. Much the same applied to the army men who ruled neighbouring Uruguay, who were forced into dubious undemocratic methods in their battles against the Tupamaro urban guerillas in the early 1970s.

Chile scored a first by democratically electing a Marxist government under the presidency of Salvador Allende Gossens (1908–73). He was eventually defeated by galloping inflation, strikes and a military uprising in 1973, during which he lost his life. Politics swung full circle, and Chile was thereafter governed by a right-wing military group.

After increasing apathy among politicians in the 1960s and fears of a communist takeover, the army stepped in to rule Brazil with a succession of generals. They suspended many of the citizens'

INCAS and relics of their empire are much in evidence, especially in the city of Cuzco and in the 'lost city' of Machu Picchu, discovered in 1911. Most of today's people are either descended from the Incas or are MESTIZOS *(see page 51)*. Agriculture and fishing are important, and the country's great mineral wealth is fully exploited. Area: 1,285,216 sq km; population: 18,085,000; capital: Lima (4,121,500).

R **Rio de Janeiro** is the second largest city in Brazil and the former capital.

Huancayo Indians, Peru

It lost that status to newly-founded BRASILIA in 1960. With its fine beaches and mountain backdrop, Rio is one of the world's most beautiful cities and a major seaport. Population: 5,442,600.
Rio de la Plata is a major estuary on the south-east coast of the continent formed by the Parana and Uruguay rivers flowing into the Atlantic. Montevideo, capital of Uruguay, stands on the east bank facing BUENOS AIRES, the capital of Argentina, on the west bank. The English name, River

Plate, is a mistranslation of the Spanish 'River of Silver'.

S **Sao Paulo** is the largest city in Brazil and one of the fastest-growing in the world. It lies 386 km south of RIO DE JANEIRO and 48 km inland from the Atlantic. Population: 7,513,600.
Surinam, formerly Dutch Guiana, is a small independent nation in the north-east corner of the continent. It is bordered by the Atlantic, French Guiana, Guyana and Brazil. The country is divided into a flat coastal plain, an upland plateau and a heavily

forested inland area watered by fast-flowing rivers. Most of the people are of Asian, Negro or Creole (a person born in the country but of foreign descent) parentage. They live by growing bananas, sugar cane, groundnuts, coconuts, timber and citrus fruits, but bauxite is the chief export. The official language is Dutch. Area: 163,265 sq km; population: 500,000; capital: Paramaribo (200,000).

T **Tierra del Fuego** is a group of islands lying at the southernmost tip of the

Above: Brasilia, the recently built new capital of Brazil, is an architect's dream. The view shows the imposing Congress Buildings. The city was designed in the shape of an aeroplane by the Brazilian architect Oscar Niemayer.

The United States, having for a long time kept a fatherly eye on its junior continent to the south, found itself faced with increased hostility and charges of 'Big Brother' interference. Nevertheless, it has extended substantial economic aid to its less fortunate neighbours in the period since 1945. The Alliance for Progress was the name of a development programme launched in 1961 by President Kennedy. Co-signatories with the United States were 19 Latin American countries to whom the United States pledged $20,000 million in loans from 1961 to 1971. The money was to improve medical and educational facilities, establish low-cost housing, redistribute land more equitably and reform taxation. Some, but not all, of these reforms have been carried out.

All the South American nations, except Guyana and Surinam, became charter members of the United Nations but this did not entirely abolish international friction from the continent. Apart from Argentina's long-standing grievance against Britain over the sovereignty of the Falkland Islands, a potentially more serious quarrel developed between Argentina and Chile over the ownership of part of Tierra del Fuego. So critical did the situation become, that both nations were reported to be mobilizing their armed forces in the area at the end of the 1970s.

democratic rights but kept a firm hand on the economy throughout the 1970s and appeared to be on course for a prosperous future in the 1980s and beyond.

In Peru, a bloodless coup in 1975 installed South America's only left-wing military dictatorship.

Right: An Argentine *estancia* (large agricultural estate) is made up of many parts. These may differ in detail but substantially follow the pattern as shown. The most imposing house belongs to the owner, or manager, and his family. Humbler quarters are inhabited by tenant farmers and the inevitable *peons* (hired hands). Crops surround the cattle corrals, and power for the complex is provided by wind pumps and water tanks.

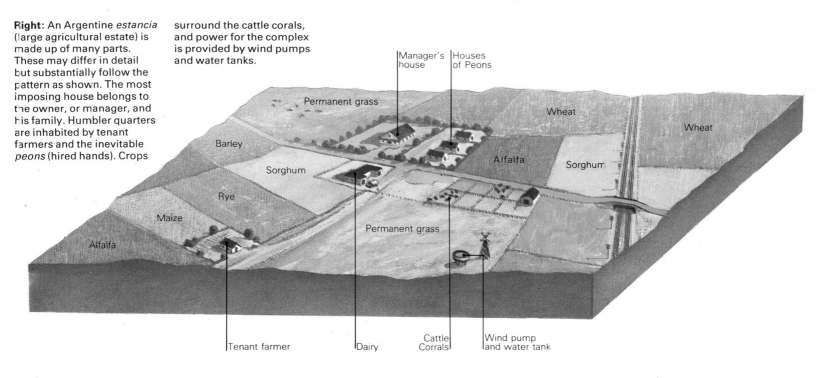

continent. Ownership is divided between Argentina (the eastern islands) and Chile (the western islands), though the boundary is in dispute. The southern tip of the archipelago is called Cape Horn. Area: 69,508 sq km; population: 20,000.
Titicaca, Lake is the highest large body of fresh water in the world. It lies in the ANDES at a height of 3,812 metres on the borders of Bolivia and Peru, and covers 8,446 sq km.

U Uruguay, one of the continent's smallest countries, is an independent Spanish-speaking nation on the east coast. Almost all the people are white, of Spanish or Italian stock and, unusually for South America, nearly all of them can read and write. Many people live in or around Montevideo, the capital and only large town. Agriculture is the main industry, with cattle and sheep most important, and flax, wheat and rice are the chief crops. Uruguay has had a long history of stable democracy, although tarnished in the 1970s with allegations of torture. Advanced social re-

forms were begun as long ago as 1903. Area: 177,508 sq km; population: 3,250,000; capital: Montevideo (1,303,500).

V Venezuela is an independent Spanish-speaking nation on the north coast of the continent. It is bordered by Colombia, Brazil, Guyana and the Caribbean Sea. The land can be divided into 4 distinct regions: the coastal lowlands, the Guiana Highlands, the mountainous north end of the ANDES, and the ORINOCO basin. Most of the people are

Shanty, Venezuela

a mixture of Amerindians, descendants of the original Spanish settlers, and post-World War II European immigrants. About 80% of the nation's income comes from petroleum (Venezuela is the fifth largest producer of oil in the world). Other important exports include iron ore, cocoa, coffee, cotton, rice, sugar, fruit and fish. Area: 912,050 sq km; population: 13,943,200; capital: Caracas (2,802,000).

Many superb West Indian islands are holiday havens for foreign tourists. But the spirit of independence and all that this means in terms of economic progress is alive in the hearts of modern West Indians.

West Indies

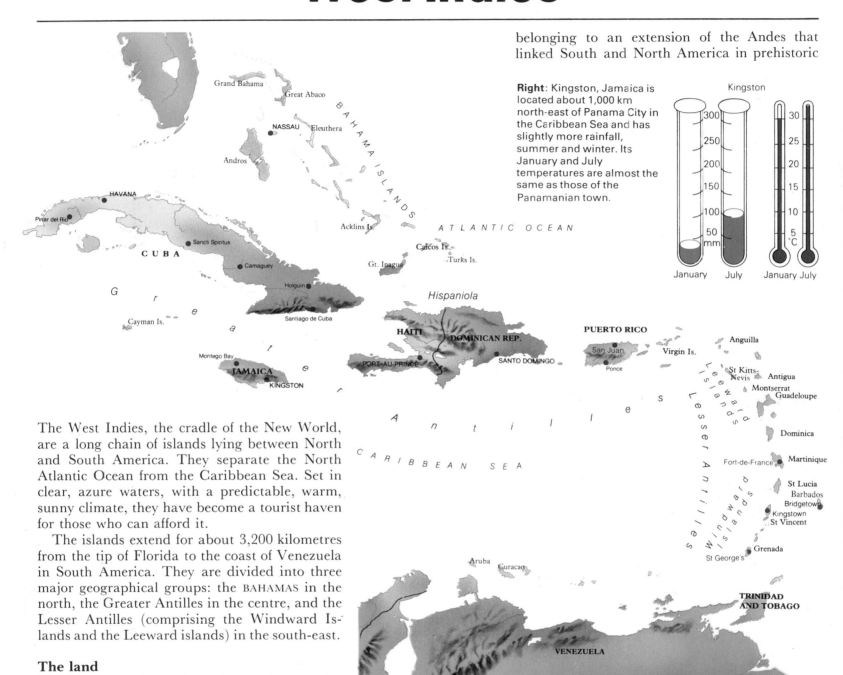

belonging to an extension of the Andes that linked South and North America in prehistoric

Right: Kingston, Jamaica is located about 1,000 km north-east of Panama City in the Caribbean Sea and has slightly more rainfall, summer and winter. Its January and July temperatures are almost the same as those of the Panamanian town.

The West Indies, the cradle of the New World, are a long chain of islands lying between North and South America. They separate the North Atlantic Ocean from the Caribbean Sea. Set in clear, azure waters, with a predictable, warm, sunny climate, they have become a tourist haven for those who can afford it.

The islands extend for about 3,200 kilometres from the tip of Florida to the coast of Venezuela in South America. They are divided into three major geographical groups: the BAHAMAS in the north, the Greater Antilles in the centre, and the Lesser Antilles (comprising the Windward Islands and the Leeward islands) in the south-east.

The land
The islands are the peaks of drowned mountains

Reference

A **Anguilla** is a small island in the Leeward group that reverted to British colonial status after briefly joining ST KITTS-NEVIS to form a self-governing state in 1967. Area: 91 sq km; population: 6,500.
Antigua is a self-governing, volcanic and coral island in the Leeward group, scheduled to become completely independent in 1979. It includes the nearby islands of Barbuda and Re-

donda. The main industries are cotton, sugar and tourism. Area: 280 sq km; population: 75,000; capital: St John's (24,900).

Antigua market

Arawak Indians were the first Indians encountered by the Spanish *conquistadores*. They then inhabited the Bahamas and Greater Antilles, and probably came from the Amazon Basin.

B **Bahamas** are a group of about 700 islands extending for about 1,000 km between Florida and Cuba, and forming an independent sovereign state. About 85% of the people are Blacks. Tourism is the main industry. Area: 13,935 sq km; population: 241,500; capital: Nassau (138,000).

Barbados is an independent island in the Windward group. Most of the people are English-speaking Blacks who rely on tourism, fishing and sugar for their income. Area: 431 sq km; population: 264,800; capital: Bridgetown (9,400).

C **Carib Indians** were a fierce tribe who inhabited the Lesser Antilles when discovered by Europeans. They fought off the Spanish but succumbed to the French and British. Their descendants are found in Dominica, St Vincent and

Central America (to which they were deported from St Vincent).
Cayman Islands are 3 small islands that lie about 288 km north-west of Jamaica. Uninteresting geographically, this British colony is known internationally as a tax-free haven. Its people are unique in the Caribbean in that they are descendants of Scottish farmers and shipwrecked pirates. Area: 259 sq km; population: 14,000; capital: George Town (4,000).
Cuba, an independent Marxist republic, is the largest island in the West Indies.

times. Many of these islands are volcanic but some are formed of coral. Most are mountainous, with lush, tropical vegetation, fertile soil and sparkling, inviting beaches.

Climate and vegetation

The islands enjoy mild winters along the coasts but inland, on the higher ground, temperatures can fall sharply. All the islands receive the trade winds. On the north-eastern shores the full force of the Atlantic surf comes rolling in, but on the western side the beaches are well protected. The rainy season extends from August to October and during that time there is a very real danger of hurricanes.

Peoples and languages

The West Indies are a melting pot of many races and nationalities. There are many Blacks, descendants of African slaves taken there by Europeans from the 1500s to the 1800s to work on the sugar plantations. These and other races have intermarried with Indians such as CARIBS and ARAWAKS to produce distinctive cultures.

In earlier days the West Indies were fought over by the major European powers, with free-ranging buccaneers capturing treasure-laden galleons as they sailed back to Europe from South America. The results of these international squabbles can be seen today in the Spanish cultures of CUBA, PUERTO RICO and the DOMINI-

Above: A street market in Jamaica offers a motley assortment of fruits and vegetables for sale. Bananas, plantains, citrus fruits, coconuts, allspice, ginger, and arrowroot are included in the display.

Below: A palm beach on Guadeloupe. An overseas French department, Guadeloupe is made up of 2 main and 5 smaller islands. The main islands are called Guadeloupe or Basse-Terre, and Grande-Terre.

CAN REPUBLIC; the French influence seen in MARTINIQUE, GUADELOUPE and the independent Black republic of HAITI; the Swedish influence in St Barthelemy; the Danish in St Thomas and St Croix; the Dutch in the NETHERLANDS ANTILLES; and the British in such islands as the Bahamas, JAMAICA, TRINIDAD AND TOBAGO, BARBADOS and others. In addition, later immigrants from China, India and the East Indies have all helped to swell the polyglot population.

Ways of life

Most of the people are farmers or fishermen. In spite of poor wages, high unemployment and the resulting low standard of living on many of the islands, the people generally adopt a fairly light-hearted, leisurely attitude towards life, helped no doubt by the soporific qualities of climate and scenery. Although most of the people are officially Roman Catholic, there are large enclaves of specific Protestant faiths, including Methodists, Seventh Day Adventists and Baptists, on some islands.

Economy

Agriculture and tourism are the two major industries of the West Indies. Sugar cane is the most important crop, in which Cuba leads, but almost all the islands harvest large quantities. Tobacco is another major source of revenue, especially for Cuba, Puerto Rico, Haiti and the Dominican Republic. Bananas and citrus fruits are grown on nearly all the islands. Among other

Most of the land is gently rolling, with fertile valleys and plains. Hurricanes are frequent. Sugar makes up 80% of the country's exports, and tobacco is also grown. About 75% of the people are white. The official language is Spanish. Area: 114,524 sq km; population: 10,100,000; capital: Havana (2,094,000).

D **Dominica** is an independent island nation in the Windward group. Most of the people, descended from African slaves, speak a French dialect, although the

official language is English. The chief crops include bananas, citrus fruits and tobacco. Area: 750 sq km; population: 79,500; capital: Roseau (12,400).

Dominican Republic is an independent Spanish-speaking republic that makes up the eastern part of the island of HISPANIOLA. The people, mainly MULATTOS *(see page 51),* farm the mountainous land to produce sugar, coffee and fruits. Nickel and bauxite are becoming increasingly important. Area: 48,442 sq km; population: 5,130,000; capi-

tal: Santo Domingo (1,063,000).

G **Grenada** is an independent English-speaking republic that lies 137 km north of Trinidad. It consists of the island of Grenada and the smaller islands of the southern Grenadines. The people depend almost entirely on agriculture. Area: 344 sq km; population: 115,000; capital: St George's (12,000).

Guadeloupe is an overseas department of France situated in the Windward Islands. It is made up of the

islands of Basse-Terre, Guadeloupe, Grande-Terre and smaller islands. Most of the people are dependent on rum, sugar, bananas and

'Papa Doc' Duvalier, Haiti

tourism. They speak a French dialect. Area: 1,780 sq km; population: 383,000; capital: Pointe-à-Pitre (42,700).

H **Haiti** is the world's oldest independent Negro republic. A mountainous, densely-populated country, it makes up the western third of HISPANIOLA. Most of the people, descended from African slaves, speak French and make a living by growing bananas, rice, sugar cane and tobacco. VOODOO is widely practised. Area: 27,750 sq km;

crops, for export or home consumption, are sisal, cacao, coffee, cotton and vegetables. Some livestock is reared in the Bahamas, the VIRGIN ISLANDS, Trinidad and Tobago and the Dominican Republic. Molasses and rum are by-products from the many sugar-refining plants. Fishing brings substantial catches around most of the islands, but especially in the Bahamas. Bauxite is mined extensively in Jamaica, and there are large quantities of natural asphalt and petroleum in Trinidad.

History and culture

When Christopher Columbus (1451–1506) arrived in the West Indies in 1492 he was greeted by Arawak and Carib Indian inhabitants. Descendants of the former have long since

Right: Pitch Lake, in Trinidad, is a natural lake of asphalt that lies in the southwestern part of the island. It has an area of more than 46 hectares and was discovered by Sir Walter Raleigh in 1595.

Below: Processed sugar for export is loaded on to boats at a Haitian port. Sugar cane is grown in the interior of the island and processed in the capital, Port-au-Prince. Coffee and sisal are the only other 2 products that are grown in any quantity.

vanished, as have those of many of their Spanish conquerors. The West Indies became a battleground for trade-hungry European powers in the 1600s and 1700s. Later, vast numbers of African slaves were imported to work on the sugar and tobacco plantations. Their descendants today form the bulk of the islands' population.

After World War II, there arose the usual procession of petty dictators who almost inevitably accompanied the setting up of independent states from colonial rule. In Haiti, Francois Duvalier, a country doctor, became president in 1957. From then until his death in 1971, he ruled as absolute dictator by means of terror and superstition. His son, Jean-Claude, succeeded him as president-for-life on his father's death.

In 1959, Cuban dictator Fulgencio Batista was ousted by Marxist revolutionary Fidel Castro.

population; 5,000,000; capital: Port-au-Prince (566,000). **Hispaniola** is the second largest island in the West Indies. It lies between Cuba and Puerto Rico. The land is divided between HAITI and the DOMINICAN REPUBLIC. Area: 76,480 sq km.

J Jamaica is an independent island nation lying 145 km south of Cuba. A beautiful mountainous country, it is one of the world's leading producers of aluminium ores. The people, more than 90% of whom are of African descent, rely also on tourism and agriculture for a living. Jamaica is a member of the Commonwealth. Area: 10,962 sq km; population: 2,200,000; capital: Kingston (552,000).

M Martinique is an overseas department of France consisting of a volcanic island in the Windward group. The highest peak is Mont Pelee, an active volcano that erupted disastrously in 1902. Most of the people are Blacks or MULATTOS *(see page 51)*, and speak French. They export rum, sugar, fruit, tobacco and vegetables. Area: 1,100 sq km; population: 339,800; capital: Fort-de-France (124,800).
Montserrat, one of the Leeward Islands, is a British colony. It rejected self-government in 1966. The mountainous, volcanic land is intensively cultivated and planted mostly with cotton. Area: 98 sq km; population: 13,800; capital: Plymouth (1,400).

N Netherlands Antilles is a self-governing, Dutch-speaking group of 5 main islands (Aruba, Bonaire, Curacao, Saba and St Eustatius), and the southern part of a sixth (St Maarten). The capital, Willemstad

Street trader, Puerto Rico

(160,500), stands on Curacao, the main island. The chief industry is the refining of petroleum from Venezuela. Area: 993 sq km; population: 254,500.

P Puerto Rico is a self-governing commonwealth in association with the US. Its Spanish-speaking peoples, all US citizens (without a US vote) rely on tourism and industries such as canning and cement-making for their income. Area: 8,870 sq km; population: 3,600,000; capital: San Juan (896,600).

Kitts-Nevis-Anguilla became states associated with Great Britain. St Vincent joined them two years later.

In the 1970s, the desire for independence spread like an epidemic. Independence came to the Bahamas in 1973 and to Grenada a year later. In 1978 Dominica and St Lucia followed suit, and in 1979 it was the turn of St Kitts-Nevis and St Vincent (with the Grenadines). Scheduled for independence later that same year was Antigua (with Barbuda). In 1979 there was a bloodless coup in Grenada.

Many of these islands, so eager to grasp independence, are mere specks in the sunny blue sea. The heady prospect of freedom seemingly outweighs formidable economic problems. Dominica, for example, without even its own currency, with few roads, poor crops and limited tourist facilities, faces a bleak future. But each new independent Caribbean nation carries a potential vote in the United Nations. As such, they become important pawns in the power game and are therefore assiduously wooed by the superpowers.

The new government immediately initiated a programme of social and economic reforms, and in 1960 nationalized all private industry. Castro quarrelled with the United States and relied heavily on the USSR for trade and co-operation, becoming a member of Comecon *(see page 30)*. In 1962, Soviet missile bases on the island caused an international crisis. As a result, the United States severed diplomatic relations with Cuba and friction between the two nations persisted through the 1970s.

In 1958, ANTIGUA, Barbados, DOMINICA, GRE-NADA, Jamaica, MONTSERRAT, St Kitts-Nevis-Anguilla, ST LUCIA, ST VINCENT and Trinidad and Tobago formed a state within the Commonwealth called the West Indies Federation. But after Jamaica and Trinidad and Tobago withdrew and became independent, the federation was dissolved in 1962.

ANGUILLA declared its independence from ST KITTS-NEVIS in 1967 and tried to break away from Britain in 1969. But Britain sent a force to restore order in the island. In 1976 Anguilla was granted a separate constitution under the Anguilla (Constitution) Order.

In 1967, Antigua, Dominica, Grenada and St

Above: A Haitian voodoo dance is a necessary prelude to possession. Voodoo, which is a mixture of African and Christian beliefs, teaches that if a devout follower performs certain rites, he or she will be possessed by the gods. Dancing takes place on specially prepared ground that has been covered with flour by the priest.

Below: Fidel Castro, flanked by his aides, begins a tour of inspection. After more than 20 years of dictatorial rule, the revolutionary Cuban leader seems still to enjoy widespread popularity in his native land.

St Kitts-Nevis is an independent island nation in the Leeward Islands. The volcanic mountainous islands include St Christopher (St Kitts), Nevis and Sombrero. The capital, Basse-Terre (23,500), is on St Kitts. Tourism is the main industry. The islands joined with ANGUILLA in 1967, but Anguilla left the union after a few months. Area: 311 sq km; population: 60,000.
St Lucia is an independent volcanic island in the Windward group. The people speak a French dialect. Bananas and hardwood are exported. Area: 616 sq km; population: 115,300; capital: Castries (54,000).
St Vincent is an independent island nation in the Windward group. It is made

Brahmin cattle, Tobago

up of the main island of St Vincent and the smaller Grenadine Islands. The people speak English. Arrowroot and cotton are exported. Area: 389 sq km; population: 110,000; capital: Kingstown (35,000).

Trinidad and Tobago is a sovereign state made up of the two most southerly islands in the West Indies. The capital, Port of Spain (120,100), is in Trinidad. Blacks, East Indians, Europeans, Chinese and people from the Middle East make up the population. The offi-

cial language is English. Sugar, petroleum and tourism are the main industries. Area: 5,128 sq km; population: 1,200,000.
Turks and Caicos Islands is a British dependency of more than 30 islands, only 6 of which are inhabited. Salt, sponges and shellfish are exported. Area: 430 sq km; population: 8,400; capital: Grand Turk (3,000).

Virgin Islands are two groups of islands in the Lesser Antilles. (1) The Virgin Islands of the United States comprise 68 islands,

St Croix, St Thomas and St John being the chief ones. Area: 344 sq km; population: 130,000; capital: Charlotte Amalie (15,000). (2) The British Virgin Islands include Anegada, Jost Van Dyke, Tortola and Virgin Gorda. Area: 153 sq km; population: 12,000; capital: Road Town (2,600).
Voodoo is a religion combining both African and Christian beliefs.

World of Knowledge

Peoples and Places

Ron Carter

Peter Way

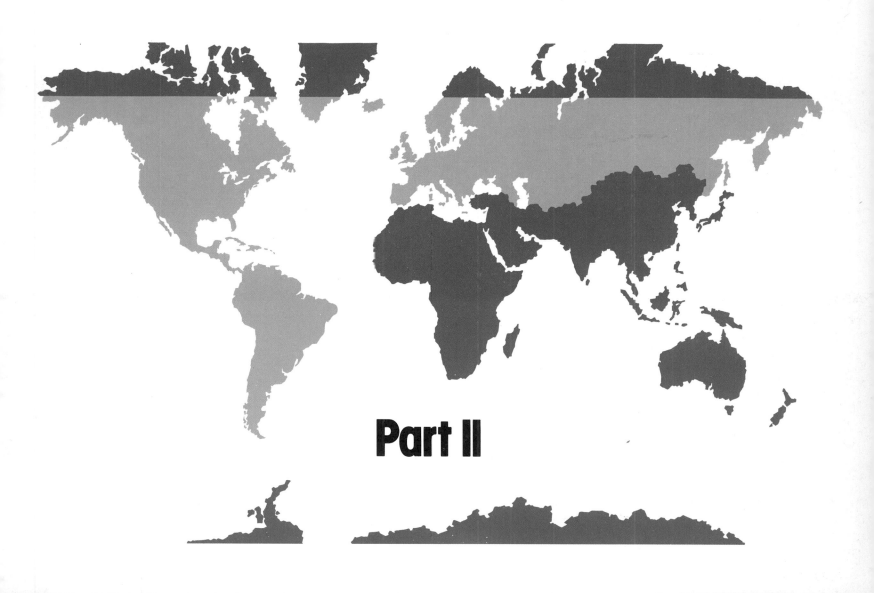

Part II

Introduction

The peoples of the world are divided by many factors, including language, politics, race and religion. Another fundamental division in the modern world is the rift between the 'haves' in the developed world and the 'have-nots' in the developing world. This rift is reflected in stark contrasts in standards of living, opportunities, life expectations, health and so on. And many experts believe that, despite aid to and investment in developing countries, the gap between the developing and the developed worlds is becoming even wider, a fact which may have grave consequences for our future. **Peoples and Places, Part II** contrasts Asia and Africa, which largely belong to the developing world, with the developed nations of Australia and New Zealand in Oceania. There is also a chapter on the polar regions — the thinly-populated Arctic and the bleak continent of Antartica, which has no permanent population. Population figures for countries are 1980 estimates based on United Nations' statistics. Populations of other political divisions, cities and towns are the latest available figures.

South-west Asia, the home of great early civilizations and the birthplace of three great religions, has recently assumed tremendous power in world affairs, largely because of the huge oil deposits which lie beneath the desert sands.

South-west Asia

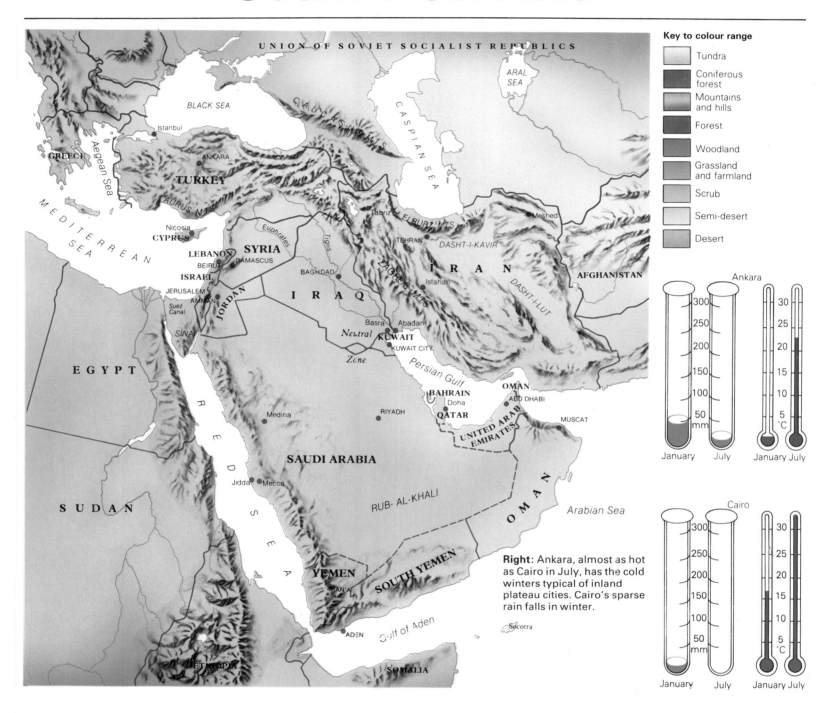

Key to colour range
- Tundra
- Coniferous forest
- Mountains and hills
- Forest
- Woodland
- Grassland and farmland
- Scrub
- Semi-desert
- Desert

Right: Ankara, almost as hot as Cairo in July, has the cold winters typical of inland plateau cities. Cairo's sparse rain falls in winter.

Reference

Street scene, Aden

A **Aden**, capital of SOUTH YEMEN, declined as an international port after independence in 1972. Population: 290,000.
Aleppo is an important city in north SYRIA. Population: 885,000.
Amman is the capital of JORDAN and the site of the ancient city of Philadelphia. Population: 770,000.
Anatolia is a plateau of Asia Minor and covers most of TURKEY.

Ankara, once a small town in Angora, was developed into TURKEY'S modern capital by Kemal Ataturk, who ruled the country from 1923 to 1938. Population: 1,900,000.

B **Baghdad**, the present capital of IRAQ, dates only from the early 1800s, when the famous historic city was destroyed by fire. Population: 3,000,000.
Bahrain, a tiny oil-producing independent emirate off the east coast of the Arabian peninsula, is an archipelago. The main language is Arabic. Area: 622 sq km; population: 294,000; capital: Manama (120,000).
Basra is IRAQ'S only impor-

tant port. Population: 450,000.
Beirut is the capital of LEBANON and was a leading commercial and cultural centre of the Middle East before civil war began in the late 1970s. Population (not allowing for war casualties and migration): 845,000.

C **Cyprus** is an island republic in the eastern Mediterranean. It had about an 80% Greek population in 1974 when a coup failed to unite the republic with Greece against the wishes of the 20% Turkish minority.

Civil war followed between Orthodox Christian Greeks and Muslim Turks backed by Turkey, which landed 40,000 troops. Following this, the northern 40% of the island became a quasi-independent Turkish state, and the southern 60% a quasi-independent Greek state. Area: 9,251 sq km; population (not allowing for migration and Turkish soldiers): 663,000; capital: NICOSIA.

D **Damascus** is the capital of Syria and one of the world's most ancient

South-west Asia includes TURKEY, IRAN, 12 Arab states, ISRAEL and CYPRUS. The region covers 4.6 per cent of the world's land area and contains three per cent of its population.

Cyprus, Turkey and Iran

The island of CYPRUS is situated in the eastern Mediterranean south of TURKEY and west of Syria. The terrain is mountainous, with the wooded Kyrenia mountains in the north and the higher Troodos mountains to the west of centre. There is a low-lying plain along the east coast. The climate is warm and dry, with some light rainfall, and is suitable for growing cotton, barley, vines and fruits.

Turkey lies at the crossroads of Europe and Asia. Most of the country is in Asia on a large peninsula between the Black, Aegean and Mediterranean seas. This comprises the large central plateau of ANATOLIA, the TAURUS mountain range in the south and the Pontic range in the north-east. European Turkey lies across the Sea of Marmara which connects northwards, through the Bosporus, to the Black Sea and southwards, through the Dardanelles, to the Aegean Sea. Along the coasts, the climate is mild and moist with temperatures ranging from 4°C in January to 27°C in July. In contrast, conditions inland are harsh and dry. January temperatures for the central plateau, for example, average

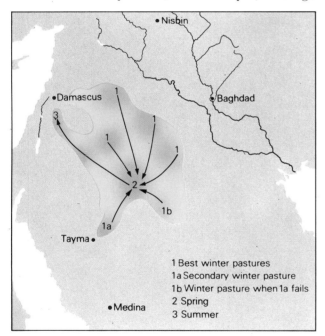

1 Best winter pastures
1a Secondary winter pasture
1b Winter pasture when 1a fails
2 Spring
3 Summer

Above: Nomads spread cooking pots in front of their tents near the border of Luristan and Kurdistan in western Iran. Their tribal loyalties extend beyond national boundaries. Life in much of rural Iran remains unaffected by the country's oil-based prosperity.

Left: Nomadism results from the need of herdsmen to find pasture for their livestock. Tribal wanderings are governed by climate and vegetation patterns well understood by the nomads. The map shows the pattern of migration followed by groups of the Bedouin Ruala tribes. The nomads normally wintered their herds in the places marked **1**. If winter rain was insufficient there, they wintered at the place marked **1a**. If, however, the rains failed there, they wintered in the area marked **1b**. Wherever they wintered, the herdsmen made for the area marked **2** in spring. They moved on in summer to area **3**. By inter-tribal agreement, the Ruala could move only within the desert area shaded. They moved across 4 countries (Syria, Jordan, Iraq and Saudi Arabia), ignoring political frontiers which are still largely unpoliced except the motorized vehicle routes.

–11°C. Vegetation reflects the pattern of climate. The west, especially along the Mediterranean, is naturally forested. Here pines give way to deciduous trees, grassy steppe and semi-desert eastwards towards Iran.

Most of Iran is a plateau over 1,200 metres above sea level bordered by high mountain chains. They include the rugged ZAGROS in the west and the snow-capped Elburz range to the north which rises to 5,775 metres. Natural forests cover parts of the northern and western uplands, but between them lie two vast, barren and uninhabited areas — the salt desert of Dasht-I-Kavir and to the south-east the sand desert of Dasht-I-Lut. Several small rivers flow from the mountains on to this central plateau, where most dry up in the intense heat. Temperatures may reach 55°C on summer afternoons although in parts of the country night temperatures drop below freezing even in summer. Annual rainfall varies from 100 millimetres along the Caspian coast to only 12 millimetres in the deserts. Here, violent winds often swirl the salt and sand into dangerous storms. The population lives mainly in farming settlements or towns in the long, narrow, fertile valleys between the mountains. A fertile strip of coastland also borders the low-lying Caspian Sea.

The Arab lands and Israel

The Arab territories of Asia seldom rise more than 1,000 metres above sea level. They comprise

cities, being more than 4,000 years old. Population: 835,000.
Dead Sea, a salt lake on the Jordan-Israel border, lies 397 metres below the level of the Mediterranean. Area: 1,020 sq km.

E Euphrates River is an important river of South-west Asia formed by the confluence of the East and West Euphrates in eastern Turkey.

G Gaza is a small strip of PALESTINE on the Mediterranean coast north

of Egypt. It came under Israeli occupation in 1967.
Golan Heights, a hill region of south-west Syria, came under Israeli occupation in 1967.

Iran (formerly Persia) is mostly a vast plateau over 1 km above sea level, surrounded by high mountains. Much of the country is desert or too mountainous for cultivation, but it has large oil reserves. When world petroleum prices rose steeply in 1973, the country's overseas earnings soared. The resulting wealth

Carpet weaving, Iran

remained largely in the hands of the Shah whose ambition was to make Iran a great nation again by industrialization and building up military strength. Resentment against the Shah's policies, especially by devout Muslims opposed to westernization, exploded into open rebellion in 1978-79. Only about 55% of the people are Persian, while some 35% are of Turkic origin, such as the Kurds. The main language is Persian written in Arabic script. Area: 1,648,000 sq km; population: 37,859,000; capital: Tehran.

Iraq is a mostly desert Arab republic. It has a fertile region between the EUPHRATES and TIGRIS rivers which was the site of 3 great civilizations (Sumer, Babylonia and Assyria). The country has a varied economy which is dominated by its income from petroleum. Over 60% of Iraqis are Sunnite Muslims and 30% Shi'ite; some 3% are Christians of various sects. Politically the country has been unstable since the assassination of its last king in 1958. It is a strong supporter of the Arab cause against

the Arabian peninsula and its borderlands northwards to the Mediterranean and Mesopotamia (which lies between the EUPHRATES and TIGRIS rivers). Arabia is mostly an arid, barely populated sand desert with grassland and palms in the more fertile areas. The RUB AL KHALI, a desert in the south, is called the 'Empty Quarter'. SAUDI ARABIA occupies the bulk of the peninsula, with NORTH YEMEN and SOUTH YEMEN in the south-west, OMAN in the south-east and the smaller UNITED ARAB EMIRATES, QATAR, BAHRAIN and KUWAIT in the east.

From this austere heartland the early Arabs pushed northwards to enter a comparatively fertile, crescent-shaped belt of grasslands and date palms. Along this 'fertile crescent' the northern Arab states of IRAQ, JORDAN, SYRIA and LEBANON later developed. ISRAEL, like PALESTINE

Above: Riyadh, the modern capital city of Saudi Arabia, has developed in 2 generations from a desert outpost to one of the world's most important commercial centres. Skilled workers from many countries have gone to work in Saudi Arabia on short-term contracts, attracted by high pay.

Left: Irrigation and scientific farming have restored fertility to barren areas of the Middle East, once part of the ancient 'fertile crescent'. The picture shows an Israeli experimental site near the River Jordan.

and Canaan before, lay along this belt between the Mediterranean and the Jordan Valley.

The dominating climatic feature of the Arab lands is the general lack of rain. July day temperatures may rise to 52°C inland, then fall drastically at night. In winter, inland temperatures often fall below zero at night.

Peoples of South-west Asia
Almost the whole of South-west Asia is Islamic in religion except for Israel which is mainly Judaist and southern Cyprus where people practise Orthodox Christianity.

The Cypriots
The southern 60 per cent of CYPRUS is occupied by Greek Cypriots who in 1973 comprised 79 per cent of the population. Most of the rest are Turkish Muslim Cypriots, and due to friction between these two communities they have been rigidly separated since 1974. Farming is the main activity for about 35 per cent of the people. Village houses are simple, but the towns have new buildings and often luxury tourist hotels. The trend is towards a more modern way of life. This is seen most clearly in the style of dress the younger people are now adopting. They have largely discarded the old-style Greek and Turkish costumes of their parents and grandparents.

Turks and Iranians
The Turks are mostly a Mongoloid people

Israel, but was much preoccupied in the 1970s by an internal war between its Arab and Kurdish peoples. The main language is Arabic, with Kurdish the chief minority language. Area: 434,924 sq km; population: 13,150,000; capital: BAGHDAD.

Isfahan was the 16th century city of Shah Abbas I. Despite industrialization, the old architecture still survives. Population: 570,000.

Israel, being mainly non-Arab, non-Muslim, and having only small known petroleum deposits, is the 'odd man out' among the mainland states of South-west Asia. The Israeli republic came into being in 1948 after Britain acknowledged the demands of the Jews for an independent homeland in PALESTINE. Four wars with surrounding Arab states (1948, 1956, 1967 and 1973), with intervening periods of 'no war no peace', have dominated the country's brief history. Jews make up 90% of the population of pre-1967 Israel. The other 10% is mostly Muslim Arab, with some Christians. The main languages are Hebrew,

Mosque, Isfahan.

Arabic and English. Area: 20,770 sq km (but another 68,600 sq km of Arab territory was occupied by Israel after the 1967 war); population: 3,900,000; capital: Jerusalem.

Istanbul (in Europe) is Turkey's biggest city. As Byzantium it was once the capital of the Byzantine empire. Later, as Constantinople, it became the capital of the Turkish empire. Population: 2,930,000.

Jerusalem, holy to Jews, Christians and Muslims, is the capital of Israel, which took control of the old part of the city only in 1967. Population: 330,000.

Jidda (Jedda) is the main business city of SAUDI ARABIA. Population: 670,000.

Jordan is an Arab kingdom in South-west Asia. It expanded in 1948 to absorb the region of PALESTINE known as the WEST BANK (of the Jordan River). The country has borne much of the brunt of the Arab-Israeli conflict. The West Bank, for example, was occupied by Israel following the 1967 war. AMMAN, the capital, is the only major city. Area: 97,740 sq km; population: 3,153,000; capital: Amman.

Jordan River separates the WEST BANK from Jordan's

much stronger than in Turkey and only four per cent of the people are Christians, Jews or Zoroastrians. The Arabic script has been retained for the Persian language. Persians are of Indo-European descent and the name Iranian means Aryan. But only about 60 per cent of Iranians are Persians, the rest are mainly Turks with some Kurds and Arabs who live along the borders.

The Arabs

North of Arabia, the Arabs have intermixed with other peoples, especially in Syria and Lebanon, while in the south there has been a Negroid admixture. Up to 1900, the Arabs were mainly nomadic herdsmen living a primitive life under Turkish rule. Permanent settlements were few and small in scale away from bustling cities such as DAMASCUS, ALEPPO, BEIRUT, AMMAN, BAGHDAD and BASRA. Bedouin tribes wandered from oasis to oasis in search of water and pasture for their herds. Women held a very low position in Arab society. Diet was poor and disease ensured that people did not live long. But the discovery and exploitation of petroleum beneath the sand transformed this way of life – gradually at first, then with remarkable speed. Arab states are now among the wealthiest in the world. They have embarked on a programme of rapid modernization, buying expertise from industrial nations. Standards of living have gone up, education increased and the position of women improved.

related to the medieval Tartars, but they are intermixed with earlier inhabitants of Asia Minor such as the Hittites and the Greeks. Kurdish tribes occupy a region called Kurdistan which straddles the borders of TURKEY, IRAN and IRAQ, and make up about seven per cent of Turkey's population. Arabs, Armenians, Greeks, Georgians, Jews and Circassians form smaller minorities.

During the 1900s, Turkey has undergone some dramatic changes. From an oriental empire, it has developed into a westernized state. Western dress was promoted and women officially discouraged from wearing the veil. In modern cities, such as ISTANBUL, ANKARA and Izmir, women now have near equality with men. About 60 per cent of all workers are still farmers. One of the most significant changes to the country came in 1928 when the Turks replaced the Arabic script with the Roman alphabet. The language therefore became easier to write, so this was a great boon to education.

Like Turkey, Iran has undergone considerable social change in the 1900s. But the great size of the country and the remoteness of many settlements have slowed the pace of development. There are several modern western-style cities such as TEHRAN, ISFAHAN and Abadan, but nearly half of the population lives outside towns, often in mud-built houses. The same proportion are either farmers or nomadic herdsmen. Islam is

Above: An open-air *souk* (market place) in Saudi Arabia serves as the main market for locally-produced commodities such as dates, wheat and wool.

Below: Turkey, once the overlord of Arabia, has fallen behind in prosperity. Here farmers beat out linseed by hand. Many men have emigrated from Turkish farms to find work in western Europe.

East Bank. It rises in SYRIA and flows 600 km to empty into the DEAD SEA.

K **Kurdistan**, a mountainous area with no clearly defined borders, covers about 190,000 sq km where south-east Turkey, north-west Iraq, and north-east Iran come near together. It is the homeland of the Kurds, whose repeated efforts to found an independent state have been unsuccessful.
Kuwait was one of the first of the small Arab emirates to rise from poverty to riches on its income from pet-

roleum. The transformation took place between 1946 and 1961, in which year it gained independence from Britain. Then holding 20% of the world's known oil reserves, Kuwait had already become the world's richest country, even before the vast increase in oil prices began in the 1970s. Two areas called the Neutral Zone, totalling 5,698 sq km, were created in 1922 along the Kuwaiti-Saudi Arabian border. But they were divided between the 2 countries in 1966. It is now known as the Partitioned Zone. The main lan-

guage of the country is Arabic, although English is also spoken. Area without the Partitioned Zone: 17,818 sq km; population: 1,282,000; capital: Kuwait City (population 250,000).

L **Lebanon** is a small republic in South-west Asia. It has a mainly Arab population divided almost equally into Muslims and Christians. The Christians are subdivided into Maronites, Greek Orthodox, Armenians, Greek Catholics and Protestants. Muslims are subdivided into Sunnites

and Shi'ites. There are also Druses, a group whose secret religion is based on aspects of Islam and Christianity. The country occupies

Beirut, Lebanon

roughly the same area as ancient Phoenicia. It has a mixed economy and 26% of the gross national product normally comes from finance and commerce. The varied religions, corresponding roughly to cultural groups, have given the Lebanese a vigorous society. However, group rivalries, worsened by the presence of Palestinians in the country, exploded into multi-sided civil war in the late 1970s. In the capital, BEIRUT, some 50,000 lives were lost. Lebanon's second city, Tripoli, has some 210,000 people.

The Israelis
Since 1948 the Israelis have created a Western-style state superimposed on the more traditional Palestinian way of life that had much in common with Syrian and Lebanese society. Because most of the Arab Palestinians left the country when Israel gained independence, 85 per cent of the population are Jews. The rest are Muslims, with a few Christians and Druses. Hebrew and Arabic are the official languages.

The economy
Petroleum dominates the economy of South-west Asia although not all countries possess deposits. SAUDI ARABIA, IRAN, KUWAIT, IRAQ, the UNITED ARAB EMIRATES, QATAR, OMAN and BAHRAIN all have substantial reserves of petroleum which account for about 75 per cent of their income. LEBANON, JORDAN, NORTH YEMEN, SOUTH YEMEN and CYPRUS have not found oil, but SYRIA, TURKEY and ISRAEL each possess small reserves.

The importance of oil
Towards the end of June 1978, world petroleum production totalled 22,373 million barrels. (As defined by OPEC a barrel equals 35 imperial gallons or 159 litres.) OPEC is the Organization of Petroleum Exporting Countries to which many oil exporting countries, especially in south-west Asia belong. South-west Asia produced about 30-34 per cent of this total, the USA and the USSR another 35 per cent and the rest of the world produced the remainder. The Americans consumed all their own output and imported much more, while the Russians consumed about 75 per cent and exported most of the rest to communist countries. Consequently Japan and the major western powers relied heavily on Iranian and Arab oil to maintain the economies of the chief non-communist industrial nations. Understandably, the Iranians and Arabs had different interests than their customers. The Iranians especially took account of the fact that their oil reserves were limited. (At the 1978 level of production, their known petroleum reserves would run out by about the year 2010.) When in power, the Shah of Iran proposed to use the oil wealth to industrialize his country, thereby

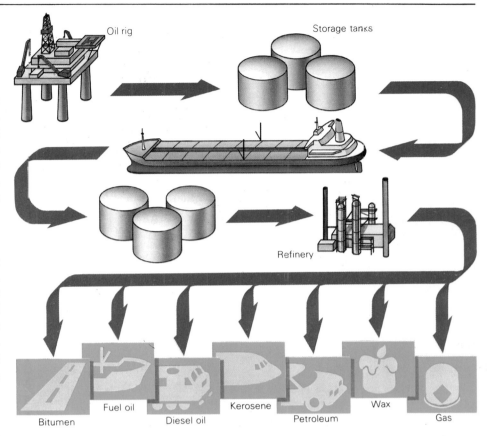

Above: Petroleum, the main commodity of South-western Asia, is extracted from ocean or inland oilfields. Once extracted, it is stored in tanks locally, awaiting transport by tanker to storage tanks in the importing country. From there it goes to the refinery, where it is broken down by distillation in fractioning towers. There, crude oil, heated to a vapour, rises through the towers. Differing kinds of oil condense at varying levels, and are piped off for further refinement or processing. The plan shows the different qualities of oil. Light fuel gas is at the top of the tower; heavy bitumen at the bottom.

Below: The burning off of surplus gases gives colour to desert oilfields. Petroleum from this site at Ras Tanuna, near Bahrain, contributes towards making Saudi Arabia the world's third largest petroleum producing nation after the USSR and the United States.

The main language is Arabic, but French and English are widely used. Area: 10,400 sq km; population (not allowing for war deaths and migration): 3,347,000; capital: BEIRUT.

M Mecca, along with Riyadh, is the joint capital of SAUDI ARABIA. It is the birthplace of Muhammed and the focal point of the Islamic religion. Each year thousands of pilgrims visit the Kaaba — a small, stone building in the Great Mosque. Population: 438,000.

Pilgrims' tents, Mecca

Medina, SAUDI ARABIA, is the second holiest city of Islam. Muhammed lived and died here after he fled Mecca in AD 622. Population: 235,000.

N Nicosia is the capital of Cyprus. Population (before the Greek coup and Turkish invasion of Cyprus in 1974): 147,000.
North Yemen, a little-visited Arab republic in the south-west corner of Arabia, has an almost 100% Muslim Arab population about equally divided between the Sunnite and Shi'ite sects. The people along the coastal strip are partly Negroid. Asn'a and Taiz are the only large towns. The economy is mainly agricultural. Area: 195,000 sq km; population: 7,732,000; capital: SAN'A.

O Oman (formerly Muscat and Oman) is an independent sultanate in the south-east corner of the Arabian peninsula. Until 1970, it was socially and economically among the world's least advanced countries. In that year, the sultan was replaced by his son, who began to use the income from petroleum for the advancement of the nation. Oman is barren except for its narrow fertile coastal plain. The Arab population is descended equally from north and south Arabians. Black Africans live along the coast,

and there are also important Iranian, Pakistani, Indian and European minorities Nearly everybody is a Muslim. The main language is Arabic although Urdu, Baluchi, Hindi and English are spoken. Area: 212,457 sq km; population: 894,000; capital: Muscat (Masqat) (14,000).

P Palestine is the homeland of the biblical kingdoms of Israel and Judea. It was largely occupied by modern Israel following 4 Arab-Israeli wars (1948, 1956, 1967 and 1973). The dispossessed Palestinians

creating the basis of a sound economy after the oil had run out. The Arabs put as their priority the conflict with Israel. In 1973 their oil was used as a weapon against the industrial nations to try to force them to give more political support against the Israelis. Simultaneously with the outbreak of the fourth Arab-Israeli War in October 1973, petroleum prices soared. During the next year prices quadrupled and by the end of 1978 they had increased sevenfold. However, the Arabs were paid in American dollars that had lost over half their purchasing power through world inflation, caused largely by the rise in oil prices. Nevertheless, the increase in wealth that had come to Arab rulers was enormous. But it remains to be seen how effective the plans to develop their countries prove.

Countries outside the oil-rich belt

Those countries which produce little or no oil have considerable problems in balancing their economies. Usually they have to be supported by a range of activities. Syria receives 'rent' for the Iraqi pipeline that crosses the country to take oil to the Mediterranean. Jordan exports phosphates, potash and cement, while Lebanon's income derives mainly from commerce and finance. Exports of fruit and vegetables, wines, cement, clothing and footwear are important to the Cypriot economy. However, both Lebanon and Cyprus were seriously disrupted by civil war in the 1970s. Turkey endures particular problems in that exports of cotton, fruits, minerals and cereals pay for only about 30 per cent of its imports. Fortunately, money sent home from migrant workers in Western Europe helps to balance the budget. North Yemen produces salt, cotton and farm products, and nearly half its exports go to China. South Yemen is also mainly agricultural, but Aden is still a transit port for the trade of nearby countries.

Despite its lack of petroleum, Israel is comparatively rich, however, about 30 per cent of its income is spent on defence. The Israelis have achieved remarkable progress economically. Between 1955 and 1977 the area of cultivated land was doubled through irrigation, and atomic energy has been developed and minerals worked. But exports pay for only 47 per cent of imports so tourism and money from Jews living abroad help to keep the country solvent.

Above: Many Iranian women continued to wear the veil outside their own homes despite the efforts of the last 2 Shahs to westernize the country between 1925 and 1978. In 1979, followers of Ayatollah Khomeini tried to persuade Westernized women to go back to the veil.

Below: Jerusalem's 'Wailing Wall' is a remnant of King Herod's temple. The wall has strong emotional significance for Jews. It is grooved horizontally where generations of Jews have gashed their foreheads to bewail the destruction of the temple.

History and culture

Some 2,500 years ago Persia became the first of the great empires. It reached a peak of Islamic culture under Shah Abbas in the early 1600s, then declined. By 1907, Persia was practically under the control of Russia and Britain and soon after, the British Anglo-Persian Oil Company began developing the country's petroleum. This foreign occupation speeded political change and the collapse of the dynasty. In 1925, Reza Khan, commander of the Persian Cossack brigade, became the first shah of a new dynasty. During World War II, Persia suffered another British-Russian occupation. This resulted in the forced abdication of Reza and the succession of his son, Mohammed Reza Pahlavi. Under this shah, Persia (renamed IRAN), nationalized its oil and from 1973 accumulated the great wealth with which the shah proposed to industrialize the country. The social changes which wealth brought were resisted by Muslim leaders who organized rebellion against the shah's economic and foreign policies in 1978-79. The Shi-ite Muslim leader Ayatollah Khomeini returned from exile in 1979 to establish an Islamic republic.

Turkey and its successor states

The Turkish empire spread across three continents to reach its height under Suleiman the Magnificent in 1520-66. Although Turkey declined, it held the whole of south-western Asia

west of Persia. Further decline saw Cyprus lost to British rule in 1878, and defeat in World War I finally destroyed its empire. France took SYRIA and LEBANON and Britain took PALESTINE, JORDAN and IRAQ. By 1924, Ibn Saud, head of a family allied to the Muslim Wahhabi sect, had hammered most of Arabia into the kingdom of SAUDI ARABIA. World War II speeded the departure of France and Britain from South-west Asia and brought independence to the northern Arab states. The last remaining sultanates of the Arabian peninsula became fully independent by 1971. The Bedouin nomadic shepherds were fast disappearing into the prosperous towns, while trucks and aircraft replaced camels. Despite social change, the Islamic religion strengthened.

Palestine and the emergence of Israel

The Jews had been scattered as minority groups in many countries for 1,800 years when a movement began in the late 1800s to set up a Jewish national home in PALESTINE – their Biblical homeland. Little came of this idea until World War I. Then, having secretly promised the Arab's independence to gain their support against the Turks, the British further agreed to Jewish settlement in Palestine, which was then populated mainly by Arabs. Matters came to a head after World War II. Many of the surviving Jews in Europe made their way to Palestine. They endured barely tolerable conditions in 'hell ships' which managed to smuggle them into the country past the British blockade. As the last British soldiers left Palestine in 1948, the first Arab-Israeli War began. Israel survived this war and three others in 1956, 1967 and 1973, despite the overwhelming numbers of their Arab opponents. The 'Palestinian problem' has continued to dominate South-west Asian affairs politically as oil has done economically. In 1979 Egypt became the first Arab country to sign a peace treaty with Israel, but other Arab states condemned Egypt and a permanent peace is still sought. Israel and the territories it captured in the 1967 war, has a sizeable Arab Muslim minority. On its borders, particularly with Jordan and Lebanon, live the dispossessed Arab Palestinians whose families fled from Israel in 1948. They continue to fight a guerrilla war against Israel in the hope of retrieving some of their former lands.

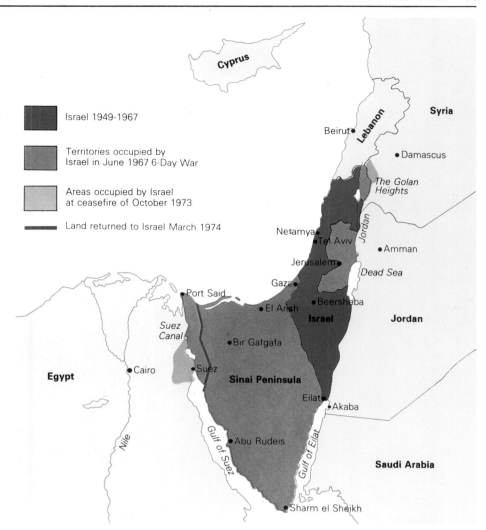

Israel 1949-1967

Territories occupied by Israel in June 1967 6-Day War

Areas occupied by Israel at ceasefire of October 1973

Land returned to Israel March 1974

Above: The first Arab-Israeli war (1948) left Israel in possession of roughly the old Palestine area except the West Bank (of the Jordan River). In the third Arab-Israeli war (1967), Israel occupied the West Bank, the Golan Heights, and the Sinai Peninsula.

Right: Following the Israeli invasion of Egypt in 1967, the Suez Canal was blocked by sunken ships. Egypt claimed Israeli bombers sank the ships; Israel charged Egypt with deliberately sinking them along with floating docks.

T Taurus Mountains, a range in southern Turkey, rise to over 3,600 km.

Tehran is the capital of IRAN. It is a modern city of international importance, as well as being an industrial and railway centre. Population: 4,300,000.

Tel Aviv is ISRAEL's biggest city and an important centre of business and industry. A modern town, dating back only to 1906, it has absorbed the city of Jaffa. Population: 440,000.

Tigris River rises in Turkey and flows 1,900 km through Iraq to unite with the EUPHRATES RIVER and finally empties into the Persian (Arabian) Gulf.

Turkey, situated partly in Europe but mainly in Southwest Asia, occupies roughly the region once known as Asia Minor. Turkey's varied economy has not achieved the prosperity of most European states and many people leave the country to find work abroad. The main language is Turkish, and Kurdish and Arabic are the minority languages. Area: 780,576 sq km; population: 44,160,000; capital: ANKARA.

Kemal Ataturk and wife

U United Arab Emirates became an independent emirate in 1971 following British withdrawal from the 6 emirates of Abu Dhabi, Dubai, Sharjah, Ajman, Umm al Qaiwain and Fujairah. A seventh emirate, Ras al Khaimah, joined in 1972. Petroleum dominated the economy of this rich federation, which is governed by its leading families. The mainly Arab population has important Iranian, Pakistani and Indian minorities. Area: 83,600 sq km; population: 229,000; capital: Abu Dhabi.

W West Bank is that part of PALESTINE west of the JORDAN RIVER taken by JORDAN in 1948 and occupied by ISRAEL in 1967.

Z Zagros Mountains run north to south-east along the borders of IRAN with TURKEY and IRAQ. The peaks rise from 2,750 to 4,550 metres above sea level.

Southern Asia is one of the world's most densely-populated regions. It has considerable natural resources, but the population explosion and ancient traditions have made it difficult for governments to raise living standards.

South Asia

Southern Asia includes AFGHANISTAN, PAKISTAN, INDIA and BANGLADESH; and the southern islands of SRI LANKA and MALDIVES. The region covers only 3.8 per cent of the world's land area but has 20.4 per cent of its population.

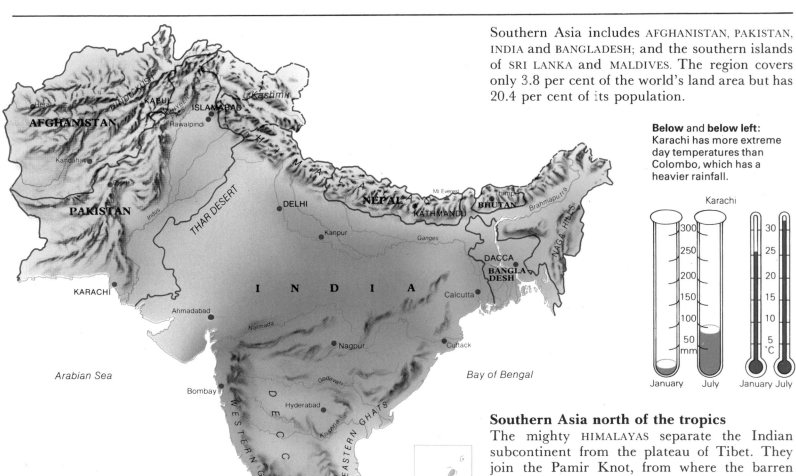

Below and **below left:** Karachi has more extreme day temperatures than Colombo, which has a heavier rainfall.

Karachi

Colombo

Southern Asia north of the tropics

The mighty HIMALAYAS separate the Indian subcontinent from the plateau of Tibet. They join the Pamir Knot, from where the barren Hindu Kush sweeps south-west into Afghanistan, and smaller ranges extend into Pakistan almost to the Arabian Sea. In the plains south of the Himalayas flow several great rivers including (from west to east) the INDUS, Sutlej, GANGES and BRAHMAPUTRA. All except the Ganges rise in Tibet. Oaks, conifers and rich meadows are found on the lower slopes of the northern mountains, changing to dense evergreen forests eastwards towards Assam. The fertile river valleys of Bangladesh and India grow enough grain to sustain a dense population but are subject to disastrous flooding. Bangladesh grows

Reference

A **Adam's Bridge** is a chain of shoals between south-east India and north-west Sri Lanka, nearly 50 km in length. In Hindu mythology, the 'bridge' was built by the divine hero Rama to enable his Indian armies to attack Sri Lanka.

Afghanistan, a landlocked republic, lies between IRAN (*see page 68*), PAKISTAN and the USSR. The Hindu Kush, together with other ranges and barren plains, cover most of the country. Only the valleys are fertile. Consequently, Afghanistan is a poor country. In origins the people are about 50% Pathan, a tall Caucasoid people, and 50% Mongoloid, especially Uzbek, Hazara and Tadzhik. About 72% of the gross national product comes from agriculture and 85% of the people live outside towns. Previously stable, Afghanistan had 2 coups in the 1970s and by 1979 was in a state of insurrection. The chief cities include KABUL, the capital, Kandaha, Herat and Mazar-i-

Sharif. The main languages are Pushtu, spoken by the Pathans, and Dari, a Persian dialect spoken by Tadzhiks and Hazaras. Uzbeks speak a form of Turkish. Area: 647,497 sq km; population: 21,858,000; capital: Kabul.

Ahmedabad is the capital of Gujarat state, INDIA. Population: 1,850,000.

Ajanta, site of 30 Buddhist rock-hewn caves from 1,200 to 2,200 years old, is an important tourist site in west-central India.

Amritsar in north-west India is the site of the Golden Temple of the Sikhs. Population: 540,000.

B **Bangalore** is the capital of Karnataka state, India. Population: 1,250,000.

Golden Temple, Amritsar

Bangladesh, a republic surrounded by the Bay of Bengal and INDIA, was the province of East PAKISTAN until independence came following civil war with the West Pakistanis in 1971. The revolt against the Pakistani government had been sparked off by a devastating tidal wave caused by a cyclone that killed about 250,000 people. Climatic misfortunes have dominated this small state, 50% of which is covered by the deltas of the GANGES and BRAHMAPUTRA rivers. The rivers cause disastrous

mainly rice, but as the soil becomes drier westwards towards Pakistan and Afghanistan, wheat becomes the main crop. Only two per cent of Afghanistan can be cultivated and only the southern 25 per cent of Pakistan – the plain formed by five rivers – is fertile. East of the Indus and north of the Tropic of Cancer, lies the dry, sandy THAR DESERT, covering more than 250,000 sq km of Pakistan and India. The rain-drenched southern slopes of Bhutan's mountains are thickly forested. Despite their height, the fertile valleys of Nepal are sunny and warm for much of the year.

Tropical Southern Asia

The DECCAN, a fertile plateau where crops are grown and animals grazed, covers most of tropical India south of the NARBADA RIVER. Its western edge rises from 900 to 1,500 metres as the Western Ghats, a mountain range that borders the coastlands along the Arabian Sea. Here the chief city and port is BOMBAY. Several rivers flow from the Western Ghats eastwards into the Bay of Bengal notably the GODAVI. Although dry for much of the year, they often flood the country during the rainy season, especially in mid-June to September. The Eastern Ghats of north-eastern Deccan rise to between 450 and 600 metres. The Malabar coast of south-western India contains evergreen rain

Above: Rice farmers protect themselves from India's monsoon rains by wearing short straw 'coats' to cover their heads and backs.

Below: Despite the high altitudes, valleys in the Nepalese Himalayas benefit from good soil, regular rainfall, and generous sunlight. Farmers grow rice in the monsoon season and wheat in the dry season.

forest. The island of Sri Lanka lies 70 kilometres across the Gulf of Mannar, almost connected to south-eastern India by ADAM'S BRIDGE. Once all forested, it now has large areas of savanna, grasslands and fernlands. The low-lying triangular-shaped island rises to over 2,400 metres south of the central area, and several small rivers flow seaward passing through forests and rubber and tea plantations.

The 2,000 mainly uninhabited coral atolls (islands) of Maldives are grouped into 12 clusters. They lie only two to 24 metres above sea level but are protected from the Indian Ocean by barrier reefs. Islanders grow coconut palms, fruit trees and millet and are excellent fishermen.

Climate of Southern Asia

Most of Southern Asia has a monsoon climate. Westerly winds bring a wet season, lasting in places from May to October, and a 'dry' season from November to April. However, this dry season's rain can be heavy at times, especially in Assam and Bangladesh in the north, and in Sri Lanka in the south. The rain gradually phases out as the peak of the dry season approaches. The sub-continent has great variations in rainfall. For example, Jacobabad near Quetta in Pakistan has only 100 millimetres of rain a year, but Cherrapunji in Assam, north of Bangladesh, has over 100 times as much. The populated areas of Afghanistan have a dry, healthy climate, with about 300 millimetres of rain annually.

The coastal areas of Bangladesh and West

---

floods, yet also provide the fertility to grow rice, tea and jute, which are the mainstays of the economy. Bangladesh has a population density of about 625 people to the sq km, 7 times the world average. DACCA, the capital, and CHITTAGONG are the largest cities. Nearly all the people are Bengali; 87% are Muslim and 12% Hindu. Bengali is the language spoken. Area: 143,998 sq km; population: 90,670,000; capital: Dacca.
Benares, see Varanasi.
Bhutan, lying between India and China, is a remote coun-

try. The southern plains, only 50 metres above sea level, rise northward to the HIMALAYAS, where mountain peaks reach 7,300 metres. It has been dominated politically in the past by India, but Bhutan's king began to open his land-locked Buddhist kingdom to the rest of the world in the mid-1970s. Most of the people are Bhutanese (Bhotias) of Tibetan descent, although about 25% are Nepalis. There are few towns and nearly all the inhabitants live in the countryside. The main language is Dzongka, with Nepali and

tribal dialects also spoken. Area: 47,000 sq km; population: 1,311,000; capital: Thimpu (population 9,000).
Bombay is INDIA's main port to the West and capital of the Maharashtra state. Population: 7,000,000.
Brahmaputra River rises in south-west Tibet, where it is called Tsangpo, and flows about 2,900 km through northern India and Bangladesh. Here it becomes the River Jamuna, and merges with the GANGES.

C Calcutta is the capital of West Bengal State

and is the largest city in INDIA. With access to the Bay of Bengal along the Hooghly River, it is a major port, handling jute and iron

Chowringhee, Calcutta

among other products. With Howrah, its satellite town, it is also a major industrial centre. Road and rail routes converge on the city. Population: 8,500,000.
Chittagong is the second city and principal port of BANGLADESH. Its annual rainfall is one of the heaviest in the world. Population: 580,000.
Colombo is the capital, business centre and chief port of SRI LANKA. Population: 725,000.

D Dacca is the capital of BANGLADESH. It is situated

Bengal, India, comprise the Brahmaputra-Ganges delta region, which is very fertile but prone to devastating floods and cyclones (vast, inward-spiralling winds of great force). The Maldive islands near the Equator, are hot and humid.

Temperatures in KABUL, Afghanistan, range from about 3°C in January to 25°C in July. In the Kathmandu Valley region of Nepal, temperatures range from 10°C in January to 26°C in July. But they can drop to −40°C in Nepal's highest Himalayan peaks. In Pakistan, northern India and Bangladesh, January temperatures usually exceed 17°C and July temperatures go well above 27°C. Temperatures range between these extremes in tropical India and Sri Lanka.

Right: Highly-decorated heavy vehicles ford a shallow waterway by the Indus River, near Islamabad, capital of Pakistan. Decoration of vehicles, especially with religious motifs, is common in Pakistan. A favourite symbol is the hand of Fatima, believed to ward off the evil eye.

Peoples and ways of life

INDIA is the giant of Southern Asia, occupying 64 per cent of its land area and containing 76 per cent of its people. About 63 per cent of all Southern Asians are Hindus and most of the rest are Muslim. Other religions (roughly in order of numbers) include Buddhists, Sikhs, Christians, Jains, Lamaists, Zoroastrians and Jews. Nowhere else in the world is there such a variety of active religions practised as part of daily life. Farming is the dominant occupation of the region where most people live in villages. Incomes are low but money matters much less in Southern Asia where much of what is consumed is either home produced or obtained by barter.

Styles of dress

The cultural heartland of Southern Asia is the territory once contained in the Indian Empire which lasted for over 2,000 years until 1947. Despite the antagonism of Hindus and Muslims, the old empire had a cultural unity still evident in its ways of dress. Women generally wear the *sari,* an unsewn length of coloured cloth, except for special groups such as the trouser-wearing Sikh women of the Punjab. Richer women also wear a *choli,* a blouse-like garment. In contrast most men wear a cotton turban and a *dhoti,* a single length of white cotton cloth worn as a loincloth that can also be thrown over the shoulders. These styles of dress are prevalent in the million villages that house 80 per cent of India's population. They are also worn in Sri Lanka, but to a lesser extent in the colder,

Left: India's hereditary caste system takes 2 forms. *Jati* divides society into hundreds of castes based on occupations. Alongside it, *Varna* divides people into *brahmans* (priests), *kshatriyas* (rulers and warriors), *vaisyas* (merchants and craftsmen), and *sudras* (unskilled labourers). 'Outcastes' or 'untouchables' are outside the caste system.

on the Burhiganga River with an outport at Narayanganj. Population: 1,200,000.
Darjeeling is a hill station in West Bengal, India, and the surrounding area is famous for its tea. It lies 2,165 metres above sea level. Population: 55,000.
Deccan is a large plateau in INDIA between the NARMADA and Krishna rivers, and more generally the area south to the sea. The plateau rises to the west where it is bounded by the Western Ghats (1,500 m). In the north-east, the Eastern Ghats rise to 600 metres, while to the north

the Vindhya, (1,200 metres) and other mountain ranges separate the Deccan from the northern plains.
Delhi, capital of INDIA, is situated on the Jumna River.

Lutyens building, Delhi

It comprises Old Delhi which was largely rebuilt in the 17th century and New Delhi which was designed mainly by Sir Edward Lutyens and completed in 1929. Population: 5,000,000.

E Eastern Ghats *see* Deccan.
Ellora is the site of 34 Buddhist, Hindu and Jain cave temples 1,000 to 1,500 years old. It lies in west central India The site has a complete rock-cut temple.

G Ganges River rises in the Indian HIMALAYAS and

flows south and east through India, where it is regarded as sacred, especially at VARANASI. It flows through West Bengal and Bangladesh, forming a vast delta before emptying into the Bay of Bengal. Its total length is about 2,500 km.
Godavari River rises in north-east Maharashtra, India, and flows about 1,450 km southeast across the DECCAN to empty into the Bay of Bengal through several tributaries.

H Himalayas (Himalaya), a huge mountain range

forming the northern border of the Indian subcontinent, extends for 2,400 km from Kashmir in the west to Assam in the east. The range covers most of Nepal, Sikkim, Bhutan and south Tibet. Its average height is 6,000 metres, but Mount Everest, the world's highest mountain, towers 8,848 metres. K2 (also called Godwin-Austen or Dapsang), the world's second highest mountain rises to 8,616 metres.
Hyderabad is the largest city of Andhra state, India. Population: 1,400,00.

landlocked countries of the north. Many Pakistani women wear trousers like the Sikhs, especially in cities, or, like Afghan village women, a black garment with small eyeholes that covers them from head to toes. Orthodox Muslims believe that women should always be hidden from men except their near relatives. In the cities of Southern Asia, most men now wear western dress. More distinctive styles of dress are worn in Bhutan and northern Nepal, which come under Tibetan influence.

Villagers and city dwellers

In the villages, houses are often built of mud, in a square, windowless style, but brick or stone may be used in some areas. Streets are unpaved and usually unlit except in the more prosperous areas. Women still carry water on their heads for a kilometre or more in some parts. In areas remote from towns, villagers have been used to looking after themselves for many generations and continue to do so. Indian villages have the *panchayet* (rule by five) system whereby a group of elected councillors (ideally five) meet and decide communal matters in the village. The Indian state governments often support the *panchayets*, giving them money perhaps to buy a radio or install oil lamps to light village meeting places at night. The most precious possessions of village families are often their cooking pots and brass water containers, which may be inherited.

City life is a world apart, where newcomers from the villages fight for jobs that will bring a

Above: Colourful religious festivals are frequent throughout India. In the Hindu festival shown, worshippers fly pennants bearing sacred signs such as the swastika—one of the earliest-known symbols of several Asian religions.

Left: Houses built of mud and straw accommodate many millions of Indian villagers. When a village is near a town, some members of the family may work in the town to increase their income, which can be used to buy a radio, a bicycle, or other factory-made goods.

little money to ward off starvation. Home for many in the cities is a pitch on the pavement at night, sufficiently big to lay a bedding roll and perhaps play a game of cards with a neighbour before trying to sleep through the all-night bustle. The caste system that once decided a Hindu's status in life from birth, is fast breaking down in the turmoil of city life. High caste Brahmins and outcaste 'untouchables' stand crushed together in the packed trains that carry them from the cheaper suburbs to their jobs in the centres of great cities such as Calcutta and Bombay. For many families, city life holds only the promise of a room in a slum with half the food eaten by a village family. However, with caste discrimination long banned by law, there is now the chance of rising by merit into the growing

India is the world's second most populous country. It is a federal republic of 22 states and 9 territories of vastly different size. Nagaland state has only 620,000 people while Uttar Pradesh has 106,000,000. Indians range from the light skinned Kashmiris of the north to the dark Tamils of the south. About 83% of Indians are Hindus, 11% Muslims, 2% Sikhs, 2% Christians, and 0.5% Jains. Other communities include Zoroastrians, Buddhists and Jews. The Hindu caste system, once dominant, is

Village barber, India

now breaking down. Despite its very great population, India is not so crowded as some other Asian countries. Although its people are among the world's poorest, India is rich in potential resources. Food production could probably be doubled by the use of fertilizers, the adoption of better methods of agriculture and the implementation of hydro-engineering projects to prevent disastrous flooding. Until recently, economic progress has been severely hampered by the passive opposition of traditionalists. Over 80% of India's people live in some 750,000 villages, yet the country has some of the most populous cities and biggest industries

in the world. It has the largest steelworks in the Commonwealth and the world's most productive film industry. Few go hungry in the villages, but in the cities, workless people may starve. Indian cities with over a million people include CALCUTTA, BOMBAY, DELHI, the capital, MADRAS, HYDERABAD, BANGALORE, AHMEDABAD and Kanpur. About 44% of India's gross national product comes from agriculture, 23% from mining and manufacturing, and 16% from commerce and communication. It has the most exten-

sive rail system in Asia. There are 14 official languages: Assamese, Bengali, Gujarati, Hindi, Kannada, Kashmiri, Malayalam, Marathi, Oriya, Punjabi, Sanskrit, Tamil, Telegu, and Urdu. However, English is the general language of communication between educated Indians. Hundreds of local languages and dialects are spoken. Thirty years of rule by the Congress Party ended in 1977, when Indira Gandhi, daughter of Jahalawal Nehru, India's first prime minister, was defeated in a general

maize and barley crops while India and Pakistan are leading cotton countries. With Bangladesh they produce much tobacco for home consumption. Nepal grows rice in the monsoon season and wheat in the dry season. Bangladesh produces much of the world's jute and Sri Lanka and India a large percentage of the world's rubber and tea. Mechanization is improving. India, for example, has some 220,000 tractors, but Bangladesh has only 2,500.

The region has over 500 million domesticated animals, 50 per cent of which are cattle found mainly in India. Water buffaloes, for example, are widely spread, especially in rice-growing areas. And India, Pakistan and Afghanistan raise most of the 80 million sheep kept. Pigs are reared in India and Nepal, but not in Muslim countries. Poultry are kept everywhere.

Southern Asia produces very little petroleum

Left: Cows, especially sacred to the Hindus, roam freely through the streets of India's great cities. Few cows are sufficiently nourished to produce milk. These brahmin humped cattle seek food in a Bombay street.

Above: India desperately needs more dams such as the Tungabhadra Dam on the Deccan Plateau in Karnataka state, which irrigates over 750,000 hectares and controls floods. The 600-km long Tungabhadra River is formed by the confluence of the Tunga and Bhadra rivers.

middle class. Education too, can be bought cheaply by those who have the stamina to cram in the many night classes run by poor teachers.

Economy

The economy of Southern Asia is fairly uniform, though patterns change in the mountain regions of the north where crop farming is difficult. But differences are determined as much by the differing lifestyles of Hindus and Muslims as by geography.

Crops, animals and industry

Small-scale agriculture dominates the economy except in SRI LANKA, where the rubber and tea estates have been brought under government control. The average Indian farm, for example, comprises only two hectares compared with 45 hectares in Britain and 150 hectares in the USA. INDIA and BANGLADESH lead in rice production, and India, PAKISTAN and AFGHANISTAN in wheat.

India and Afghanistan also grow important

and outside India has few large industries. Reflecting its size, India ranks as an important producer of coal, iron ore and steel. A giant steel mill near CALCUTTA is among the world's biggest, and the country has the largest chemical fertilizer plant in Asia. India also makes its own vehicles, has the most extensive rail system in Asia, and has a nuclear power station near BOMBAY. The

---

election that was fought with much bitterness. Area: 3,287,590; Population: 662,961,000; Capital: Delhi.
Indus River rises in southwest Tibet and flows 2,900 km through Kashmir and Pakistan into the Arabian Sea. Its river basin is nearly 1,000,000 sq km in area. The Indus Valley civilization developed within this basin about 4,500 years ago and lasted for about 1,000 years.
Islamabad, the newly-built capital of PAKISTAN, was planned as a city of outstanding modern architecture. Population: 75,000.

K **Kabul** is the capital of Afghanistan. It once commanded the strategic mountain passes through which many invaders gained entrance to the Indian subcontinent. Population: 650,000.
Kanpur, India, is an industrial city and transportation centre on the GANGES RIVER in Uttar Pradesh. Population: 2,400,000.
Karachi, the former capital of PAKISTAN is the country's biggest city and main port. Population: 4,700,000.
Kashmir, borders Tibet and Sinkiang-Uighur and is the

northernmost region of the Indian subcontinent. In area, it is the size of France. It was claimed by both India and Pakistan at independence in 1947. After war in 1947–49,

Kashmiri with hookah

Pakistan occupied the west and India the east. Area: 222,800 sq km; population: 5,500,000.
Kathmandu the capital of NEPAL, is an unmodernized town with many temples of unique architecture. The similar towns of Patan and Bhadgaon lie nearby. Population: 185,000.
Khyber Pass was for hundreds of years the gateway to the Indian subcontinent for invading armies. About 53 km long, it is situated on the Afghan-Pakistan border in the Safed Ko range, an offshoot of the Hindu Kush.

L **Laccadive Islands,** with Minicoy and Amindivi, form an Indian territory 320 km off the south-west coast of India. Area: 28 sq km; population: 30,000.
Lahore is the capital of Punjab province and a leading cultural centre in northeast PAKISTAN. Population: 2,500,000.

M **Madras** is the biggest city of southern INDIA and is the capital of Tamil Nadu state. Population: 2,500,000.
Maldives is an independent republic in the Indian Ocean.

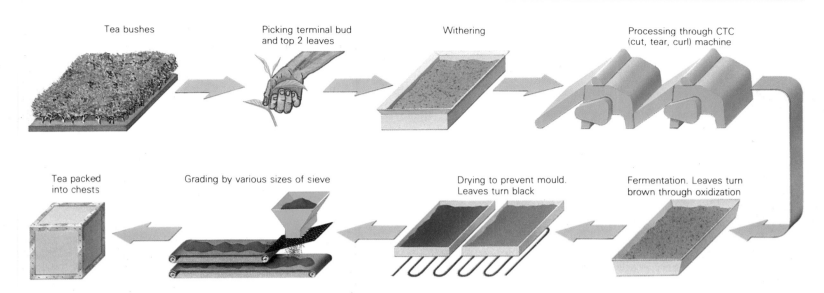

Tea bushes | Picking terminal bud and top 2 leaves | Withering | Processing through CTC (cut, tear, curl) machine

Tea packed into chests | Grading by various sizes of sieve | Drying to prevent mould. Leaves turn black | Fermentation. Leaves turn brown through oxidization

great rivers of the subcontinent have been harnessed to provide irrigation, produce electricity and reduce flooding. In 1979, India sought Russian aid in an ambitious project to link India's waterways by a huge canal network.

The problem of population
India, Pakistan, Bangladesh and Sri Lanka are bedevilled by a basic problem that troubled countries such as Britain during the time of their early industrialization. As the standard of living rises, more babies survive to swell the population, so consuming the extra production that brings about the higher standard of living in the first place. Indian governments, for example, have tried to solve this problem by persuading people to have less children. In fact India's annual rate of population increase slowed from 2.4 per cent to 2.1 per cent in the ten years ending 1976, representing two million less mouths to feed each year. However, except for Bangladesh, Southern Asia is less densely populated than either Japan or South Korea, which have much higher standards of living.

The potential wealth of India
Despite Southern Asia's poverty, it has the resources to become a prosperous region. It has a wealth of fertile land and rich mineral reserves. Food production could certainly be doubled because tradition often stands in the way of

Above: Stages in the processing of tea are shown. The best quality tea comes from leaves picked from the end of the branch; the very best tea, 'pekoe tip', comes from the leaf bud at the end of the branch. Picked leaves are left on trays in racks for 1 or 2 days to dry—a process called 'withering'. The leaves are then crushed to bring out the flavouring juices. Some tea is then allowed to ferment before drying to become black tea. Green tea is unfermented. After drying the tea is graded and packed into tea chests for export. Indian and Sri Lankan teas are sent to London for the skilled process of blending.

Right: Salt, excavated by simple machinery, lies ready for processing at a mine head in Pakistan. The mineral has played an important part in the history of the Indian subcontinent. Taxes were sometimes levied in salt during the time of the British Raj.

progress. For example, India has millions of cows which, being holy to Hindus, wander freely even into city streets. These half-fed animals consume valuable food but are too undernourished to produce much milk and too sacred to be eaten. The cow dung, which if applied to the land could increase fertility, is instead collected and patted into 'cakes' to provide fuel to burn under domestic cooking pots.

It comprises some 2,000 coral islands situated nearly 600 km off south-east India. About 220 islands forming 12 clusters are inhabited. Fishing is the mainstay of the economy. The people are mainly Muslims of mixed Indian, Sinhalese and Arab descent, and they gained independence from Britain in 1965. Area: 298 sq km; population: 134,000; Capital: Malé (15,000).

N Naga Hills border the Indian state of Nagaland and north-west Burma and rise about 3,000 metres.

Narbada (Narmada or Nerbuddha) River, which rises in the Maikala Range of Madhya Pradesh, divides north INDIA from the DECCAN. It flows 1,290 km roughly east to west to empty into the Gulf of Cambay. The river is sacred to Hindus.
Nepal is a landlocked Hindu-Buddhist mountain kingdom lying between India and Tibet. It was cut off from the rest of the world until the 1950s. The Nepalese are mainly descended from migrants from India, Tibet and Central Asia. Only 4% of the people live in

towns, which include KATHMANDU, Patan and Bhadgaon, all in the fertile Kathmandu Valley. The main

Patan, Nepal, fruit stall

language is Nepali but there are also Tibeto-Burman and Indian languages and dialects. Area: 140,797 sq km; Population: 14,082,000.

P Pakistan broke away from INDIA at independence in 1947 because its 86% Muslim population feared Hindu domination. The Islamic Republic of Pakistan was first divided into western and eastern regions, separated by 1,600 km of India. The two regions separated following civil war in 1971, East Pakistan becoming BANGLADESH. In the

past, Pakistan was the north-western frontier of the Indian subcontinent through which many invaders passed. Consequently, Pakistanis are of mixed origins. Like India, Pakistan is a poor country. Much of the land is too dry or too mountainous to be productive and 80% of the people live in villages. Leading cities of Pakistan include KARACHI, LAHORE, Shah Faisalabad, HYDERABAD, Rawalpindi and the small adjacent newly-built town of ISLAMABAD, the capital. In its first 30 years of independence Pakistan ex-

Agricultural inefficiency is bound up with the land system. Many farmers have inherited family debts. Apart from owing money to landlords and moneylenders, they also have to borrow from them at very high interest rates in order to buy the vital seeds and tools needed to carry on working the land. New hope came in the mid-1970s when the governments of India and Pakistan promised land reform. The first groups of tenant farmers were given possession of the land they tilled and the opportunity to borrow the capital needed at reasonable rates of interest from government agencies.

History and culture
Southern Asia has been the home of several great civilizations. The earliest, the Indus Valley culture, flourished some 4,000 years ago in what is now PAKISTAN. A Buddhist-Hindu-Jain-based civilization reached its height about 2,300 years ago and has left many traces, especially at ELLORA and AJANTA. Beginning in the AD 700s, Islam dominated the area for 1,000 years as a

Above: The Khyber Pass now has a good road connecting Pakistan to Afghanistan. This narrow ravine, forms the strategic gateway to the plains southward.

Below: Mrs Sirimawo Bandaranaike, the world's first woman prime minister, led the government of Sri Lanka during 1960-65 and again during 1970-77.

result of several invasions of India from the direction of Afghanistan, through the strategic KHYBER PASS. For about 200 years up to 1947, Britain controlled much of the area, often through local rulers. The many religions of the subcontinent have been mainly responsible for moulding its deep and diverse culture.

Political problems of the new states
At independence in 1947, the Indian empire split into India, where Hindus predominated, and Pakistan, which was mainly Muslim. The multiracial island of SRI LANKA (then Ceylon) gained independence in 1948. Pakistan comprised a western region and a smaller, eastern region, separated by 1,600 kilometres of Indian territory. Control of the northern region of KASHMIR, with its mainly Muslim population but Hindu ruler, was disputed by INDIA and Pakistan and eventually led to war in 1947–49. A cease-fire arranged by the United Nations left Kashmir divided between the two countries. India lost a brief border war with China in 1962 and fought another inconclusive war against Pakistan over Kashmir in 1965–66. Resentment in East Pakistan over its alleged exploitation by West Pakistan increased in 1971 following a disastrous cyclone that hit the East Pakistan coast in late 1970. Disease and famine followed, and between 200,000 and 500,000 died. The East Pakistanis claimed that most of these deaths happened because the western-based Pakistani government neglected its duty to arrange speedy relief. Anger exploded into rebellion, military repression and finally civil war. Following a third Indo-Pakistani war, East Pakistan became the independent republic of BANGLADESH in late 1971. Following a coup, General Zia assumed power in Pakistan in 1977. The former prime minister, Zulfikar Ali Bhutto, was executed in 1979, allegedly for complicity to murder.

In Sri Lanka, Mrs Bandaranaike, became the world's first woman prime minister, ruling in 1960–65 and again in 1970–77. In India, Mrs Ghandi, the daughter of the country's first prime minister, Jawaharlal Nehru, headed the government from 1966 to 1977 when she was replaced by the Janata Party government led by the veteran politician Morarji Desai. BHUTAN moved towards full independence and Maldives became independent from Britain in 1965.

perienced several military takeovers of government and fought 3 wars with India. KASHMIR remained in dispute between the two countries, but agreement was reached on the disposal of the vital Indus Valley waters in 1960. The main languages are Urdu and English, Punjabi, Sindhi and Baluchi are spoken regionally. Area: 803,943 sq km; population: 81,450,000; capital: Islamabad.
Poona, India, is a main centre of Marathi culture. It is a commercial centre. Population: 900,000.

S Sri Lanka, formerly Ceylon, is an island republic off the south-east coast of India. About 66% of Sri Lankans are Buddhist Sinhalese and most of the rest are Tamils who are mainly Hindu. However, Christians form about 8% of the population. Minorities include the Muslim Moors (descended from Arabs), Burghers (Eurasians) and Veddahs (descendants of the earliest known inhabitants) who now live in remote forests. Tea, rubber and coconuts are the mainstay of the country's economy. The

main languages in Sri Lanka are Sinhalese, English and Tamil. Area: 65,610 sq km; Population: 15,568,000; Capital: COLOMBO.

T Thar Desert (Great Indian Desert) is a sandy wasteland in north-west India and south-east Pakistan. It is bounded by the Aravalli Hills, the Indus and Sutlej rivers, and the Arabian Sea. It covers about 2,600,000 sq km.
Thimpu is the capital and largest town of Bhutan and was established only in 1961 around some old temples. It

stands 2,500 metres above sea level. Population: 9,000.

Pilgrims at Varanasi

V Varanasi (formerly Benares), the holiest city of Hinduism, is a centre for pilgrims. It stands on the GANGES RIVER in north-east INDIA. Population: 750,000.

W Western Ghats (see DECCAN).

Eastern Asia is dominated by two contrasting nations, the industrial colossus of Japan and the world's most populous nation, communist China. Both nations are now adjusting to their vital roles in world affairs.

Eastern Asia

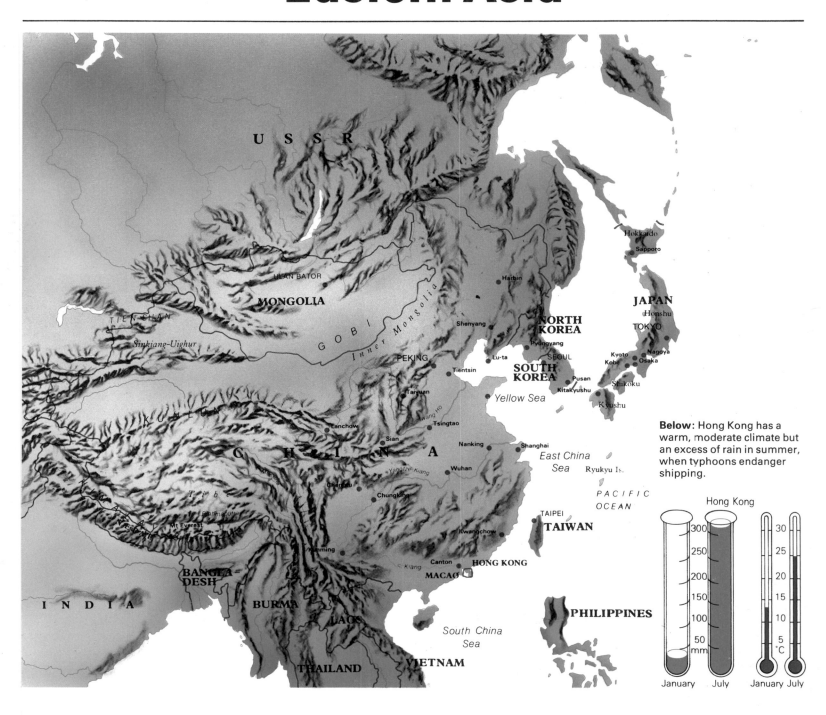

Below: Hong Kong has a warm, moderate climate but an excess of rain in summer, when typhoons endanger shipping.

Hong Kong

January July   January July

Reference

A **Ainu** people, numbering about 16,000, are the survivors of a white people of Caucasoid race who may have been the original inhabitants of JAPAN. They are now confined to north-east Japan.

C **Canton**, see KWANG-CHOW.
China is the world's most populous country and also the third largest in area. The People's Republic of China is

bigger than all Europe and is divided into 21 provinces and 5 autonomous (self-governing) regions. Szechwan province alone is larger than France and has more people than France, Belgium and the Netherlands combined. Yet the population density of China is less than the average for Asia and its annual rate of increase is well under the world average. China's age-old culture is rooted in the Confucian-Taoist and Buddhist traditions, but some 5% of the population is Muslim. However, religion

as such now has little influence on Chinese affairs. China's economy — once among the world's poorest — has improved considerably since the ending of over 20 years of civil and foreign wars in 1949. In that year, a communist government was established under Mao Tse-tung. Mao was revered almost as a god, especially during the 'cultural revolution' in 1966-69. Opponents of his policies were attacked as 'revisionists'. But reverence for his inward-looking objectives declined rapidly after his death in 1976. China

then increased its contacts with the non-communist world and gave priority to the modernization of its economy. Although China's industry is growing rapidly, agriculture is still the basis of the economy. Steel pro-

duction, for example, had by 1978 reached only 30% of Japan's output. About 94% of China's people are 'Han' Chinese and the remainder include Tibetan, Manchu, Mongol, Korean, Uighur, Hui, Yi Chuang and Maio

Great Wall of China

Eastern Asia comprises the mainland countries of CHINA, MONGOLIA, NORTH KOREA and SOUTH KOREA; the European enclaves of HONG KONG and MACAO; and the island countries of JAPAN and TAIWAN. The region covers 8.85 per cent of the world's land area but holds 26 per cent of its population.

China, Mongolia and Korea

The Manchurian Plain, east of the Great Khingan Mountains in north-east China, and the North China Plain in the valley of HWANG HO southeast of PEKING, comprise China's best agricultural land. Westwards lies the Loess Highlands, an area made fertile by loess, yellow dust blown by winds from Central Asia. Loess washed away by the Hwang Ho (Yellow River) accounts for the name of that river and of the Yellow Sea into which it empties. Southwards, across the Tsinling Mountains, lies the vast, fertile Yangtze Plain where about seven per cent of the world's people live in the basin drained by the YANGTZE KIANG. Southwards again, the land becomes hilly. Westwards lies the great black plateau of TIBET, source of the Hwang Ho and

Below left: The bleak steppes of Mongolia can barely sustain settled agriculture, which was almost unknown in the country before 1955. Stockraising is the main occupation.

Below: The 'boat people' of Macao, Portugal's tiny enclave on the Chinese mainland, live mainly by catching and selling fish. Their fishing boats are also their homes. Often, boat people of Macao continue to live on the waters of the South China Sea from choice rather than from necessity.

Yangtze Kiang. The Himalayas tower along the southern edge of the plateau, forming a mighty wall against the Indian subcontinent. West of Tibet, the Karakoram Range runs through Jammu and Kashmir to join the PAMIR KNOT, from where the TIEN SHAN range branches northeast into China's Autonomous Region of SINKIANG-UIGHUR. The Tien Shan forms the northern edge of the Takla-Makan, which extends to the KUNLUN SHAN and Altyn Tagh ranges that rise along the northern fringe of the Tibetan Plateau. North-east of the Takla-Makan, across the Turfan depression, which is over 150 metres below sea level, lies the Dzungarian basin. North-east again, extending into Mongolia, lie the Altai Mountains. This range extends into the Plateau of Mongolia, and south of this lies the bleak GOBI. This desert extends into China's autonomous region of INNER MONGOLIA. North and South Korea form a peninsula off north-eastern China, extending almost to Japan. The YALU RIVER, which rises in the Chang-pai Shan range in China, forms most of the border between North Korea and China before emptying into Korea Bay.

(Meo) peoples. China has some of the world's most populous cities, including SHANGHAI, PEKING, TIENTSIN, SHENYANG, CHUNGKING, LU-TA, KWANGCHOW (Canton), WUHAN, HARBIN, SIAN, NANKING and TSINGTAO. These 12 cities have a combined population roughly equal to that of Britain or Italy. About 20 million Chinese live outside China in addition to 4.5 million in HONG KONG and 18 million in TAIWAN — an offshore state which China claims as part of the homeland. Thirty per cent of the people live in the YANGTZE

KIANG basin. Wheat is the main crop in the north and rice in the south. Chinese is written in a standard non-alphabetical script and spoken in many dialects of which Mandarin is the official one. Minority languages include Tibetan and Uighur (a Turkic language). Area: 9,596,961 sq km; Population (including Chinese residents abroad): 911,573,000; capital: Peking.
Chungking is a city in southern China and the country's former wartime capital. Population: 3,000,000.

G Gobi is a windswept, basin-shaped desert in central Asia covering 1,250,000 sq km. A plateau over 1,000 metres above sea level, it straddles south-east Mongolia and north-east China, and is surrounded by mountains. A few nomadic tribes roam the desert and there are a few settlers. The Turk-Siberian railway passes through it to Peking.

H Harbin, a city in China's former province of Manchuria, is an important transportation centre. Population: c. 2,000,000.

Hindu Kush, an offshoot of the PAMIR KNOT, divides east Afghanistan from north-west Pakistan. Its highest peak, Tirich Mir, rises to 7,705 metres.
Hiroshima, in west Honshu, Japan, was largely destroyed in 1945 by the first atomic bomb to be dropped on a city. Population: 650,000.
Hokkaido, nothernmost of Japan's 4 main islands, contains only 5% of its population, including most of the AINU people. Area: 78,073 sq km; population: 6,200,000.
Hong Kong is a British colony on the coast of south

China and has a 98% Chinese population. Most of the people live crowded on Hong Kong island or in Kowloon, a city on the mainland. Beyond Kowloon, covering most of Hong Kong's area,

Floating restaurant, Hong Kong

The tiny Portuguese enclave of Macao, a peninsula and two islands, lies on the east side of the Si Kiang (West River) of southern China. Hong Kong, a British enclave on the Chinese mainland and some 230 islands, lies east of Macao on the Chu Chiang (Pearl River).

Japan and Taiwan

Japan is an archipelago off the north-east Asian mainland. It is made up of four main islands which are (north to south) HOKKAIDO, HONSHU, SHIKOKU and KYUSHU. The country is very mountainous and has about 200 volcanoes, some still active. The highest mountains, the Japanese Alps, rise to 3,779 metres at Mount Fuji (Fujiyama) an inactive volcano in central Honshu. Japan is on the 'ring of fire', an earthquake belt that rings the Pacific and has over 1,000 earth tremors a year. A great earthquake that struck Tokyo in 1923, together with the resultant fire and tidal wave, killed over 100,000 people. Nowhere in Japan lies more than 150 kilometres from the sea and the country has no long rivers. Instead, thousands of swift-flowing streams flow down from the mountains to the coasts.

South-west from Japan and part of the same archipelago, the RYUKYU ISLANDS (owned by Japan) extend in an arc towards Taiwan. They are hilly and infertile. Taiwan, like Japan is mountainous and earthquake-prone.

Natural vegetation of Eastern Asia

Forest land forms the natural vegetation of eastern China. Hardwoods and conifers predominate in the extreme north-east (near the USSR border), and the deciduous oaks along the North China Plain. These give way to evergreen oaks towards the south. Tropical rainforest once covered the southern coastal region and Hainan Island. Mountain plants and desert grasses cover much of Tibet below the snow line. Most of the vast area between Kashmir and eastern Mongolia is desert. Grassland, steppe and meadow predominate in the long region extending from the north-eastern border of Tibet north-eastwards through Inner Mongolia to the USSR. Deciduous trees predominate in the north of Korea, giving way to bamboo and evergreens in the south. The natural vegetation of Japan and Taiwan is similar to that of eastern China.

Above: Japan's sacred Mount Fujiyama, an exhausted volcano 100 km south-west of Tokyo, is still the site of Shinto pilgrimages. In the foreground, rice dries within sight of Fujiyama's snow-capped peaks.

The climate of Eastern Asia

China's climate is much affected by monsoons. These winds carry warm, moist air inland from the sea in summer. In winter, they are reversed, blowing cold, dry air seawards from central Asia. Summer temperatures average about 27°C over much of China, rising to over 37°C in the Takla Makan and Gobi desert regions, but averaging only 15°C in Tibet. January temperatures for north and central China and Tibet fall to an average of about –7°C in winter, and on the Plateau of Mongolia drop to an average of about –24°C. China's coastlands vary less than these extremes. Generally, the south-east coast has a warm, subtropical temperature for most of the year; inland extremes are greater between summer and winter and between day and night.

Japan's climate is affected by two ocean currents. The Japan Current, flowing northwards along the southern and eastern coasts of the country, keeps southern Japan and eastern Taiwan warmer than the Chinese mainland opposite. However, the Oyashio Current flows south to bring cold northern waters to the coasts of north-western Japan. July temperatures aver-

---

lie the New Territories, so called because they were occupied by the British later than Hong Kong island. They are due under treaty to be returned to China in 1997. Hong Kong has a dynamic economy prospering from banking, commerce, shipping and manufacturing, and from acting as an outlet for Chinese trade. It is largely dependent upon China for water and food, although the land is intensively farmed. The Confucianist-Taoist-Buddhist religion is not a strong force. Most of the people are refugees, or children of refugees, from China. Area: 1,045 sq km; population: 4,689,000; capital: VICTORIA.

Honshu is Japan's largest island and contains about 78% of the country's people. Area: 227,415 sq km; population: 92,030,000.

Hwang Ho (Yellow River) is the second longest river of China. It rises in north-east Tibet and flows about 4,700 km through Chinese territory to the Yellow Sea, draining more than 1,000,000 sq km. The yellow colour of the river and sea results from the presence of loess, a fine yellow dust, which is carried in the water.

▎Inner Mongolia is an Autonomous Region of CHINA bordering the Mongolian People's Republic. Area: 1,177,500; population: 16,000,000.

▎Japan, an island empire in North-east Asia, has within 100 years developed from a medieval state to the world's third greatest industrial nation. Although Japan's density of population is 10 times that of the world average, only 15% of its land can be cultivated and there are few natural resources. Consequently most of its food, petroleum, coal and timber

Sumo wrestling, Japan

have to be imported. Japan's wealth is based mainly upon the export of vehicles, electronic and telecommunications equipment, instruments, man-made fibres, ships and other manufactures. More than 60% of all Japanese now live in cities, which include TOKYO, the capital, OSAKA, YOKOHAMA, NAGOYA, KYOTO, KOBE, KITAKYUSHU, SAPPORO, Kawasaki and Fukuoka. These 10 cities have a population equal to that of Canada's. Despite industrialization, the Japanese still value ancient traditions

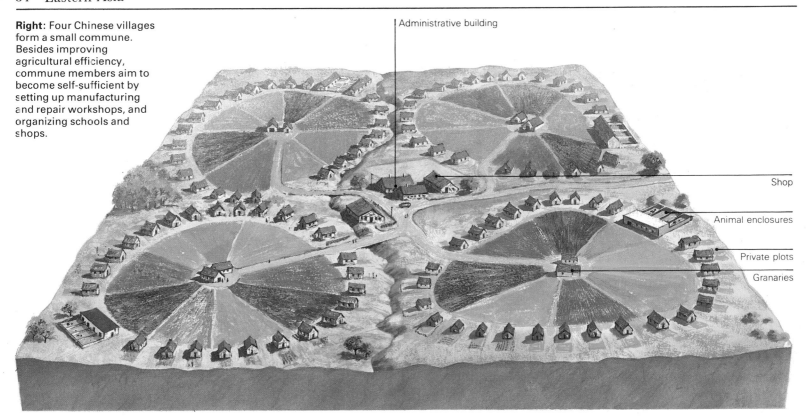

Right: Four Chinese villages form a small commune. Besides improving agricultural efficiency, commune members aim to become self-sufficient by setting up manufacturing and repair workshops, and organizing schools and shops.

Administrative building

Shop

Animal enclosures

Private plots

Granaries

age 16–22°C in northern Japan, rising above this in the south and up to 30°C in Taiwan. January temperatures of 15–18°C in Taiwan drop to 4–8°C in the southern tip of Japan and fall further northwards to below –6°C in northern Hokkaido.

China receives most of its rainfall in summer. Its annual precipitation (rain and snow) gradually decreases from above 1,500 millimetres in south-east China to about 500 millimetres in central China and below 100 millimetres in Mongolia. Korea's annual precipitation varies from 550 millimetres in the north to 1,400 millimetres in the south. The driest part of Japan, eastern Hokkaido, receives about 1,000 millimetres of precipitation; the wettest part, the south-eastern coast, receives more than 3,000 millimetres a year. Most of Taiwan receives 1,000 millimetres of precipitation annually and mountain areas up to 5,000 millimetres.

Peoples and ways of life

Almost all the 1,100 million people of Eastern Asia are of the Mongoloid race and over 80 per cent are Chinese. Traditionally, Buddhism was

the dominant religion of the whole area, alongside the earlier established religions of Taoism and Confucianism in China and Taiwan, and Shinto in Japan. Koreans practised all four of these religions and others too, including Christianity. About 5 per cent of China's people are Muslims. However, religion now has little influence in the communist republics of China, Mongolia and North Korea.

Life in the Chinese communes

China has always been an agricultural country. It was also once a land where bandits, warlords, oppressive landlords and tax collectors kept the peasants perpetually poor. Although poverty did not disappear after the communist victory in 1949, these four age-old enemies of the peasants did. Also famine and flooding — the twin scourges — were greatly reduced by an urgent programme of public works. At first, the communists seized the land and redistributed it to those that tilled it. During the 1950s, each tiny family farm was merged into a cooperative (a group of farms organized as a larger unit) to gain the benefits of large-scale production. The

Below: To use chopsticks, grip one at the base of the thumb; then the second chopstick is held by the top of the thumb and the forefinger, to be deftly manipulated with the rigidly-held first chopstick.

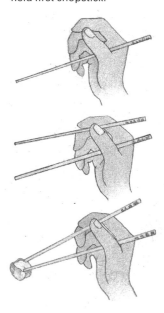

founded upon the national religion of Shinto, which for most people is fused with Buddhism. Following defeat in World War II, Japan retained its monarchy but renounced the claim that its emperor was a god. Over 99% of the people are Japanese and speak Japanese, but some 16,000 AINU people live in the north-east. Area: 372,313 sq km; population: 118,747,000; capital: Tokyo.

K Kitakyushu is a city in north KYUSHU, Japan. It was formed in 1963 by combining the former cities of

Kokura, Moji, Tobata, Wakamatsu and Yawata. Population: 1,150,000. **Kobe,** a leading Japanese city, is also the port for OSAKA. Population: 1,400,000. **Kun Lun** is the longest mountain system of Asia, extending over 3,000 km into Tibet from the PAMIR KNOT. It rises over 7,700 metres. **Kwangchow** (formerly Canton) is an important river port in south CHINA. It is situated on the Canton River to the north-west of Hong Kong. Population: 4,000,000. **Kyoto,** the capital of Japan for 1,000 years until 1868, is

a leading cultural centre. Population: 1,580,000. **Kyushu** is the south-westernmost of Japan's 4 main islands. It contains 13% of the total population, to make it the most densely populated island with 420 people to the sq km. But none of the largest Japanese cities are situated here. Area: 36,555 sq km; Population: 15,470,000.

L Lhasa is the capital of Tibet and one of the world's most remote cities. It contains the Potala Palace, once the winter residence of

the Dalai Lama, head of the Lamaist religion. The population was formerly 70,000, but many Tibetans have fled and more Chinese have moved in since 1965. **Lu-ta** (formerly Lushun-Talien), China, comprises the old naval port of Port Arthur and the old commercial port of Dairen. The city is situated in the south of Laiotung province on Korea Bay. Population: 4,500,000.

M Macao is a Portuguese possession on the Chinese mainland. It lies about 65 km west of Hong

Kong. Apart from its 2 small offshore islands, it is almost entirely urban and has the

Cathedral ruin, Macao

Right: Chinese food is much favoured internationally and has many regional varieties. The Cantonese meal shown includes tea, bean curd, rice, sweet and sour pork, and spring rolls. Cantonese food forms the main cuisine of Hong Kong.

Below: Korean food, like Korean culture generally, has been heavily influenced by both China and Japan. The Korean meal shown includes tea, vegetables, rice, and rice sweetmeats.

tres were set up under management committees formed by commune members.

The Mongolian way

In Mongolia, communist since 1924, livestock farming forms the basis of the economy with over 20 million animals. The Mongolians are traditionally nomadic, but since the mid-1950s they have been organized mainly into ranch cooperatives. Some settled agriculture has been introduced and mining and manufacturing is developing. The ranch cooperatives have shops, schools, clubs and medical and veterinary facilities.

Right: The Chinese girl (*left*) wears the padded trouser suit and hairstyle of Canton. The Japanese girl (*right*) is dressed in the *kimono*, still worn by Japanese of both sexes in their own homes. The Korean girl (*centre*) comes from a country heavily influenced by both China and Japan.

cooperatives, which could afford better fertilizers, tools and machinery, developed into collective farms in which the private ownership of farms by individual families disappeared. In 1958, with China fully committed to the ideals of Chairman Mao Tsetung, rural affairs took another turn. The collective farms began to amalgamate into even larger units. Spurred on by Maoist leaders, the farmers set up people's communes in which the work and daily life of the people was closely integrated and the collective good of the commune was supposed to be put above family ties. Communal workshops, living quarters, eating places, nurseries and even communal shopping, washing and sewing cen-

Right: The Japanese meal includes tea, rice, and vegetables like the Chinese. Uniquely Japanese is *sushi* (rice balls with seaweed, filled with egg), and *tempura* (sea-food fried in batter).

world's highest population density — 18,500 people to the sq km. Over 60% of the people live in Macao City. Once the most important European port in the Far East, Macao is now a convenient outlet for the trade of China, which strongly influences the territory's government. The languages spoken are Chinese, Portuguese and English. Area: 16 sq km; Population: 295,000; capital: Macao City.
Mongolia is a remote communist republic in east central Asia and has the lowest population density of any

country — 1 person to 1 sq km. It is a bleak, landlocked area of high plateaux and mountains, with the GOBI in the 'south-east. About 700 years ago, the Mongolians dominated most of Asia and eastern Europe, but their empire disintegrated leaving their homeland isolated. They are a nation of stock-raisers whose communist government has settled most of them in vast ranches since the 1950s. The only large city is ULAN BATOR. Mongolians are traditionally Shamanist and Buddhist, but religion now has little

influence in the country. The main language is Khalkha Mongolian, but Turkic is also

Mongolian tribesman

spoken. Area: 1,565,000 sq km; Population: 1,675,000; capital: Ulan Bator.

N **Nagasaki** is an important port and industrial centre on KYUSHU, Japan. At one time it was the only port open to foreigners. The city was badly damaged by the second atomic bomb in 1945. Population: 470,000.
Nagoya, on HONSHU, is one of Japan's biggest industrial cities. Population: 2,252,000.
Nanking 'Southern Capital' has been the capital of CHINA on several occasions, the last being in 1946-49. The

city is situated on the YANGTZE KIANG, about 260 km from its mouth near Shanghai. The port handles much of the river traffic and important industries include textiles and fertilizers. Population: 2,000,000.
Nara, a town east of Osaka, was the capital of Japan in 710-784. It still preserves buildings of the period. Population: 165,000.
North Korea is a communist republic in north-east Asia. It separated from the southern part of Korea in 1945, following 35 years of Japanese occupation. The

Traditionally Japanese houses are delicately structured with sliding doors and the minimum of furniture. Beds and tables are close to the floor, which is never walked on without first taking ones shoes off. Even modern apartments keep much of the traditional style, although the charcoal-burning earthenware heating pots have mostly been replaced by gas or electric heaters. Although western dress is usually worn on the streets, the *kimono*, a loosely-tied robe of cotton or silk, is worn at home. Almost all Japanese combine to some extent the national religions of Shinto and Buddhism in their everyday lives.

The Koreans and Taiwanese

Korea, under Chinese influence for hundreds of years, was occupied by Japan between 1895 and 1945. Socially, the country reflects both Chinese and Japanese influences. Economically, the communist north has similarities with both China and the USSR, while the non-communist south has points of contact with an earlier stage of Japanese development. The Taiwanese traditional way of life was not destroyed by communism, but rather eroded by the effort to achieve a Western-style economy.

Economy

Farming occupies 65 per cent of all the workforce in China and Mongolia, 50 per cent in North Korea, 35 per cent in South Korea and Taiwan

The Japanese

In the 100 years 1868–1968 Japan changed from a feudal, medieval country to the world's third richest nation. Seventy-five per cent of all Japanese now live in towns and cities. Although in many ways the Japanese have Westernized even more than some European peoples, old values and traditions still survive, ensuring the continuation of Japan's most ancient culture. Elders and people in superior positions are respected more than in the West; bowing and ultra-polite forms of address, for example, have been retained. Feelings and emotions are kept private rather than being displayed.

Rice remains the basic food but is now part of a richer diet that includes fish (usually raw), and a variety of dishes prepared from soya bean and seaweed. Like most people in Eastern Asia, the Japanese eat from a bowl with chopsticks.

Above: Towering modern office blocks on busy Hong Kong island contrast strangely with the colony's few remaining rickshaws—now fast-disapearing oddities often bought up by wealthy trophy-seekers.

Right: The 'world's ricebowl' lies in monsoon Asia, extending from India through South-east Asia to Japan. (China and Japan are often called 'monsoon lands' although they lie north of the tropics.) The monsoon climate favours the growth of rice, which flourishes especially in Bangladesh, along the great river valleys of China, and in the fertile volcanic island of Java. Each dot represents about 250,000 tonnes of rice.

economy is heavily dependent on mining and industry. Almost all the population is Korean and speaks Korean. Over 30% live in towns, the only large city being Pyongyang. The country has a mixed religious tradition including Confucianism, Buddhism, Shamanism (belief in spirits and the powers of medicine men or shamans), Shinto and Chondokyo (a Buddhist-Christian cult). However, religion is not now dominant. Area: 120,538 sq km; population: 18,002,000; capital: PYONG-YANG.

O **Osaka** is the second city of Japan. It is noted for its many waterways crossed by 800 bridges. Population: 2,950,000.

P **Pamir Knot** is a high plateau in Central Asia where the HINDU KUSH, TIEN SHAN, KUN LUN and Himalaya ranges meet to form a 'knot'. Called 'the roof of the world', the plateau straddles parts of Afghanistan, USSR, China, India and Pakistan. It rises in places to 4,600 metres and covers some 93,000 sq km.
Peking is the capital of CHINA

Imperial Palace, Peking

and one of the world's 6 most populous cities. Historically, there were 4 cities in Peking before 1912. The Outer City was Chinese while the Inner City was reserved for the Manchu conquerors of China. Within this the Imperial City and the Forbidden City were accessible only to members of the Manchu dynasty and their retinue. Peking is now a single city, but its historic buildings still stand. Population (including surrounding rural area): 9,000,000.
Pusan is the chief port of SOUTH KOREA. It lies on its south-east coast opposite Japan. Population: 2,125,000.

Pyongyang is the capital of NORTH KOREA. Founded about 3,000 years ago, it was once the capital of all Korea. Population: 2,200,000.

R **Ryukyu Islands** are a group of about 100 Japanese islands lying between Japan and Taiwan. They include Okinawa, scene of one of the bloodiest battles in World War II. Population: 2,200,000.

S **Sapporo** is Japan's northernmost large city. It was planned in Western style. Population: 1,150,000.

but only 20 per cent in Japan. Trade and industry predominate in Hong Kong. The per capita income (i.e. the average income per person) in the region is only ten per cent of that in USA, but great variations exist between countries. For example, the per capita income of a Japanese is about 65 per cent of that of an American, while, at the other extreme, per capita income in China is little more than 3 per cent of that in the United States. However, the cost of living is low in China because of subsidized necessities such as housing. Hong Kong and Taiwan are the richest places in eastern Asia after Japan.

China – rousing the sleeping giant
In 1949, when the Communist Party took control of the economy, China was a 'sleeping giant'. The new leaders hoped to transform the country into an economic superpower within a short period, but their 'Great Leap Forward' failed in 1958–60. Even so, by 1977 China led in the world production of rice, millet, sweet potatoes, tobacco and jute. It came second in maize, barley, soya beans, groundnuts and tea; and third in wheat, cotton fibres, potatoes and tomatoes. Rice, grown mainly in the south, and wheat, grown in the north, accounted for over 50 per cent of all the food produced.

China, the world's third largest coal producer, mined in 1977 the equivalent of 75 per cent of the coal output of the United States. With Bolivia, China also led in antimony. Its crude oil production equalled 20 per cent of Saudi Arabia's and crude steel output was nearly 25 per cent of that of the United States or Japan.

Left: Japanese technology, non-existent in 1868, now challenges that of Western countries for supremacy in a world of shrinking markets. The picture shows a ship under construction at Yokohama.

Below: Japanese companies provide housing, holidays, medical facilities and pensions. The 'father-figure' employer even arranges marriages between employees and provides facilities to care for their children—who may become the next generation of employees. Promotion often depends on age, service and loyalty rather than ability.

But the electricity consumed reached only five per cent of that used in the USA. China's small manufacturing industries were developing fast but foreign trade remained negligible.

Japan — economic superpower
In 1976, Japan, with a gross domestic product equalling $562 billion, moved near to overtaking the USSR and becoming the world's second richest country, with imports totalling $70 billion and exports topping $80 billion. Japan was surpassed as a trading nation only by the United States and West Germany and excelled in the manufacture of cars and electronic devices.

Street scene, Seoul

Seoul (Kyongsong) is the capital of SOUTH KOREA and a leading commercial, cultural and industrial centre. The city was occupied by North Korean forces in 1950 and again in 1953. It underwent considerable reconstruction when the war ended in the same year. Population: 6,500,000.
Shanghai lies on the Whangpoo River, on the central coast of China. It grew from a small fishing port to become the world's largest city in only 130 years. This was developed as an international outlet for Chinese trade, mainly by the British, French and Americans, who occupied and ran it until World War II. Despite its being the world's most populous city, its importance has declined under communist rule. Population (including nearby rural areas): 12,000,000.
Shenyang (formerly Mukden) is the capital of China's Liaoning province. It was the leading city of the region once called Manchuria. Population: 5,000,000.
Shikoku is the smallest and only non-volcanic island of Japan's 4 main islands. It has only 4% of the country's population. Area: 18,257 sq km; population: 5,035,000.
Sian, as Chang-an, was an ancient capital of China. Population: 2,000,000.
Sinkiang-Uighur is CHINA'S north-westernmost Autonomous Region. It has fewer than 10,000,000 people living in its 1,646,800 sq km owing to the barrenness of the land.
South Korea is a republic in north-east Asia. It was separated from NORTH KOREA in 1945 after 35 years of Japanese occupation. South Korea has twice as many people as North Korea crowded into less territory. It also has only 30% of the mineral resources of the North but its people are richer. Ethnically, the population is almost 100% Korean and Korean is the main language. South Korea has the same religious traditions as the North, but religion plays a more important role. It also has a 5% Christian minority which is mainly Protestant. Cities include SEOUL, PUSAN, Taegu, Inchon and Kwaniu. Area: 98,484 sq km; Population: 38,512,000; capital: Seoul.

T **Taipeh** is the capital of TAIWAN. It contains in its museum many of the cultural treasures of China taken there by the retreating Nationalist armies in 1949. Population: 2,250,000.

In contrast to China — the agricultural giant — it is the industrial colossus of the east. By 1977 it had become the world's second or third largest producer of crude steel, pig iron, copper, aluminium, cadmium, zinc, magnesium and synthetic rubber. Despite this impressive record, Japan has few mineral resources and is self-sufficient only in lead, sulphur and zinc. Nearly all minerals and 98 per cent of petroleum have to be imported. Japan's barren islands, on which only 15 per cent of the land can be cultivated, have to support a population density of 320 to the square kilometre (3.5 times that of China). It is densely forested, and half the farmland is allotted to rice. Most farmers own their own land.

The smaller economies

During the 1950s and 1960s, Hong Kong became a 'pocket-sized trading giant', marketing a vast range of products manufactured either in Hong Kong or in China. These were eagerly bought throughout the world because of their cheapness. During the 1970s, prosperity brought the end of cheap labour and saw a rise in prices. First Taiwan, then South Korea, set out to undercut Hong Kong. By 1977, both countries had a flourishing foreign trade greater in value than China's. North Korea, which in the 1960s had a higher per capita income than South Korea's fell behind by the late 1970s. South Korea had by this time manufactured its own make of car, the *Pony*. The two Koreas and Taiwan have valuable mineral deposits and are heavily forested.

Above: Pharmaceutical stores set up in Maoist China became efficient but highly utilitarian. Cosmetics were considered unnecessary. Beauty treatment became part of the trend towards femininity only after Mao's death.
Below: Mao's 'Little Red Book', revered like a sacred work by China's soldiers and workers, was downgraded after his death.

Agriculture remains highly important despite industrialization. Much of Macao's income comes from tourism, with gambling casinos especially important.

History and culture

CHINA has the world's longest continuous civilization (still unbroken for 3,500 years), which is to some extent the parent of the Japanese and Korean cultures. For a century or so, around the AD 1200s to 1300s, MONGOLIA held the world's largest empire. Although art and culture generally continued to flourish in Eastern Asia, by the 1800s the region materially had fallen into decline when compared to Europe and the United States. From the mid-1800s, the West used its superior technology to dominate Eastern Asia. The Japanese quickly saw that the only way to repel Western domination was to outdo the westerners in the technology that gave them their advantage.

The transformation of Japan

In 1868, in a 'palace revolution' led by the god-emperor, JAPAN threw off feudalism and strove to become a modern state in the quickest possible time. The Japanese leaders studied Western countries carefully and took the best points from each. For example, after Germany defeated

Taiwan (also known as Formosa) is a breakaway island province of CHINA. Occupied by Japan in 1895-1945, it became the final retreat of the defeated armies of Nationalist China when China fell to the communists in 1949. The Nationalist soldiers, once a threat to mainland China, are now all well past military age. The Taiwan government still claims to represent all China and the Peking government claims Taiwan. However, for practical purposes Taiwan is now an independent republic shunned by most of the world diplomatically, but not commercially. Over 98% of the people are Chinese and the Confucianist-Taoist-Buddhist tradition is stronger than in China or HONG KONG. The island has about 180,000 aboriginal people ethnically related to Indonesians. It is a prosperous state which earns about 35% of its gross national income from industry. The main language is Mandarin, but other Chinese dialects are spoken. Area: 35,962 sq km; population: 16,800,000; capital: TAIPEH.

Tibet, at times in the past an independent or semi-independent state, became an Autonomous Region of China in 1965. It is a high, cold, bleak plateau in south central Asia containing the world's highest mountains and hundreds of lakes, many of salt. Poor soil and harsh climate render most of Tibet unfit for crop farming, but yaks, animals related to cows, provide food, clothing and transportation. Many important rivers rise in Tibet, including the YANGTZE, Mekong, Salween, Indus and Brahmaputra. Area: 1,221,600 sq km; popula-

tion: 1,300,000 (1965). Since 1965, about 85,000 Tibetans are believed to have left and some 500,000 Chinese have settled there. Capital: Lhasa

Tibetan monk in India

(50,000 in 1953).
Tien Shan, a mountain system mainly in Chinese SINKIANG-UIGHUR, extends about 2,400 km north-east from the PAMIR KNOT. Pobeda Peak rises to 7,444 metres above sea level.
Tientsin, China, was once a leading centre of foreign trade, but it has now diminished in international importance. Population: 5,000,000.
Tokyo is the capital of Japan and the world's most populous city after SHANGHAI. It contains about 10% of Japan's people. It is a Wes-

France in the Franco-Prussian war of 1870–71, Japan hastily replaced its French military advisers with Germans. In less than 40 years, Japan achieved victories against both China and Russia resulting in territorial gains and 'spheres of influence' and became the most important ally of the British Empire. Rapid social and economic advance in Japan brought internal political stresses, that found release in overseas wars and conquests in Korea and China. In 1941–43, Japan finally challenged the whole of the West, seizing its empires in the Pacific area. However, the dropping of the atomic bombs on HIROSHIMA and NAGASAKI by the USA in 1945, brought the total defeat of Japan. Between 1945 and 1951 it came under American occupation. The pace of social and economic change accelerated during the following quarter century, during which Japan became one of the world's richest nations.

The Chinese revolutions

Revolution brought the end of 3,500 years of Chinese dynasties during the last days of 1911. But the republic set up in 1912 barely survived the political dissension, civil wars and Japanese invasions of the next 37 years. From 1925, the *Kuomintang* (nationalists) tried to rule China but had to fight the Japanese and the Communists led by Mao Tsetung. Mainland China finally fell to the communists in 1949, and the nationalists retreated to China's offshore island of TAIWAN. Protected by the United States, Taiwan developed into a prosperous, independent state.

China did not become fully communist for several years after 1949, but Mao was determined to implant his own form of communism — or Maoism — at almost any price. But the failure of the Great Leap Forward led to criticism of his policies by other leaders in the early 1960s. Mao's reply was to create a 'cultural revolution' in which China's youth, spearheaded by 'red guards', attacked all those who disagreed with Mao's ideas. Even the President of China was toppled, and the economy was severely disrupted. A secret power struggle continued into the 1970s. Meanwhile, China's former ally Russia became its rival, then its enemy. Gradually China moved towards friendship with its old enemy, the United States. Towards the end of his life, Mao's god-like status diminished. After his death in 1976, his policies began to be changed

Above: A Japanese priest beats the gong at a Shinto festival. Shinto involves the worship of an infinite number of *kami* (nature spirits). It has almost no foreign adherents, but nearly every Japanese practises Shinto, often alongside another religion, usually Buddhism.

rapidly. His successor as chairman was Hua Guofeng. But the man seen to be leading China away from Maoism and towards greater democracy and economic efficiency was the first vice-premier, Deng Xiaoping, a survivor of persecution during the 'cultural revolution'.

Korea, Hong Kong and Macao

The collapse of Japan in 1945 brought northern Korea under Russian occupation and southern Korea under American occupation. The Russians and Americans quit in 1948–49, leaving the country divided at the 38th parallel of latitude between a northern pro-Russian government and a southern pro-American government. Civil war followed in 1950–53 in which United Nations forces led by Americans aided the south, and Chinese forces aided the north. About a million soldiers and a million civilians died in the war. Since the armistice of 1953, North Korea and South Korea have been separate republics.

The Portuguese took Macao in about 1557 and in 1887 the Chinese recognized it as Portuguese territory. Britain took the tiny island of HONG KONG by force in 1842 and Kowloon on the mainland in 1860. It leased the larger New Territories from China for 99 years in 1898. China was content to leave the two enclaves under foreign rule.

---

ternized city much rebuilt after World War II. The city area has a density of about 16,000 people to the sq km (nearly double that of New York and over 3 times that of London). Tokyo is a leading world business centre. Jammed with vehicles, it has developed serious problems of pollution. Population: 9,250,000.
Tsingtao is one of China's chief industrial cities. Population: 1,700,000.
Turkestan is a vast area in Central Asia with no precise boundaries. It extends into China, the USSR and Af-

ghanistan. The PAMIR KNOT and the TIEN SHAN mountains divide the region into East Turkestan, which covers most of Chinese SINKIANG-UIGHUR, and West Turkestan, which belongs to the USSR except for a small area lying across the border in Afghanistan. Area: 2,600,000 sq km.

U **Ulan Bator** (Red Hero) is the capital of Mongolia and contains nearly 25% of the country's people. Population: 380,000.

V **Victoria** is the capital of HONG KONG and the col-

ony's main business centre. Population: 625,000.

W **Wuhan,** in central China, was formed

Unloading Yangtze barges

from the former cities of Hankow, Wuchang and Hanyang. Population: 3,000,000.

Y **Yalu River** rises on the northern border of NORTH KOREA and forms its frontier with China, flowing 800 km to the Sea of Japan.
Yangtze Kiang is China's longest and most important river. It rises in the KUN LUN Mountains nearly 5 km above sea level and flows 5,000 km through Tibet and China into the Yellow Sea. More than 30% of China's population live in the

1,800,000 sq km drained by the Yangtze and its tributaries. Many people live in house boats. The river is navigable for ocean-going ships for 1,000 km inland.
Yokohama, a leading port of Japan about 30 km south of Tokyo, is connected to the capital by the industrial suburb of Kawasaki. The 3 places form the world's largest urban complex. Population: 2,600,000.

South-east Asia has been the scene of tremendous upheavals since the withdrawal of European colonial administrations. War has scarred the face of several South-east Asian countries.

South-east Asia

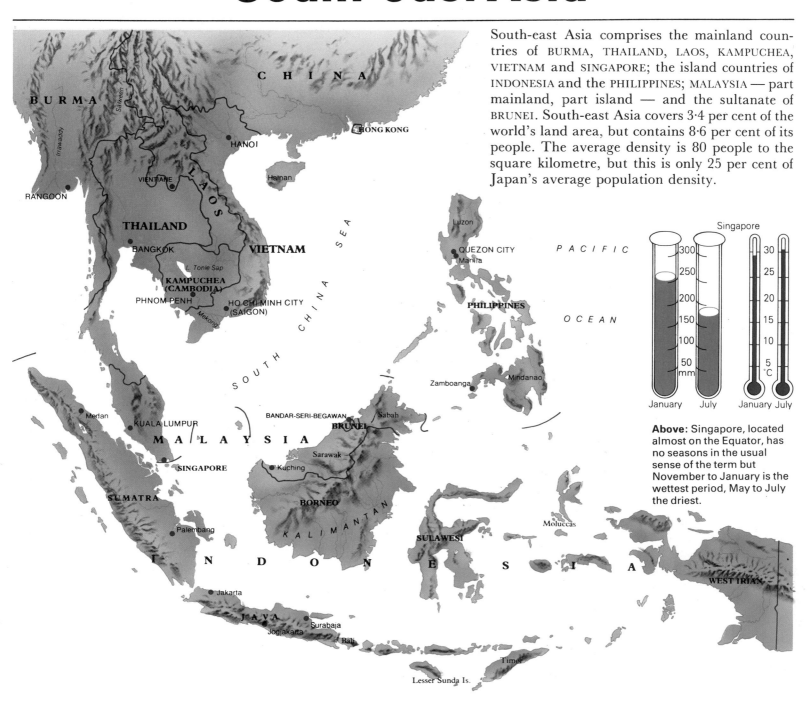

South-east Asia comprises the mainland countries of BURMA, THAILAND, LAOS, KAMPUCHEA, VIETNAM and SINGAPORE; the island countries of INDONESIA and the PHILIPPINES; MALAYSIA — part mainland, part island — and the sultanate of BRUNEI. South-east Asia covers 3·4 per cent of the world's land area, but contains 8·6 per cent of its people. The average density is 80 people to the square kilometre, but this is only 25 per cent of Japan's average population density.

Above: Singapore, located almost on the Equator, has no seasons in the usual sense of the term but November to January is the wettest period, May to July the driest.

Reference

A Angkor, in north-west KAMPUCHEA, is the site of the spectacular civilization of the Khmers.

B Bali is one of the smaller Indonesian islands. Its beauty has made it a favoured tourist spot. Population: c. 3,000,000.
Bandung, an Indonesian city in east Java, was the site of the first Afro-Asian conference in 1955. Population: 1,400,000.

Bangkok is the capital and only large city of THAILAND. It lies on the Chao Phraya River which separates it from the older city of Thonburi, now a suburb. Combined population: 4,000,000.
Borneo is the world's third largest island and is divided between BRUNEI, INDONESIA and MALAYSIA. Area: 752,000 sq km.
Borobudur is a huge Buddhist monument in east Java, dating from the late AD 700s.
Brunei is an oil-rich sultanate on the north coast of Borneo. It opted to remain a

British protected state rather than to join MALAYSIA in 1963. The small capital, Bandar Seri Begawan, has impressive Islamic architecture and the fast-growing population includes mainly Malays, Chinese and Dyaks. Area: 5,800 sq km; population: 217,000.
Burma is a socialist Buddhist republic and has undergone continuous internal unrest since independence in 1948. In 1963-75 it was almost cut off from the outside world. The country's main problems have arisen because 25% of its popula-

tion are non-Burmese. Several groups, notably the

Tribal girl, Shan, Burma

Karens, have gone to war to resist attempts to 'Burmanize' them. Under General Ne Win, the army has tried to rule the country as a socialist state, and the minority peoples, such as the Chinese, Indians, Bengalis and Karens have been encouraged to emigrate. Burma is a leading rice-producer. Its only large cities are RANGOON, Mandalay, Moulmein and Bassein. The main languages are Burmese, Chinese and Indian, but there are also local languages and dialects. Area: 676,552 sq km; population:

The mainland states

Mainland South-east Asia has several mountain ranges running north-south, with river valleys parallel between them. Two main mountain chains extend from China to separate Burma from its neighbours. The IRRAWADDY and SAL-WEEN rivers flow from Upper Burma southwards into the Bay of Bengal. Mountains cover northern Thailand between the Salween and the MEKONG RIVER, which forms most of the long Thai border with Laos. The high, dry Korat Plateau comprises eastern Thailand. Central Thailand is a low, flat valley formed by several rivers that flow into the Gulf of Siam. The long narrow 'tail' of tropical and mountainous southern Thailand extends 800 kilometres southwards to Malaya.

Laos lies between the Mekong River and the Annamese Mountains, one of several ranges that cross north and east Laos. The country's only good farmland lies in the lowland of the Mekong and its tributaries. Mountains separate Kampuchea from its neighbours except in the southeast, where the fertile plain extends through Vietnam to the South China Sea. In the dry season, the Tonle Sap River flows southwards from the shallow, fish-laden TONLE SAP into the Mekong at PHNOM PENH.

The island states

Indonesia consists of over 13,000 islands, the largest being KALIMANTAN (southern BORNEO), SUMATRA, WEST IRIAN (western New Guinea Island), SULAWESI, JAVA and the MOLUCCAS. The small but famous island of BALI lies east of Java. From north-east Sumatra, Indonesia extends some 5,000 kilometres to the border of Papua New Guinea. The East Malaysian states of SARAWAK and SABAH, and the sultanate of Brunei lie in Borneo, north of Kalimantan. Large rivers cut through the tropical rainforest of mountainous inner Borneo, and the coastlands are low swampy plains. Indonesia generally, is mountainous, volcanic, thickly forested and cut by many rivers with swampy banks.

More than 7,000 islands make up the Philippines, the largest of which are LUZON in the north and MINDANAO in the south. The islands are mountainous and volcanic, with thick forests and fertile plains. Forty per cent of the country's rice crop grows on its largest lowland plain, north of Manila. Many rivers, flowing from the mountains to the sea, often flood during the rainy season. Few are navigable except by rafts or small boats.

Climate of South-east Asia

The tropical climate of South-east Asia is mainly determined by the monsoons and by closeness to the sea and the Equator. Mean temperatures at sea level average about 27°C. The annual range increases from about 2°C in Singapore to about 11°C on the high ground of northern Burma. Indonesia, which is bisected by the Equator, receives about 1,750-3,500 millimetres of rain a year. Some areas get half these amounts, but in West Irian, for example, the figures are double. Singapore receives about 2,400 millimetres, spread throughout the year. Northwards, most rain falls between May and October, averaging about 1,500 millimetres. The Philippines is subject to typhoons. Generally, the natural vegetation of South-east Asia is tropical rainforest, but palms, rattans and orchids abound.

Peoples and ways of life

South-east Asia has a greater diversity of peoples and cultures than anywhere else in the world of comparable area. Burmese are mainly akin to Tibetans. Most other peoples in mainland South-east Asia are ethnically close to Chinese, but only

Below: Rice terraces at Banaue, in Luzon island in the Philippines, have been carefully cultivated for some 2,000 years. Forty per cent of the country's rice crop is grown in the fertile plain north of Manila, which includes Banaue. The distant figures are farmers transplanting young rice shoots.

33,821,000; capital: Rangoon.

C **Cebu** is the chief city of Cebu island which lies in the south central PHILIPPINES. Its offshore island of Mactan is where the explorer Ferdinand Magellan (1480-1521) was killed. Population: 450,000.
Chiang Mai, in north THAILAND, is the country's second city. It is a leading cultural and tourist centre. Population: 117,000.

E **East Timor** is part of Timor island lying north-west of Australia. Once a Portuguese possession, it was occupied by Indonesia in late 1975 following rebellion and civil war. Area:

Villagers of Timor

14,925 sq km; Population: 750,000.

H **Hanoi** is the capital of VIETNAM. Situated on the Hong River (Red River) it was badly damaged during the Vietnam war. Population: 1,300,000.
Ho Chi Minh City is the largest city of VIETNAM and was formerly the capital of South Vietnam under the name of Saigon-Cholon. Population: 2,000,000.

I **Indonesia** is a republic lying between India, China and Australia. It consists of about 3,000 islands extending over 5,000 km west to east. More than 60% of the population lives crowded on the volcanic but fertile island of JAVA, where the population density is nearly 800 to the sq km (25 times the world average). The main language is Bahasa Indonesia, a form of Malay. About 90% of Indonesians are Muslims, and some 5% Christian, especially on SUMATRA. BALI has its own form of Hinduism. Other main islands include KALIMANTAN and SULAWESI. After gaining independence from the Netherlands by war in 1949, Indonesia was ruled by President Sukarno for 18 years, during which time the economy failed to prosper.

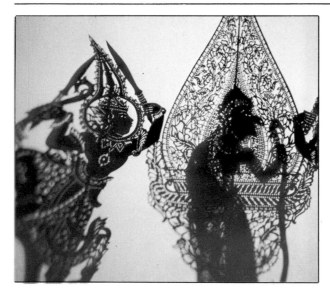

distinctive flat straw hat with concave sides. Street and village markets are highly colourful and shortly after dawn, Buddhist monks may be seen presenting their alms bowls to traders for food.

The only large cities in the region are BANGKOK, where the main airport of South-east Asia is sited, RANGOON, HO CHI MINH CITY, HANOI and PHNOM PENH (depopulated in the late 1970s). Small cities like Mandalay (north Burma), CHIANG MAI and VIENTIANE — market and craft-manufacturing centres for the surrounding countryside — are more typical of the region.

Malaysia and Singapore

MALAYA (Western Malaysia) has many of the features of the countries to its north; 30 per cent of its people, the Chinese, are Buddhist and Taoist. Malaysia is richer than all its neighbours except Singapore, and its prosperous towns, mostly Chinese in population, are flourishing trading centres. About 45 per cent of the people of Malaysia are Malays, and nearly 50 per cent are Muslim. There are large minorities descended from immigrants from the Indian sub-continent, together with some Eurasians in Malaya. Sarawak and Sabah contain many people ethnically related to Malays. Singapore, one of the world's largest ports and business centres, has a 76 per cent Chinese population, almost entirely urban. In Brunei, more than 50

38 per cent are so in Malaysia. There, as in Indonesia and the Philippines, the dominant ethnic group is Malay. Farming is the main occupation except in Singapore. The average income per head of population (per capita income) in the region is about 4·5 per cent of that in the United States, or seven per cent of Japan's, but there are great variations. For example, Singapore has three times the per capita income of Malaysia; six times that of the Philippines and Thailand; and between ten and 20 times that of the other countries (except oil-rich Brunei).

Life in mainland South-east Asia

The predominant religion of mainland South-east Asia (except Malaysia) is Buddhism. Although religious beliefs are strong, especially in Thailand and Burma, they do not dominate daily life so much as on the Indian subcontinent. Thailand, particularly, is dotted with thousands of colourful temples, many with monasteries in which a large proportion of Thai boys spend a period as monks as part of their education. Traditional dress in the region is the *sarong*, a one-piece garment that wraps round the body. Worn by both sexes, the *sarong* takes various forms, and the Burmese version is called the *longyi*. Western dress is now more common for men, and women too, often wear trousers and blouses. The conical straw hat, a shield against sun and rain, is especially popular in Vietnam. Thai peasants and street vendors often wear a

Child drying rice, Java

Left: A performer dances in a temple play featuring the demon Barong in Bali, Indonesia's most popular tourist island. The Balinese practise a unique form of Hinduism which dominates all aspects of their lives. The island has some 30,000 temples, many in private homes.

Sukarno's rule resulted in economic chaos and the massacre of some 250,000 people in 1965-66, mainly Chinese charged with being communist. Indonesia's second president, Suharto, sought to improve the country's prosperity by closer relations with the West. More than 60% of Indonesia is forested and the chief occupations are forestry and agriculture. Area: 2,027,087 sq km; population: 154,712,000; capital: Jakarta.
Irrawaddy River flows about 2,100 km through

Burma to enter the Bay of Bengal near Rangoon.

J Jakarta, INDONESIA's capital, is a port and sprawling city in north-west JAVA. The number of people living there has been boosted by migrants from the countryside. Population: 6,000,000.
Java is the fourth largest but most populous of the Indonesian islands. It contains the capital, JAKARTA. Rice cropping and other farm and forest products are the mainstay of the economy. Area: 130,510 sq km; population: 100,000,000.

Jogjakarta is a Javanese city prominent in Indonesian culture. Population: 425,000.

K Kalimantan is Indonesia's largest island territory and forms much of BORNEO. It is almost the size of France. Area: 500,000 sq km; population: 6,500,000.
Kampuchea (formerly Cambodia and the Khmer Republic) has been a communist republic since the capital, PHNOM PENH, was captured in 1975 at the end of a civil war. From 1975 the communist government depopulated the towns to force almost all civilians into the countryside to grow food. It was an unpopular policy that killed many thousands of

people. The population is about 87% Buddhist and Khmer, with Vietnamese, Chinese and Cham minorities. Khmer is the main language but French is also spoken. Area: 181,035 sq km; population (not accounting for wartime and subsequent casualties): 9,329,000; capital Phnom Penh.
Kuala Lumpur is the capital of MALAYSIA. It is a mainly Chinese city located in a tin-mining and rubber area. Population: 600,000.
Kuching, a largely Chinese river town, is the capital of

Family unit | Communal storage space | Inner verandah | Outer verandah | Rush or grass roof | Movable bamboo screen | Outer walkway

Above: The longhouse, a multi-family living unit built of bamboo and other forest products, is the home of the Land Dyaks and Sea Dyaks, 2 of the communities found in multi-racial Sarawak, East Malaysia. Communal life takes place on the outer and inner verandahs, both of which extend the full length of the 'house' which may have from 6 to 100 'doors'. The 'doors' represent the number of private living units, corresponding to the number of families, which lead off the inner, covered verandah. Access to the longhouse is often only by boat along the river.

SARAWAK, Malaysia. Population: c. 82,000.

Labuan is a small island off Sabah and part of MALAYSIA. Area: 75 sq km; population: 20,000.
Lake Toba is a huge lake in north SUMATRA that contains Samosir Island, home of the Batak people.
Laos, once known as the 'kingdom of a million elephants', is a landlocked Buddhist country in Indo-China. It was a kingdom until 1975, when it became a communist state after many years of civil war. This was

Laotian cart

part of the larger pattern of the Indo-China wars. Only 50% of the people are Lao. The several minorities include mountain tribes who follow local religions mixed with Buddhism. Lao, French and tribal dialects are the languages spoken. Area: 236,800 sq km; population: 3,690,000; capital: Vientiane.
Luzon is the northernmost large island of the PHILIPPINES. It produces 40% of the country's rice crop north of Manila. Area: 104,688 sq km; population: 22,000,000.

Malacca, once the greatest port in South-east Asia, is now a small town in Malacca state, MALAYSIA. Population: 115,000.

Malaya became the western part of MALAYSIA in 1963, 6 years after its independence from Britain. It is composed of 9 sultanates (Johore, Kedah, Kalantan, Negri Sembilan, Pahang, Perak, Perlis, Selangor and Trengganu) and 2 other states (Malacca, Penang and Province Wellesley). Area: 131,587 sq km; population: 11,700,000.
Malaysia is a kingdom divided into east and west by a 1000-km stretch of the South China Sea. West Malaysia comprises Malaya while East Malaysia comprises SARAWAK and SABAH. SINGA-

PORE became a member state of Malaysia in 1963 but seceded in 1965. Malays form about 45% of the population, Chinese 38%, and Indo-Pakistanis 9%. About 8% of the people descend from tribes such as the Land or Sea Dyaks of Sarawak and the Dusuns or Kadazans of Sabah. A variety of languages are spoken including Malay, English and Chinese, besides several indigenous languages and dialects. Islam, the state religion, is practised by almost all Malays. Other important religions include Buddhism,

Above: Bangkok, Thailand's capital and a leading city of South-east Asia, is built around a network of waterways. Vendors sell fruit and other commodities from the city's 'floating market'. Despite its popularity with tourists, the floating market is fast disappearing as a result of rapid urbanization. The straw hats of the vendors are unique to Thailand.

per cent of the people are Malays; the Chinese come next, and there are Land and Sea Dyak communities.

Indonesia and the Philippines

Indonesia is 90 per cent Muslim in religion and predominantly Malay ethnically, with Papuan and Chinese minorities. The island of Bali has its own form of Hinduism and some five per cent of the population are Christian, especially in northern Sumatra. Indonesia has many of the features of other South-east Asian countries, but its way of life also resembles to some degree that of Muslim areas in the Indian subcontinent. The huge capital of JAKARTA has attracted millions of people from the surrounding countryside to form straggling settlements in and around the city. SURABAJA and BANDUNG are the only other large cities. JOGJAKARTA is a cultural centre.

The Philippines is 83 per cent Roman Catholic, reflecting its 400 years of Spanish rule. About nine per cent of the people are Protestant, a result partly of 44 years of American domination. The five to seven per cent in the extreme south, who are Muslims, have never fully accepted foreign or Christian rule. Manila is by far the largest of several cities which are mainly medium-sized. However, only 30 per cent of Filipinos live in urban areas. The Philippines combines, to some extent, the characteristics of other South-east Asian countries, but its Christian religion and the common use of the English language give it cultural links with the West.

Economy

The general diversity of South-east Asia carries over into its products. Agriculture, forestry and fishing form the basis of the economy, together with mining and small-scale manufacturing. Between 50 per cent and 75 per cent of workers in every country except Singapore work on the land as farmers.

Farm and forest products of South-east Asia

Many agricultural and forest products are found throughout this tropical region. They include the following (the countries in brackets are the main producers): rice (Indonesia, Thailand and Burma); sweet potatoes, sugar, maize, pepper (Indonesia and Malaysia); groundnuts, soya beans, tea and coffee (Indonesia); coconuts and pineapples (Philippines); copra, cinchona (Indonesia and Laos); tapioca, from cassava or manioc (Indonesia, Malaysia and Thailand); cotton (mainland states); tobacco, palm oil (Indonesia and Malaysia); rubber (Malaysia, Indonesia and Thailand); timber and bamboo.

Teak is found mainly in Burma and Thailand, and mahogany in the Philippines. The Philippines is also known for *abaca*, a tall plant from which fibres are taken for Manila hemp. Burma is noted for sesame seeds and Laos for citrus fruits, *cardamom* (a kind of ginger) and opium. Laos and Indonesia produce *benzoin* (gum benjamin) used for perfumes, incense and friar's balsam. Kapok grows in Indonesia, the Philippines and KAMPUCHEA; and jute in Thailand.

Stockraising and fishing

Water buffaloes, including carabaos in the Philippines, are reared for transport and

---

Taoism, Hinduism, and Christianity. Its wealth grew by exporting rubber and tin, although palm oil is now even more important. Malaysia's cities include KUALA LUMPUR, Georgetown (generally called PENANG), Ipoh and KUCHING. Area: 329,749 sq km; population: 13,791,000; capital: Kuala Lumpur.
Manila is the largest city and port of the PHILIPPINES. It has a spacious central area flanked by densely-populated environs. Population: 1,770,000.
Mekong River rises in east

Tibet and flows about 4,200 km through China, Burma, Laos, Thailand, Kampuchea and Vietnam.
Mindanao is the southernmost large island in the PHILIPPINES. It is mainly unexploited economically. Area: 94,628 sq km; population: 9,700,000.
Moluccas are a group of islands in eastern INDONESIA. They were controlled by the Dutch from the mid-1600s to 1949. Area: 86,286 sq km; population: 1,285,000.

P **Penang** (Pinang) is an island off north-west

MALAYSIA and one of the former 'Straits Settlements'. It is now part of Malaysia.

Igorots, Luzon, Philippines

Philippines is an island republic comprising over 7,000 islands, but only about 730 of the larger ones are inhabited. The biggest islands, LUZON and MINDANAO, comprise 70% of the country's land area and contain 65% of its people. Filipinos are of Malay descent with Mongoloid, Indonesian and Spanish admixture. Filipino, based on Tagalog, and English are the two languages spoken. Filipinos are about 80% Roman Catholic — a result of 300 years of Spanish rule (1565-1898) — and 10% Protestant. In the south,

especially around the city of ZAMBOANGA and in the Sulu Archipelago, some 7% are Muslims (or 'Moros'). The Moros have never ceased to rebel against Christian rule, whether by Spaniards, Americans (1898-1942) or Filipinos (since 1946). American rule was effectively ended by the Japanese occupation in 1942-45. Following political unrest and increasing lawlessness, President Marcos imposed martial law in 1972, which was endorsed by later referenda. About 60% of the land is forested. About 30% of the

farmwork, especially in rice paddies. Cattle are raised for transport and for meat. However, Muslims do not eat pork, which the Chinese and Vietnamese much prefer, and many Buddhists either do not eat beef or are vegetarians. The leading beef countries of the region are Indonesia and the Philippines while Vietnam and the Philippines lead in pork production. Only Indonesia produces sizable quantities of mutton — the meat preferred by most Muslims. The leading fish and sea-food countries include Indonesia, the Philippines and Vietnam.

Minerals, petroleum and manufacturing

South-east Asia is rich in a wide variety of minerals. Vietnam and Indonesia have sizable coal reserves and Malaysia and Thailand are among the world leaders in tin. Burma, and to a lesser extent Thailand, are rich in precious metals and stones. Vietnam and Kampuchea extract iron and manganese. Indonesia is the most important producer of crude oil in the region, followed by Malaysia. Brunei's wealth also derives from oil and Singapore profits from oil refining.

Singapore, lacking land, has only three per cent of its workforce employed in farming but 20 per cent in manufacturing. It specializes in ship building and repairing, electronics, textiles and food, rubber and timber processing. It is one of

Left: Singapore has grown rapidly to become a major international financial centre. The picture catches a lively moment at the Singapore Stock Exchange.

Above: Sprouting coconut seedlings will reach 30.5 metres as mature trees. Copra, the dried kernel of the fruit, is a valuable source of oil.

the world's leading banking, trading and tourist centres. All other South-east Asian countries have less than ten per cent of their workforces employed in manufacturing, except the Philippines (11 per cent). Small crafts, such as wood and stone carving, rattan work, jewellery making, silverwork, spinning and weaving of silk and cotton, and pottery work, flourish throughout the region. These are mainly dependent upon local materials and customs.

History and culture

The countries of mainland–South-east Asia were heavily influenced by Indian seaborne visitors

---

gross national product comes from agriculture and forestry and 17% from mining and manufacturing. Manila is the largest town. Area: 300,000 sq km; population: 49,051,000; capital: QUEZON CITY.

Phnom Penh is the capital of Kampuchea. It became a 'ghost city' following its evacuation forced by the communist government in 1975 at the end of civil war. Its population in 1974 was about 2,000,000, including refugees. The population began to return to the city in 1979.

Q **Quezon City**, the official capital of the PHILIPPINES, adjoins Manila. Population: 1,000,000.

R **Rangoon** is the capital of Burma and the site of the Shwe Dagon, a Buddhist shrine constructed over 2,400 years ago. Population: 2,250,000.

S **Sabah**, formerly British North Borneo, became part of MALAYSIA in 1963. Population: 740,000.
Saigon, see HO CHI MINH CITY.
Salween River rises in Tibet and flows 2,400 km

through China and Burma.
Sarawak, once ruled by the 'white rajahs' of the English Brooke family, became part of MALAYSIA in 1963. Area:

Village in Sabah

125,206 sq km; population: 1,280,000.
Singapore is an important city and republic at the southern tip of the Malay peninsula. Having very little territory or resources, the country has concentrated on commerce, finance, shipping and manufacturing. Singaporeans are 76% Chinese, 14% Malay, and 8% Indo-Pakistani in origins. Some Europeans and Eurasians also live in the country. Malay, English, Chinese and Tamil are the main languages spoken. The various religions are not dominant.

Singapore has a high population density of 4,000 people to the sq km. Area: 581 sq km; population: 2,427,000.
Sulawesi (formerly Celebes) is INDONESIA's third largest island. It is well forested and has a small population for its size. Area: 189,484 sq km; population: 11,000,000.
Sumatra is the second largest of INDONESIA's islands. Area: 473,607 sq km; population: 25,000,000; capital: Medan.
Surabaja is a port in northeast JAVA and INDONESIA's

over 2,000 years ago. Later, this influence was superseded by the Chinese who also immigrated to the region. Arab traders brought Islam to INDONESIA, MALAYSIA and the southern PHILIPPINES by the early 1400s. Christian Europeans arrived in South-east Asia a century later. Eventually, the whole area fell under European rule except THAILAND. By the late 1800s, Britain held BURMA, present-day Malaysia and SINGAPORE; France had taken LAOS, KAMPUCHEA and VIETNAM, the Netherlands ruled Indonesia; and Spain held the Philippines until 1898 when they were seized by the United States. Japan occupied the whole region in 1942-45, forcing Thailand into alliance, but independence came to all countries between 1946 and 1965, except that BRUNEI chose to remain a British-protected sultanate.

Post-war events in the mainland states

Since World War II, mainland South-east Asia has been in a state of turbulence. Burma, for example, a mountainous land with many rebellious tribes, has experienced an unbroken series of rumbling, rather than violent, revolts since independence in 1948. The greatest upheaval was in Vietnam where people endured 30 years of bloody warfare. A colonial war against France forced the French to leave, and the country was partitioned along the 17th parallel of latitude in 1954. In the north the communists, led by Ho Chi Minh, took control of government while the south was acknowledged as an independent entity. Civil war developed as a result of the north's attempts to unify Vietnam. The USA heavily supported the South Vietnamese while communist countries gave limited assistance to the north. Victory came to the north in 1975 after America had withdrawn its troops. But Communism was not accepted by everyone and hundreds of thousands of people, including many from the Chinese minority, quit the country.

By the end of the Vietnam war, neighbouring Laos and Kampuchea had been dragged into the fighting and were under communist governments. In Kampuchea, the Khmer Rouge (Red Khmer government forces) depopulated all the towns, forcing the population to toil in the countryside. Such unpopular policies led to further civil war and some two million people are reported to have died in the war and its

Above: The agony of Vietnam began with the Japanese occupation in 1940, and fighting continued even after the communist triumph of 1975. The picture shows a Vietnamese refugee group during the war in the early 1970s, before American troops pulled out.

Below: U Thant was Secretary-General of the United Nations during 1962-72. Although he proved a popular choice in this most international of jobs, his own country, Burma, remained isolated from the rest of the world.

aftermath. However, in 1979, anti-Khmer Rouge communists, heavily supported by Vietnamese forces, ousted the Khmer Rouge government. In contrast to all these disturbances Thailand has remained relatively peaceful.

Malaysia and the island states

In Malaya, the British fought a gruelling war against guerillas before independence came in 1957. In 1963, it joined with Singapore, Sarawak and Sabah to form Malaysia, but Singapore dropped out to become an independent country in 1965. The existence of Malaysia was challenged by Indonesia, which pursued a policy of 'confrontation' (limited war) against it until 1967. Indonesia achieved its independence from the Netherlands only by war between 1945 and 1949. It annexed West Irian in 1962-63 and EAST TIMOR in 1975.

The Philippines gained independence from the United States peacefully in 1946, but a Huk (communist group) rebellion ensued until the mid-1950s. Increasing lawlessness in the country, which won Manila the nickname of 'Dodge City East', led President Marcos to declare martial law in 1972. This was retained, following approval by national referenda. The situation was complicated by the continued revolt against the Manila government by the Muslim minority in the south of the country.

---

main naval base. Population: 2,000,000.

T **Thailand** (formerly Siam) is the largest country of mainland South-east Asia. It is also the only South-east Asian country never to have been under European rule, so it has kept its culture vigorous and independent. Over 90% of the population is Buddhist and distinctive temples dominate the landscape. Most of the people are Thai, but 10% are Chinese and 2% Malay. About 1% belong to the northern hill tribes which

Elephant in Thailand

include Meo, Lisu, Lahu, Yao, E-Kaw, Shan and Karen. Thai is the main language but Chinese, Malay and tribal dialects are also spoken. Area: 514,000 sq km; population: 47,978,000; capital: Bangkok.

Tonle Sap is a lake in KAMPUCHEA fed by the MEKONG RIVER. It varies between 2,500 and 25,000 sq km in area, according to season, and is rich in fish.

V **Vientiane** is the capital of LAOS. Population: about 185,000.

Vietnam, a war torn country in South-east Asia was finally united in 1976 after more than 30 years of wars. It then became a single communist republic and many Vietnamese fled abroad. Over 85% of the people are Vietnamese who follow Confucianist-Taoist-Buddhist cults. Some 5% are Catholic. Vietnamese is the main language, but Chinese, Khmer, French and English are also spoken. Rice farming is the dominant occupation. Area: 329,556 sq km; population (not allowing for migration); 52,159,000; capital: Hanoi.

W **West Irian** (Irian Barat), the western part of the island of New Guinea, was transferred from Dutch to Indonesian rule by 1963. Population: 1,200,000.

Z **Zamboanga** is the chief market town of the southern PHILIPPINES in southwest MINDANAO and a main centre of the Moro people. Population: 250,000.

Africa, formerly called the 'Dark Continent,' has emerged into the light of
independence in the last 30 years. However, political independence has left many
complex problems in its wake.

Africa

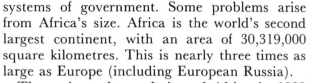

Africa is a continent in transition. By 1945 only four African countries, EGYPT, ETHIOPIA, LIBERIA, and SOUTH AFRICA, were independent. The rest were ruled by either Belgium, Britain, France, Italy, Portugal or Spain. But since then, a 'wind of change' has blown throughout Africa. By the end of 1978, African nations occupied over 30 per cent of the seats in the United Nations General Assembly. This large representation gives Africa a powerful voice in world affairs.

The emergent nations of Africa have faced many economic, political and social problems since they achieved independence. Some problems have been caused by poverty and some by the fact that nearly three out of every four Africans are illiterate. Disunity and rivalries have arisen in many countries because of ethnic, language and religious differences, and these factors have led to military coups and the adoption of autocratic, rather than democratic,

Below: Dar es Salaam is the capital and chief port of Tanzania. As the centre of communications, education and industry, it has grown rapidly, attracting talented people from all over the country. In the 1980s, the capital will be relocated at Dodoma, which is closer to the geographical centre of the country.

systems of government. Some problems arise from Africa's size. Africa is the world's second largest continent, with an area of 30,319,000 square kilometres. This is nearly three times as large as Europe (including European Russia).

The estimated population of Africa in 1980 was 458 millions. In terms of population, Africa comes third among the continents, after Asia and Europe, which are both much more densely-populated than Africa, where the average population density is only 15 people to every square kilometre. This low population density results from the fact that vast tracts of burning-hot desert and dense tropical forests are virtually uninhabited. However, Africa's population is increasing rapidly, by about 2.7 per cent per year. At this rate, the population increases make it difficult for African countries to achieve real advances in the standards of living of their people.

Land Features

Most of Africa consists of vast plateaux. About 60 per cent of the continent is more than 370 metres above sea level. These plateaux are especially pronounced in the African countries south of the equator, where 50 per cent of the land is over 900 metres above sea level. Coastal plains are mostly narrow and Africa generally lacks deep inlets. The high plateaux near the coasts once made inland travel difficult. This factor was important in discouraging Europeans from exploring the interior until the 1800s.

The highest mountains, MOUNT KILIMANJARO and MOUNT KENYA, are extinct volcanoes. Other igneous (cooled molten rock) massifs are the Ahaggar, Darfur and Tibesti mountains in the north and the Cameroon mountains in west-central Africa. The lofty Ruwenzori range in east-central Africa, however, is an uplifted block bordering the massive East African rift valley,

Above right: The lofty Drakensberg range in southern Africa is the uplifted rim of the African plateau. In Lesotho, it reaches its maximum height of 3,482 metres above sea-level. The Drakensberg, also called Quathlamba, extends for about 1,600 km.

Above left: This bleak desert region lies in the Sahara, in southern Tunisia. The world's largest desert, the Sahara covers more than 25% of Africa, and is nearly as big as the United States. Other large tracts of southern Africa are deserts or semi-deserts.

Left: The Kerio River flows through the Chebloc Gorge in Kenya. During the rainy season, African rivers may become raging torrents, sweeping away large amounts of silt and sand. However, in the dry season, many rivers are reduced to a trickle or dry up completely.

while the DRAKENSBERG range in southern Africa is an uptilted plateau rim. Africa is mostly an ancient landmass. The only fold mountains are the ATLAS MOUNTAINS in the north-west and the Cape ranges of South Africa.

Much of Africa's scenery is spectacular. This is particularly true of the East African rift valley. This deep gash in the Earth's crust, which runs from Mozambique to the Red Sea, was caused by continental drift (two landmasses drifting together, apart, or past each other). It extends through the Red Sea into Syria, in south-west Asia. Parts of the rift valley are bounded by steep walls and it contains many great lakes, including TANGANYIKA and NYASA. But Africa's largest lake, VICTORIA, is not in the rift valley. It occupies a shallow depression in the plateaux between two arms of the rift valley in KENYA, UGANDA and TANZANIA. Three of the world's longest rivers, the NILE, ZAIRE (formerly the Congo) and NIGER, are in Africa. Their courses are interrupted by rapids and waterfalls as they descend from the plateaux.

Climate

Africa is divided almost equally from north to south by the equator and over 60 per cent of the continent is in the tropics. It is the hottest continent and the world's highest air tempera-

---

Antananarivo, formerly Tananarive, is the capital of MADAGASCAR. Population: 400,000.

Aswan High Dam, on the NILE in EGYPT, controls flood-water, and its turbines generate electricity. It was inaugurated in 1968.

Atlas Mountains are in north-west Africa. The highest peak is 4,165 metres above sea-level, in MOROCCO.

B **Bamako**, capital of MALI, stands on the River NIGER. Population: 400,000.

Bangui is the capital of the CENTRAL AFRICAN EMPIRE. This

river port has a population of 302,000.

Banjul (formerly Bathurst) is the capital of GAMBIA. Population: 43,000.

Bantustans (or homelands) are areas in SOUTH AFRICA designated for the black African population. The 10 Bantustans cover a combined area which represents 13% of South Africa. One Bantustan, Transkei, became independent in 1976 and another, Bophuthatswana, in 1977. But only South Africa recognizes them.

Benin (formerly Dahomey) became independent from

France in 1960. This republic has 50 ethnic groups, the Fon being the largest. Because so many languages are spoken, French remains the official one. Farming is the chief industry and palm products are the main exports of this poor nation. Area: 112,622 sq km; population: 3,557,000; capital: PORTO NOVO.

Bissau is the capital and chief port of GUINEA-BISSAU. Population: 65,000.

Bophuthatswana, see BANTUSTANS.

Botswana, formerly British Bechuanaland, became an

independent republic in 1966. Most people belong to

Herero people, Botswana

one of the branches of the Tswana group, although about 30,000 Bushmen live in the dry KALAHARI desert. The Tswana are mostly cattle-herders in the east. The recent discovery of minerals, notably diamonds, is changing the economy. Area: 600,372 sq km; population: 804,000; capital: GABORONE.

Brazzaville, on the River ZAIRE, is the capital of CONGO. Population: 290,000.

Bujumbura, on Lake TANGANYIKA, is the capital of BURUNDI. Population: 100,000.

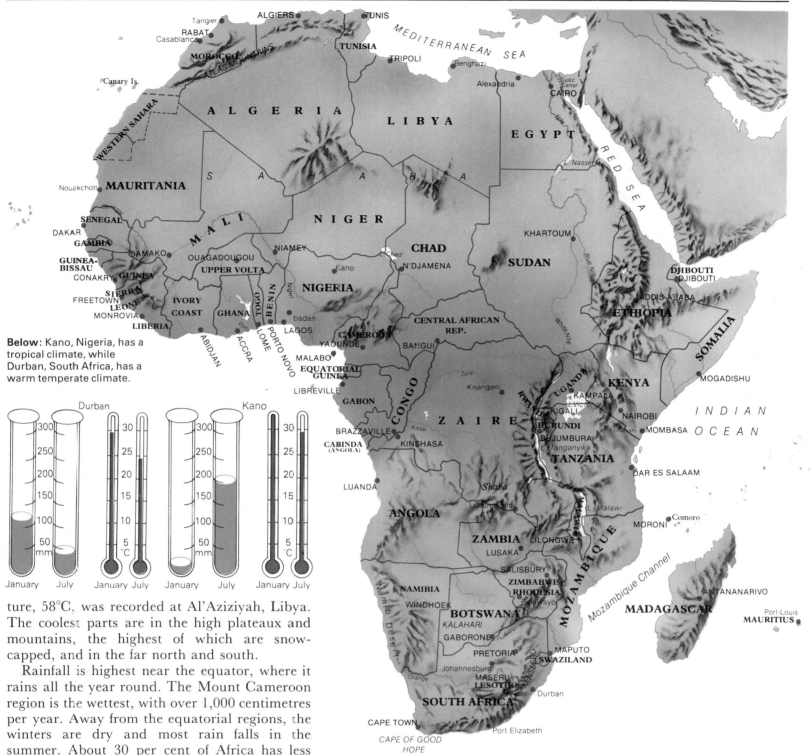

Below: Kano, Nigeria, has a tropical climate, while Durban, South Africa, has a warm temperate climate.

Durban

Kano

ture, 58°C, was recorded at Al'Aziziyah, Libya. The coolest parts are in the high plateaux and mountains, the highest of which are snow-capped, and in the far north and south.

Rainfall is highest near the equator, where it rains all the year round. The Mount Cameroon region is the wettest, with over 1,000 centimetres per year. Away from the equatorial regions, the winters are dry and most rain falls in the summer. About 30 per cent of Africa has less than 25 centimetres of rain per year. Low rainfall combined with a high rate of evaporation have caused large deserts to form. In the north is the SAHARA, the world's largest desert. In the south,

---

Burundi, an overpopulated, remote republic, was part of the Belgian Ruanda-Urundi until 1962. The tall Tutsi people (Hamites), who form 15% of the population, ruled Burundi as a monarchy, but the mwami (king) was deposed in 1966. The Hutu, a Bantu-speaking group, form 85% of the population. They are mostly subsistence farmers. Coffee is the chief export. Area: 27,834 sq km; population: 3,864,000; capital: BUJUMBURA.

C **Cairo**, Africa's largest city and capital of EGYPT,

is on the NILE. This historic city was founded in AD 969. Population: 5,715,000.

Cameroon is a republic, consisting of former French

Mohammed Mosque, Cairo

Cameroon and part of British Cameroon. French and English are both official languages. The population is extremely diverse. Sudanese Negroes, Hamitic Fulani and Arab Choa live in the grassy north, and many Bantu-speaking groups live in the forested south. Most people are poor farmers. Coffee and cocoa are exported. Area: 475,442 sq km; population: 7,042,000; capital: YAOUNDE.

Canary Islands form two Spanish provinces in the Atlantic Ocean. Area: 7,273 sq km; population: 1,170,000.

Cape Town is the legislative capital of SOUTH AFRICA. This major port has a population of 1,097,000.

Cape Verde Islands, formerly Portuguese, became an independent republic in 1975. These volcanic islands are in the Atlantic, west of Senegal. Area: 4,033 sq km; population: 329,000; capital PRAIA.

Casablanca, a major seaport in MOROCCO, has a population of 1,506,000.

Central African Empire is a poor, inland nation. The largest ethnic groups are the Banda and Baya, who are

farmers in the wet south. Coffee and cotton are exported. Formerly French, the country became an independent republic in 1960. It was made an empire in 1976. Area: 622,984 sq km; population: 1,637,000; capital: BANGUI.

Chad, formerly a French territory, became an independent republic in 1960. The arid north contains Sudanese Negroes and Berber Tuaregs. The poor Negroid peoples of the south are mostly farmers, but some are fishermen in LAKE CHAD. Cotton is the main export.

the Namib is a total desert, while the large KALAHARI is a semi-desert. Mediterranean zones, with mild, moist winters and hot, dry summers, occur in the north and along the south-west Cape coast. South Africa also contains the temperate, fairly arid, high veld and a warm temperate zone in the east. This coastal zone, which extends into Mozambique, gets about 1,000 millimetres of rain per year.

Vegetation zones

The main vegetation regions in tropical Africa are the rain forests, the savanna, the deserts and the uplands. The dense rain forests flourish in the wet equatorial lowlands, which cover about 10 per cent of Africa. These forests, including coastal mangrove swamps, extend through most of West Africa from GUINEA-BISSAU to GABON. The largest rain forest is in the ZAIRE RIVER basin. Another zone is in MADAGASCAR. Savanna (tropical grassland with trees) borders onto the rain forests and is most luxuriant where the summer rains are the heaviest. As the rainfall decreases to the north and south, the savanna merges into dry scrub and desert.

The uplands of tropical Africa contain a series of sub-zones determined by altitude. A typical sequence is savanna at the base of a mountain, merging into mountain rain forest, upland grassland, moorland then tundra and, on the highest peaks, permanent snow and ice.

Above: Cheetahs, one of the animals which roam the African savanna, are shown here in Nairobi National Park, which is a short drive from the capital of Kenya.

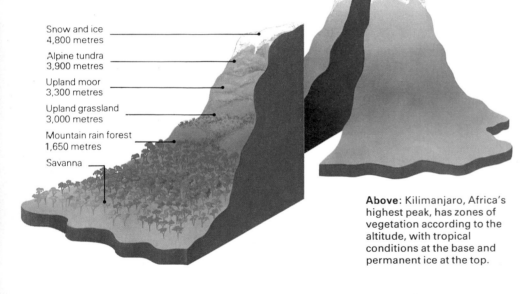

Snow and ice
4,800 metres

Alpine tundra
3,900 metres

Upland moor
3,300 metres

Upland grassland
3,000 metres

Mountain rain forest
1,650 metres

Savanna

Above: Kilimanjaro, Africa's highest peak, has zones of vegetation according to the altitude, with tropical conditions at the base and permanent ice at the top.

In the Mediterranean climate regions of northern and south-western Africa, the plants are adapted to the summer drought. The characteristic vegetation is maquis, consisting of shrubs and low trees, such as myrtle and olive, which are drought-resistant. Two other distinctive regions occur in southern Africa. The high veld is a grassland region with few trees. The warm temperate zone in south-eastern Africa, however, is largely forested.

Wildlife

The wildlife of Africa is extremely varied, although some species are threatened by poaching and, especially, by the spread of people into areas which were once the sole preserve of animals. The main animal regions, each with its own abundant and characteristic fauna, are the forests, the savanna and the uplands. National parks and reserves in these zones attract an increasing number of tourists, who bring much-needed revenue to many African countries.

The population of Africa

Africa has the highest birth rate of any continent,

Area: 1,284,000 sq km; population: 4,473,000; capital: N'DJAMENA.
Chad, Lake, is a shallow lake in an inland drainage basin, mostly in CHAD. The maximum area is 25,600 sq km.
Comoro Islands are an independent island republic in the northern Mozambique Channel. Area: 2,171 sq km; population: 347,000; capital: MORONI.
Conakry is the capital and main seaport of GUINEA. Population: 526,000.
Congo is a republic which became independent from

France in 1960. The main peoples are the Bakongo, Teke, Bobangi and Gabonais – all Bantu-speaking groups. Most are subsistence farmers, but timber and timber products are the main exports. Congo's government describes itself as Marxist. Area: 342,000 sq km; population: 1,540,000; capital: BRAZZAVILLE.

D Dakar, capital, chief seaport and industrial centre of SENEGAL, has a population of 581,000.
Dar es Salaam is the capital and chief seaport of TAN-

ZANIA. Population: 522,000.
Djebel Toubkal, in MOROCCO, is the highest peak in the ATLAS MOUNTAINS. It is 4,165 metres above sea level.

Market in Dakar, Senegal

Djibouti, formerly French Somaliland and, later, the Territory of the Afars and Issas, became an independent republic in 1977. This hot, dry country exports cattle and hides from its capital, Djibouti (pop. 62,000). The main peoples, the Issas (a Somali clan) and the Afars (Danakils), are Muslims. Area: 22,000 sq km; population: 118,000.
Dodoma, a town in central TANZANIA, will become the nation's capital in the 1980s. Population: 24,000.
Drakensberg, a mountain range bordering the central

plateau in SOUTH AFRICA and LESOTHO, reaches 3,482 metres above sea level.
Durban is a major seaport in Natal, SOUTH AFRICA. Population: 843,000.

E Egypt has been called the 'gift of the Nile.' The NILE valley covers only 4% of the land, but 99% of the people live there. A few live in the hot deserts east and west of the Nile, mainly at oases. The Nile valley was the home of the brilliant Ancient Egyptian civilization. Egypt was conquered by the Arabs in AD 640. Most people

with about 47 live births per every 1,000 people per year. But the death rate is also high, at about 21 per 1,000 per year. The high death rate is caused by several factors, including poverty, poor sanitation, inadequate health services to combat the various diseases, and poor diets. Africa's population is youthful by comparison with developed continents. In 1976 about 44 per cent of Africa's people were under 15 and only 2.9 per cent were over 65.

The average life expectation varies from region to region. The Europeans of SOUTH AFRICA and ZIMBABWE-RHODESIA live almost as long, on average, as people in Europe and North America, while Africans in tropical regions have shorter lives. For example, the average life expectation in MALI (1970-5) was 36.5 years for men and 39.6 years for women. In North Africa, people live longer. For example, in ALGERIA (1970-5), the average life expectation for men was 51.7 years and for women it was 54.8 years.

Peoples and languages

More than 1,000 languages are spoken in Africa. In some Black African countries, many languages and dialects are spoken and a European language and/or a local lingua franca must be used as an official language. For example, TANZANIA has more than 120 languages. The official languages are English and Swahili. Swahili is an East African coastal language

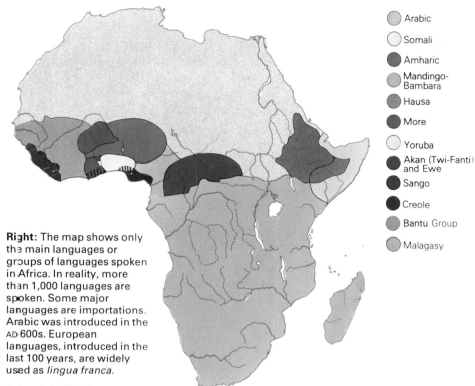

Arabic
Somali
Amharic
Mandingo-Bambara
Hausa
More
Yoruba
Akan (Twi-Fanti) and Ewe
Sango
Creole
Bantu Group
Malagasy

Right: The map shows only the main languages or groups of languages spoken in Africa. In reality, more than 1,000 languages are spoken. Some major languages are importations. Arabic was introduced in the AD 600s. European languages, introduced in the last 100 years, are widely used as *lingua franca.*

Below left: This Dogon village in Mali is built from baked mud. The walls are protected by thatched roofs. The Dogon have an elaborate philosophy based on myths and symbols. Villages are often arranged in the shape of an egg, a symbol of fertility.

Below: The diagram shows that Ghana, like many African countries, has a youthful population. More than 80% of the people are under 15, and the average life expectancy is only about 48 years.

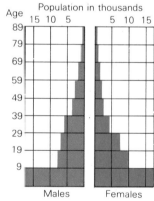

Population in thousands

Age	15	10	5		5	10	15
89							
79							
69							
59							
49							
39							
29							
19							
9							

Males   Females

which is comparatively easy to learn and has become a *lingua franca* throughout East Africa and eastern Zaire.

Ethnically, the people of Africa belong to two main groups: Caucasoids and Negroids. The Caucasoids of North Africa include the Hamitic Berbers and the Arabs, who conquered North Africa in the AD 600s, introducing a brilliant Islamic culture. The chief language in North Africa is Arabic, although some Berber tongues are also used. Many Arabs and Berbers are farmers or stock-rearers, but several cities, including ALEXANDRIA, ALGIERS, CAIRO and CASABLANCA, have populations of over a million. The Nubians of SUDAN, the Somalis and various Ethiopian groups are also basically Caucasoid, although some have Negroid features. Negroids occupy most of Africa south of the Sahara. The two largest language families are traditionally classed as the West Atlantic group in West Africa and the Bantu of central and South Africa.

The West Africans

Most of the people of West Africa, who live between the Gulf of Guinea coast and the SAHARA, speak one of the West Atlantic lan-

are now of Arab or Coptic (ancient Egyptian) origin. Most are Muslims, but there are some Coptic Christians. Egypt, a republic since 1952, is Africa's second most industrialized nation. Although cheap power supplies come from the ASWAN HIGH DAM, most people remain poor farmers. Cotton is the chief crop and export. Wars with Israel have hampered progress since 1948, but in 1979 Egypt signed a peace treaty with Israel. Area: 1,001,449 sq km; population: 42,118,000; capital: CAIRO.

Equatorial Guinea, a republic, independent from Spain in 1968, contains mainland Rio Muni and the island Macias Nguema Biyoga (Fernando Poo). The largest ethnic group is the Fang and farming is the chief industry. Area: 28,051 sq km; population: 338,000; capital: MALABO.
Eritrea has been part of ETHIOPIA since 1952. It was the scene of a secessionist war in the 1970s.
Ethiopia was the home of an ancient empire until an army group deposed Emperor Haile Selassie and set

up a socialist republic in 1974. This largely highland

Ethiopian girl, Galla tribe

nation depends on farming, and coffee is the main product. The ruling people, the Amharas, speak a Semitic language. Other groups include the Galla and Somalis, with Negroid peoples in the south-west. Christianity was introduced in the AD 300s and about half of the people are now Coptic Christians. But Muslims live in the south and east. Area: 1,221,900 sq km; population: 31,779,000; capital: ADDIS ABABA.

F **Freetown**, capital of SIERRA LEONE, was founded in 1787 as a home for

freed slaves. Population: 274,000.

G **Gabon**, a former French territory, became an independent republic in 1960. It is fairly wealthy, by African standards, because of its mineral resources, particularly oil. Forestry and farming are also important industries. The people are divided into 40 Bantu-speaking groups, the largest of which is the Fang. Area: 267,667 sq km; population: 567,000; capital: LIBREVILLE.
Gaborone is the capital of BOTSWANA. It is on the South

guages. These peoples include the Ashanti (GHANA), the ubiquitous Fula, or Fulani (spread out through SENEGAL to northern CAMEROON), the Hausa, Igbo and Yoruba (NIGERIA) and the Wolof (SENEGAL).

In the forest regions, most people are cultivators. Inland, however, the people of the savanna have a mixed arable and pastoral economy, while some are exclusively pastoralists. Traditionally, many people have lived in large villages. Some of these have developed into major cities and West Africa has a substantial educated middle class. West Africa also has great artistic traditions, especially terracotta, wood, stone and bronze sculpture.

The Bantu-speaking Africans

South of a line from Cameroon to northern KENYA lies the southern 30 per cent of Africa. Most people in this region speak one of the many Bantu languages. They include the Ganda (UGANDA), the Kikuyu (Kenya), the Kongo and Luba (ZAIRE), the Ndebele and Shona (ZIMBABWE-RHODESIA), the Tsonga (MOZAMBIQUE), the Tswana (BOTSWANA) and the Zulu and Xhosas (SOUTH AFRICA). Most Bantu-speaking people are farmers, who grow crops and rear livestock. Like the West Africans, they have artistic traditions. For example, wood sculpture is important among forest peoples and, the oral tradition of story-telling, especially in verse, has reached great heights.

Other peoples

Smaller groups in east-central Africa are the

Right: The Fulani are a widespread, essentially nomadic, cattle-keeping people. They have spread across the West African savanna from Senegal to northern Cameroon. They are a major group in northern Nigeria, where they seized power from the Hausa in the late 1800s.

Right: This Yoruba family lives in south-western Nigeria. Most Yoruba are farmers. They have important artistic traditions. The Yoruba city of Ife was a great centre for sculpture between the 1100s and 1300s.

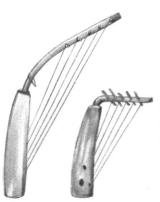

Left: Africa has its own distinctive styles of music and musical instruments. These bowharps probably originated in Egypt 5,000 years ago. The sound box is hollowed out of wood and covered with skin.

Above: A Hausa drummer. Most Hausa are Muslim farmers, who live in northern Nigeria. Their language, which has incorporated much Arabic and English, is one of Africa's richest. The Hausa founded powerful city-states between the 800s and 1800s.

Right: These Igbo (or Ibo) are playing *ayo*, a game which is popular throughout Africa. Between 1967 and 1970, many Igbo supported a secessionist movement, which tried, unsuccessfully, to establish a separate state, called Biafra.

Africa-Zimbabwe railway. Population: 37,000.

Gambia, Africa's smallest mainland nation, is a republic. It became independent from Britain in 1965. There are 5 main ethnic groups, the largest being the Mandingo. Groundnuts account for 95% of the country's exports. Area: 11,295 sq km; population: 596,000; capital: BANJUL.

Ghana, formerly the Gold Coast, is a West African republic which became independent from Britain in 1957. The people are divided into about 50 groups, the

Cleaning a shark, Gambia

largest of which is the Akan (including Ashanti, Fante and Twi). Most people are farmers and cocoa is the main export. Economic problems have dogged Ghana's progress. Area: 238,537 sq km; population: 11,603,000; capital: ACCRA.

Guinea, a republic, became independent from France in 1958. It turned for help to communist nations, but it now also enjoys good relations with the non-communist world. The main peoples are the Fulani (Peul) and Malinke. The majority are Muslims. Farming is the main industry, but bauxite and aluminium dominate the exports. Area: 245,957 sq km; population: 4,980,000; capital: CONAKRY.

Guinea-Bissau, formerly Portuguese Guinea, became independent in 1974, following a guerilla war. Farming is the main activity and groundnuts, groundnut products, palm products and copra are exported. There are about 30 ethnic groups. Area: 36,125 sq km; population: 567,000; capital: BISSAU.

Ibadan, capital of Oyo state, NIGERIA, is a manufacturing and university city. Population: 847,000.

Ivory Coast, formerly a French territory, became an independent republic in 1960. By African standards, it is stable and affluent, and the average gross domestic product per person (1976) was US $610. Coffee, cocoa and timber are the main exports and manufacturing is important, especially in Abidjan. There are about 60 groups of people. The largest are the Anji and Baule, of the Akan group. Area: 322,463 sq km; population: 5,559,000; capital: ABIDJAN.

Johannesburg, SOUTH AFRICA'S largest city, is a major financial and indust-

Below: The Hausa, Fulani and Kanuri are leading peoples of northern Nigeria, while the Yoruba are based in the south-west and the Igbo in the south-east. With over 70 million people, Nigeria has a larger population than any other African nation and its population is increasing quickly by about 2.7% per year. At this rate, the population could double in 25 years. The population of Nigeria is extremely diverse. The country has about 250 language groups in all. But the 5 groups shown here, together with 5 others (the Edo, Ibibio, Ijaw, Nupe and Tiv), make up about 80% of the population. Islam is the chief religion in the north and nearly 50% of all Nigerians are Muslims. However, Christianity and traditional religions are practised in the south. Because of its human diversity, Nigeria has suffered in the past from communal tensions. It now has a federal constitution, with a central federal government and local governments in each of the 19 states. Life is now changing rapidly in Nigeria as revenue from oil production is being used to develop the economy.

Left: The Nigerian head-dress and mask are typical of the elaborate decorations used in ceremonies and celebrations. Many of the patterns and shapes used in such objects have a religious or symbolic meaning.

Above: A Kanuri leather-worker produces goods employing traditional designs. Leather goods were one of the items in medieval trans-Saharan trade.

Left: Modern Nigerian bead work often uses forms associated with traditional African art. The abstract nature of most black African art was condemned by early European visitors as crude. But it later had great influence on such European painters as Picasso and Modigliani.

Nilotes, a mixed Hamitic and Negroid group, who are mostly cattle-owners, hunters or fishermen. They include the Dinka and Nuer (Sudan) and the Luo (Kenya). The Nilo-Hamitic group includes the Masai of Kenya and Tanzania.

Pygmies are hunters and gatherers in the equatorial rain forests, especially in Cameroon and Zaire. These short people number less than 200,000. In southern Africa, the first inhabitants, before Bantu groups arrived, were the Khoi-San. The Khoi (Hottentots) include the Nama, who are pastoralists and hunters in NAMIBIA, while the San (Bushmen) are hunters in the KALAHARI. In Madagascar, the people are mostly descendants of Black Africans from the mainland and Indonesians who settled on the island in the early Middle Ages. The official Malagasy language is related to Indonesian tongues.

Non-indigenous peoples include about five million of European origin, most of whom live in southern Africa, and about 850,000 Asians living

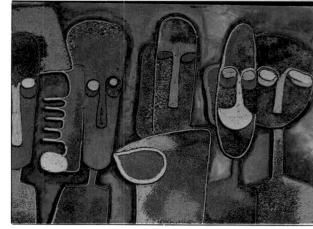

rial centre in a mainly gold-mining region. Population: 1,433,000.

K **Kalahari**, a region of semi-desert, is mainly in BOTSWANA and NAMIBIA. Some Bushmen live there.
Kampala is capital and chief commercial centre of UGANDA. Population: 331,000.
Kenya, formerly a British colony, became independent in 1963, and a republic one year later. Since then, it has enjoyed stable national government. Kenya has superb national parks. Tourism is increasing rapidly. The largest of the 40 ethnic groups are the Kikuyu and Luo, but Swahili (the lingua franca) and English are the official languages. Farming is the main industry, but only 15% of this upland nation has enough rainfall for cereal cultivation. Coffee and tea are the main exports. Area: 582,646 sq km; population: 15,951,000; capital: NAIROBI.
Khartoum, capital of SUDAN, was founded near the junction of the White and Blue NILE rivers in 1822. Population: 334,000.
Kigali is capital of RWANDA. Population: 54,000.

Kinshasa, formerly Léopoldville, is capital of

Wood carver, Lagos

ZAIRE. A major industrial city, it has 1,991,000 people.

L **Lagos** is the capital and one of the major seaports of NIGERIA. Population: 1,061,000.
Lesotho, a mountainous kingdom, formerly called Basutoland, became independent from Britain in 1966. This poor farming nation largely depends on SOUTH AFRICA, which encircles it. Many Basothos work in South Africa. Area: 30,355 sq km; population: 931,000; capital: MASERU.
Liberia became an independent republic in 1847, after having been established as a home for freed slaves by an American anti-slavery organization. Iron ore is the chief export, but income also comes from rubber and Liberia's merchant navy. Liberia has 16 ethnic groups, but the Americo-Liberian minority remains influential and English is the official language. Area: 111,369 sq km; population: 1,880,000; capital: MONROVIA.
Libreville, capital of GABON, was founded in 1849 as a home for freed slaves. Population: 251,000.

in eastern, central and southern Africa. Over two million Coloureds also live in South Africa. The Coloureds are the result of intermarriage between the early European settlers, Asian labourers and the indigenous peoples.

Substantial European populations once lived in other African countries, such as ALGERIA, ANGOLA, MOZAMBIQUE and in the cool, high plateau regions of tropical Africa. Only a few lived in the hot, tropical lowlands. Throughout Africa, Europeans had a profound effect. They introduced new ideas, encouraged economic development, set up schools and health services, created large cities and opened up isolated areas with new roads and railways. Some effects, however, were less beneficial. For example, many Africans were attracted by the cities. But, without skills, they often became almost permanently unemployed, living in poverty in sprawling shanty towns on the outskirts of the cities. Many also lost their beliefs in the values of their traditional societies. In SOUTH AFRICA, an extremely complex racial situation has arisen, in which the Europeans are trying to maintain their own culture and their control of the economy and government, despite the fact that they constitute only 17.5 per cent of the total population.

Religions
Two of the world's great religions, Christianity

Right: Christian missions provide much of the education in Black Africa and overseas missionary societies raise finance and train teachers for many schools. Christianity has had a great impact in Black Africa and the number of Christians is still increasing.

Below: Mosques in Mali are often built from mud which is plastered on to a wooden framework. Poles protruding from the walls make it easy for people to effect repairs. About 65% of the people of Mali are Muslims. Islam is the chief religion of northern Africa.

and Islam, have many followers in Africa. Christianity was introduced into ETHIOPIA in the AD 300s by Byzantine missionaries. It survived in the highlands despite the rise of Islam from the AD 600s. From the early 1800s, European missionaries converted many people in sub-Saharan Africa to Christianity and the number of Christians is still increasing.

Islam spread throughout North Africa, from Arabia, in the AD 600s. Later, many peoples of the savanna lands, south of the Sahara, became Muslims and many groups in the coastal regions of East Africa were also converted by the Arabs.

Many Black Africans, however, still follow traditional, or ethnic, religions. These religions are very varied, but all believe in a creator God or Spirit who, while remote from men, is finally responsible for all that happens to them. Between men and this Spirit are other powers, such as ancestors' ghosts and water or nature spirits that inhabit such things as stone or trees. For example, wood carvers may ask the forgiveness of a tree before cutting off a branch. Sculpture in Africa is often associated with religion and many pieces are carved for use in religious ceremonies rather than as works of art.

Economy
Most people in Africa are poor and the United Nations classifies all African countries, apart from SOUTH AFRICA, as developing nations. This distinguishes them from developed nations, such as those of Western Europe. The gross domestic product (GDP) of a country, which is the total value of all products and services, is an indicator of a nation's wealth. The countries with the

---

Libya was ruled by Italy from 1912 to 1943 and then by Britain and France until it became an independent monarchy in 1951. It became a republic in 1969. This Muslim nation is mostly desert and the mainly Arab people live on the northwest and north-east coasts. Berbers form about 5% of the population. The chief resource is oil and Libya has Africa's highest per capita gross domestic product. Area: 1,759,540 sq km; population: 2,257,000; capital: TRIPOLI.
Lilongwe has been capital

of MALAWI since 1975. Population: 103,000.
Limpopo, River, rises in SOUTH AFRICA and flows 1,440

Col. Khadafy, Libya

km to its outlet in MOZAMBIQUE.
Lomé is the capital and main seaport of TOGO. Population: 214,000.
Luanda is a major port and capital of ANGOLA. Population: 481,000.
Lusaka, capital of ZAMBIA, is a major commercial centre, being the focus for an important farming region. Population: 401,000.

M **Madagascar**, formerly the Malagasy Republic, is an island nation, which is about 400 km from the African mainland. The people of

this republic (a French territory until 1960) are mostly of African and Indonesian origin. The largest of the 18 ethnic groups is the Merina. Coffee is the main export of this chiefly agricultural nation. Area: 587,041 sq km; population: 9,303,000; capital: ANTANANARIVO.
Madeira Islands, situated off north-west Africa, form a province of Portugal. Farming and fishing are important. Area: 796 sq km; population: 251,000; capital: Funchal.
Malabo, formerly Santa Isabel, is capital of EQUATO-

RIAL GUINEA. Population: 20,000.
Malawi, formerly the British protectorate of Nyasaland, became independent in 1964, and a republic in 1966. Water covers 20% of this poor but scenic nation. The chief Bantu-speaking peoples include the Tumbuka, Nyanja-Chewa, Yao and Lomwe. Tobacco and tea are the main exports. Area: 118,484 sq km; population: 5,735,000; capital: LILONGWE.
Mali, formerly French Sudan, became an independent republic in 1960. Tuareg nomads live in the

highest GDPs are South Africa, an industrialized country, NIGERIA, a major oil-producer, and EGYPT, a partly industrialized nation.

The average *per capita* GDP is the GDP divided by the population. In Africa, in 1976, the per capita GDP averaged about US$430. This was very low compared with France ($6,550), West Germany ($7,380), and the United States ($7,890). LIBYA, with its small population and valuable oil production, had the highest per capita GDP in 1976, at $6,310. But Libya is not a developed country and most of its people are still farmers. The developed nation of South Africa had a per capita GDP of $1,340. Nigeria, whose

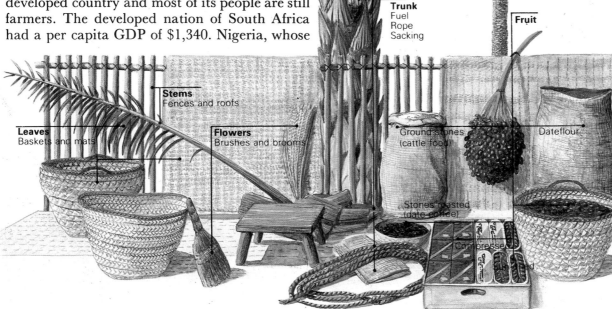

Stems
Fences and roofs

Leaves
Baskets and mats

Flowers
Brushes and brooms

Trunk
Fuel
Rope
Sacking

Fruit

Ground stones
(cattle food)

Stones roasted
(date coffee)

Dateflour

Compressed

Left: The date palm, the most characteristic plant of North Africa, thrives in hot, dry climates. It has many uses which are shown in the diagram. On the left, the leaves are woven into baskets and also mats, while the stalks are used to make fences and roofs. The flowers are made into brooms and brushes. In the centre, the trunk is a source of timber. It may be used to make furniture, such as stools. Logs are burned as fuel or made into ropes and sacking. The date, a valuable food, hangs from the tree in rich golden clusters, each of which may contain 200 dates. A commercial date palm (*right*) produces about 90 kilos of dates per season. The stones have various uses. They can be ground down to make cattle feed or roasted and used to make date coffee. Some dates are compressed and others are sun-dried. Packed in attractive case, they are exported and sold throughout the world. Some dates are dried and turned into date flour but many, of course, are eaten fresh.

total GDP was second only to that of South Africa, had a much lower per capita GDP of $380, because it is Africa's most populous nation. However, Nigeria's GDP has recently been growing faster than that of other African countries, owing to its oil exports. With its enormous resources and its large population, Nigeria is the potential economic giant of Africa.

By contrast, some nations have extremely low per capita GDPs. For example, RWANDA and UPPER VOLTA had per capita GDPs of only $110, and BURUNDI, CHAD and SOMALIA each had per capita GDPs of about $120 in 1976. One important reason for the poverty of much of Africa is that 74 per cent of the people are farmers, a higher proportion than in any other continent. In some countries, including Burundi, MALAWI, NIGER, Rwanda and TANZANIA, over 90 per cent of the people live by farming. Many farmers live at subsistence level – that is, they

Right: Farmers in southern Ethiopia use primitive wooden instruments to till the soil. Many people in tropical Africa are subsistence farmers. When the rains fail or pests destroy the crops in savanna regions, famines occur which may cause great suffering.

desert north. But most people are Black farmers in the southern, NIGER RIVER region. The largest ethnic group is the Bambara. This poor, land-locked nation exports livestock, but many animals were lost during droughts in the 1970s. Area: 1,240,000 sq km; population: 6,451,000; capital: BAMAKO.

Maputo, formerly Lourenço Marques, is the capital and a major port of MOZAMBIQUE. Population: 600,000.

Maseru, capital of LESOTHO, has a population of 30,000.

Mauritania, formerly a French territory, became an independent Islamic republic in 1960. 80 per cent of the people are of Arab or Berber descent, while the rest are Black Africans. Iron ore is the main export, but farming and fishing are the chief occupations, although much of the land is desert. In 1976 Mauritania took part of WESTERN SAHARA. But Saharan guerillas have since fought against Mauritania. Area (not including Western Sahara): 1,030,700 sq km; population: 1,481,000; capital: NOUAKCHOTT.

Mauritius, an island monar-chy east of MADAGASCAR, became independent from Britain in 1968. Indians make up over 60% of the people. Sugar is the main export of this farming nation. Area: 2,045 sq km; population: 942,000; capital: PORT-LOUIS.

Mbabane, capital of SWAZI-LAND, was founded in 1909. Population: 22,000.

Mogadishu is the capital and a major port of SOMALIA. Population: 350,000.

Mombasa is the main sea-port of KENYA. Population: 340,000.

Monrovia, capital of LIBERIA, was founded as a settlement for freed slaves in 1822. Population: 172,000.

Morocco, a kingdom in

Marrakesh, Morocco

north-west Africa, became independent in 1956. Most people are Muslim Arabs, but 30% are Berbers, who live mainly in the mountains, notably the rugged ATLAS range. Farming is the main occupation, but about 40% of the people live in cities. Phosphates are the chief export. In 1976 Morocco took part of WESTERN SAHARA. Saharan guerillas, sup-ported by Algeria, have fought Moroccan troops. Area (not including Western Sahara): 446,550 sq km; population: 17,828,000; cap-ital: RABAT.

produce only about enough food for their families and so contribute little to the GDP. Africa's chief exports are, in order of value, oil, copper, cotton, coffee, cocoa, iron ore, timber and phosphates. Although minerals are important, farming still accounts for about 60 per cent of Africa's export earnings. Africa's share in world trade is low – in 1976 it accounted for 4.6 per cent of the world's total exports and imports.

Agriculture and forestry

Although farming is the leading sector of Africa's economy, cropland covers only about 7.5 per cent of the continent. About 60 per cent of the land is too arid for any kind of agriculture and most of the rest is dry savanna, which is fit only for grazing.

In many farming areas, the rainfall is erratic and severe droughts often cause crop failure, which leads to famine. In the Sahel (dry savanna) region, south of the Sahara, several devastating years of drought in the late 1960s and early 1970s caused the deaths of millions of livestock. Water supplies dried up, plants died and the pastoralists starved. Pastoralism is a major activity throughout the savanna regions, but African livestock are generally of poor quality and pests and diseases, such as nagana, which is spread by tsetse flies, limit the grazing land. Many Africans assess their wealth by the number, rather than the quality, of the livestock they own. This leads to over-stocking, over-grazing and consequent soil erosion. In the temperate regions in the north and south of the continent, especially on European farms in South Africa, livestock-rearing is generally more scientific and more productive.

The chief food crops in Africa are: wheat in Mediterranean regions; sorghum and millet in the drier parts of the north-west; rice, cassava, sweet potatoes and yams in the rain forests; plantains (cooking bananas) in parts of East Africa; and maize in the south-eastern savanna. By world standards, yields are low and farming methods are often primitive. Many farmers are equipped only with digging sticks, hoes and

Below: Many African farmers are extremely poor and their farming methods have changed little since ancient times. To raise their standards of living, African farmers must learn new methods. Some modern techniques are shown in the picture.

1 Irrigation is necessary in much of Africa, where the rainfall is barely adequate for growing crops and is often unreliable.
2 Fertilizers renew the richness of the soil. In this way, the old method of shifting cultivation can be replaced by modern farming.

3 Storage facilities must be built so that food can be stored in good years to guard against other bad years when the crops fail.

4 Tractors and other modern farm machinery make farming more efficient and the yield per farm-worker can be greatly increased.

5 Weed killers and pesticides are essential items for combating the many problems faced by farmers in tropical Africa.

Moroni is the capital of the COMORO ISLANDS. Population: 12,000.
Mount Kenya, an extinct volcano in KENYA, is Africa's second highest mountain, at 5,199 metres above sea level.
Mount Kilimanjaro, an extinct volcano in TANZANIA, is Africa's highest mountain, at 5,895 metres above sea level.
Mozambique, formerly an overseas province of Portugal, became an independent republic in 1975, after a long guerilla war. The people of this tropical country are

mostly Bantu-speaking Black Africans, as most of the Europeans left in 1975. Farming is the main industry and exports include cashew nuts, cotton, sugar, tea and copra. Area: 783,030 sq km; population: 10,343,000; capital: MAPUTO.

Nairobi, capital of KENYA, was founded in 1899 on the Mombasa-Uganda railway line. Population: 700,000.
Namibia (SOUTH-WEST AFRICA) is an arid nation whose main resources are minerals, including diamonds, lead, tin,

uranium and zinc. Most people are Black Africans, but about 80,000 Europeans also live there. Germany ruled the area from 1884,

Bushman, Namibia

until SOUTH AFRICA conquered it in 1915. In 1919 the League of Nations mandated South Africa to rule the country. But, in 1946, South Africa refused the trusteeship which replaced the original mandate. Since then, South Africa and the UN have disputed Namibia's government and future. Area: 824,292 sq km; population: 762,000; capital: WINDHOEK.
N'Djamena, formerly Fort Lamy, is capital of CHAD. Population: 193,000.
Niamey, capital of NIGER, has 102,000 people.
Niger, formerly a French

territory, became an independent republic in 1960. Groundnuts are the main export of this extremely poor nation. Tuareg nomads live in the desert north. The Hausa, Djerma-Songhai and Fulani are the main groups in the savanna lands in the south. Area: 1,267,000 sq km; population: 5,259,000; capital: NIAMEY.
Niger, River, Africa's third longest river, rises in GUINEA and flows about 4,180 km to its outlet on the Gulf of Guinea, in NIGERIA.
Nigeria is Africa's most populous nation. It has

When world prices of such crops fall, these countries face severe economic problems.

Africa is a major timber producer, accounting annually for about 14 per cent of the world's roundwood (untreated tree trunks). However, exploitation of valuable hardwoods in the tropical forests is difficult, because the trees are scattered and transport facilities are often poor. Forestry is practised mainly near rivers and logs are floated down to the sea.

Fishing

Sea-fishing is an important industry in several countries, including ANGOLA, NAMIBIA, Senegal and South Africa, and South Africa is a major fish exporter. The production of fish from inland lakes and rivers is less than that from the sea, but it is an extremely important source of protein for the people who live around inland waters.

Mining

Mining is Africa's second most important industry. The most valuable export is crude oil and, in 1977, Africa accounted for 9.9 per cent of world production. The leading oil producers were NIGERIA (35 per cent of Africa's output), LIBYA (33 per cent) and ALGERIA (16 per cent). Algeria and Libya are also important sources of natural gas. The other oil producers are Egypt, GABON, Angola, TUNISIA, CONGO and ZAIRE. The oil-exporting nations received boosts to their economies in the 1970s, when oil prices rose sharply. Much of the revenue derived from oil sales was used to develop and diversify the economies of the fortunate few. However, oil price rises caused severe economic problems for those countries which imported oil.

wooden ploughs. The staple foods are also low in proteins which are essential for a healthy diet.

European influence has greatly affected farming techniques in many areas. From the late 1800s, Europeans introduced a cash economy into Africa and developed plantation agriculture to produce cash crops for export. Major cash crops in tropical forest regions include palm products and cocoa. Africa leads in cocoa production, yielding about 70 per cent of the world's total output. Africa also accounts for about 30 per cent of the world's coffee, which is grown on plantations in upland areas. Tea is becoming increasingly important in similar regions. The wetter parts of the savanna are ideal for groundnut and tobacco-growing and cotton flourishes on irrigated land, notably in EGYPT and SUDAN. South Africa, with European technology, produces a wide variety of tropical, Mediterranean and temperate crops. It is particularly famous for its canned fruit exports.

One major problem arises from the over-dependence of certain countries on one or two cash crops for export and, therefore, for foreign earnings. For example, cocoa accounts for over half of GHANA'S exports and SENEGAL relies on groundnuts for 75 per cent of its foreign earnings.

Above: The Argungu fishing festival is held once a year on a tributary of the River Niger, near Sokoto, in Nigeria. The river contains few fish for most of the year but, on a given date, the 'keeper of the river' says that fish will arrive. As many as 5,000 fishermen catch the Nile perch, which appear in great numbers.

Right: Gold is refined and moulded into ingots in South Africa. South Africa is the world's main gold producer and it is also fortunate in having reserves of many other minerals. Its great resources have helped South Africa to become Africa's leading economic power.

about 250 ethnic groups, including the Hausa and Fulani in the savanna lands of the north, and the Igbo (Ibo) and Yoruba in the hot, forested south. Nearly half of the people are Muslims. The rest practise Christianity or traditional religions. Because of its cultural diversity, Nigeria is governed as a federal republic, containing 19 states. Nigeria is noted for its early cultures and art, especially that of Nok, Ife and Benin. Nigeria became a united country, under Britain, in 1914. Independence was achieved in 1960.

Nigeria is now Africa's leading oil producer and is developing. But most people still depend on farming. The chief farm exports are cocoa,

Groundnut pyramid, Nigeria

groundnuts, palm oil and kernels, and rubber. Area: 923,768 sq km; population: 72,031,000; capital: LAGOS.
Nile, River, the world's

longest river, flows from the East African plateau to the Mediterranean Sea.
Nouakchott is capital of MAURITANIA. Population: 70,000.
Nyasa, Lake, is called Lake Malawi in MALAWI. It is 570 km long and has a maximum width of 80 km.

O **Orange, River**, in South Africa, rises in the DRAKENSBERG range and flows about 2,180 km to the Atlantic Ocean.
Ouagadougou is the capital of UPPER VOLTA. Population: 169,000.

P **Port-Louis** is capital and chief port of MAURITIUS. Population: 141,000.
Porto Novo is capital of BENIN. Population: 104,000.
Praia, capital of the CAPE VERDE ISLANDS., has a total population of 6,000.
Pretoria is the administrative capital of SOUTH AFRICA. Population: 562,000.

R **Rabat**, capital of MOROCCO, was founded on the Atlantic coast in 1160. Population: 368,000.
Réunion is a French island east of MADAGASCAR. Sugar is

Map legend

- ▽ Diamonds
- ● Phosphates
- ■ Coal
- ● Uranium
- ▲ Petroleum
- ● Cobalt
- ● Gold
- ● Chrome
- ● Copper
- ✳ Manganese
- ● Tin
- ● Iron Ore
- ● Lead
- ● Nickel
- ○ Bauxite

Above: The map shows that Africa is a major source of minerals. Most countries export the bulk of their mineral production, because they lack the industries to process them and use them to make manufactured goods. Problems arise when the prices paid for minerals fall. Price fluctuations can cause economic crises.

Below: The Kariba Dam was built between 1955 and 1960 across the Zambezi, which divides Zambia from Zimbabwe-Rhodesia. The 128-metre-high dam holds back a vast lake. Hydro-electricity produced at Kariba is supplied to both countries. This source of energy is vital in countries which lack fossil fuels.

Copper is the second most valuable mining commodity. ZAMBIA, Zaire and South Africa are the leading producers. Zambia is especially dependent on copper, which accounts for 90 per cent of its foreign earnings. Fluctuations in world prices for copper have caused economic problems in Zambia in recent times. Zambia and Zaire also lead the world in cobalt production.

Iron ore is mined in LIBERIA, MAURITANIA and South Africa and in smaller amounts in other countries. The development of iron-mining, except in South Africa and Egypt, has been hampered by the lack of resources to process the ore. Phosphates are mined in north-western Africa. The leading producer, MOROCCO, acquired one of the world's largest deposits in 1976 when WESTERN SAHARA was partitioned between Morocco and Mauritania. Morocco took about 60 per cent of Western Sahara to the north, which included massive deposits of phosphates at Bou Craa. GUINEA is Africa's leading bauxite producer and Nigeria and Zaire lead in tin.

South Africa has already been mentioned as a producer of copper and iron ore. But it also possesses Africa's most varied mining industry. It produces over 60 per cent of the world's gold and is a leading producer of gem-quality diamonds, although Zaire has a far greater output of mainly industrial diamonds. South Africa also has most of the continent's coal, and other important minerals include antimony, asbestos, chrome ore, manganese, nickel, platinum, thorium, uranium and vanadium.

Mining still offers great potential for Africa's future. This is because large areas have not yet been fully prospected and some known deposits are in places which are, as yet, inaccessible.

Energy

Apart from the few oil, natural gas and coal producers, Africa is generally short of fossil fuels. Much of the electrical energy is generated at hydro-electric stations at dams and along rivers. It is estimated that Africa has about 40 per cent of the world's hydro-electric potential. Major dams already supplying electrical energy include the Cabora Bassa Dam on the ZAMBEZI in MOZAMBIQUE: the ASWAN HIGH DAM on the NILE in Egypt: the Inga complex on the ZAIRE RIVER: the Kariba Dam on the Zambezi between Zambia and ZIMBABWE-RHODESIA: and the Volta Dam on

---

the chief product and rum is also exported. Area: 2,510 sq km; population: 559,000; capital: St-Denis.

Rhodesia, see ZIMBABWE-RHODESIA.

Rwanda, a remote and densely-populated republic, was part of Belgian Ruanda-Urundi until 1962. Most people are Bantu-speaking Hutus, but about 9% are Hamitic Tutsi pastoralists. Many Tutsi were killed during communal clashes in the 1960s. Rwanda's chief export is coffee. Area: 26,338 sq km; population: 4,753,000; capital: KIGALI.

S Sahara, the world's largest desert, covers about 8.4 million sq km.

Saint Helena is a volcanic British island in the South Atlantic Ocean. Area: 122 sq km; population: 5,000; capital: Jamestown.

Salisbury is capital and commercial centre of ZIMBABWE-RHODESIA. Population: 566,000.

São Tomé is a port and capital of SAO TOME & PRINCIPE. Population: 3,000.

São Tomé and Principe, formerly a Portuguese province, became an independent republic in 1975. The

main export of this island nation in the Gulf of Guinea is cocoa. Area: 964 sq km; population: 86,000; capital: SAO TOME.

Senegal, formerly a French territory, became an independent republic in 1960. The largest ethnic group is the Wolof, and Islam is the chief religion. Most people are farmers, and groundnuts and groundnut products dominate the exports. Area: 196,192 sq km; population: 5,115,000; capital: DAKAR.

Seychelles, formerly a British colony, became an independent republic in 1976. It includes about 90 islands in the Indian Ocean, east of

Cotton tree, Freetown, S. Leone

Kenya. The people are of African, Chinese, Creole, French and Indian descent. The chief export is copra. Area: 280 sq km; population: 64,000; capital: VICTORIA (pop. 23,000), Mahé island.

Sierra Leone, formerly a British territory, became independent in 1961. The country became a base for freed slaves in 1787 and the 42,000 Creoles are their descendants. But there are also 18 groups of indigenous Africans, including the Mende and Temne. Most people are farmers or pastoralists. But diamonds, iron ore, bauxite

the Volta River in GHANA. But Africa has the lowest energy consumption per capita of any continent, about 20 per cent of the world's average. And North America consumes more than 30 times as much energy as Africa per head of the population.

Manufacturing

The development of manufacturing, which generally marks the evolution of a developing nation into a developed one, has been hampered by several factors. First, there is a widespread lack of cheap energy resources. Next, most countries lack the capital required to invest in factories and machinery. Third, there is a lack of skilled workers. In most African countries, manufacturing is confined to small-scale processing of local raw materials and the production of consumer goods, such as clothes, beer and soft drinks, shoes, and so on. The development of consumer industries is restricted by the generally small home markets.

SOUTH AFRICA accounts for about 40 per cent of Africa's industrial output, and manufactures most of the continent's steel. In South Africa, manufacturing is now the leading sector of the economy, providing nearly 25 per cent of its GDP. Manufacturing accounts for more than 10 per cent of the GDP in only 14 other African nations. Of these, EGYPT is, at present, the most important. However, some nations, notably NIGERIA, ALGERIA, LIBYA and MOROCCO, have fast-developing manufacturing industries.

Transport and communications

Until the 1900s, shipping provided all coastal transport, while interior travel was arduous. Explorers and traders moved mostly on foot, with pack animals and porters to carry baggage and commodities. Sometimes, they sailed on inland waterways, but many African rivers are interrupted by rapids and waterfalls.

In the late 1800s, the railway age began. The first railways were built in the far north and south and, from the early 1900s, they were constructed in the tropics. The railways encouraged European settlement, because they enabled settlers to get their produce to the coasts. Towns on the railways became major trading centres.

Today, Africa has about 72,000 kilometres of railways. The railways of South Africa and Zimbabwe-Rhodesia, totalling about 16,000 kilometres, handle the most freight. Inland waterways, however, have mostly declined in importance. Air transport is now used to carry passengers and high-value commodities quickly over long distances. Light aircraft provide medical and other services to isolated areas.

From the 1920s, a massive road network was developed throughout Africa. Road haulage is now the chief form of transport in many areas. Most main roads remain open in all weathers, but many local dirt roads dissolve into mud after heavy rains.

The isolation of remote peoples has also been reduced by the expansion of communications, including telephones, telegraph services, and so

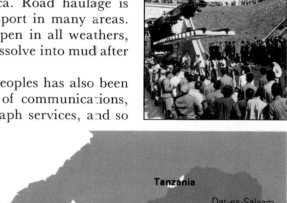

Below: The *Uhuru* (freedom), or Tanzam, railway, linking Tanzania and Zambia, was opened in 1975. It enabled Zambia to export goods through a friendly nation.

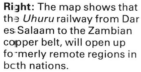

Left: Human porterage was the chief form of transport in Africa until recently, and it remains important in rural areas where foods and other goods, such as pots, are carried long distances to local markets. However, Africa's economy now depends on faster means of transport.

Right: The map shows that the *Uhuru* railway from Dar es Salaam to the Zambian copper belt, will open up formerly remote regions in both nations.

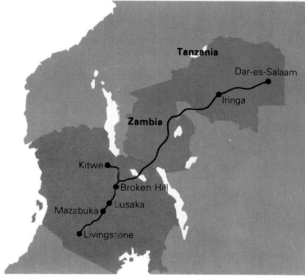

---

and rutile dominate the exports. Area: 71,740 sq km; population: 3,556,000; capital: FREETOWN.

Somalia, officially the Somali Democratic Republic, became independent in 1960 when the former British

Somali people

Somaliland united with Italian Somaliland. The land is largely arid and most people are nomadic pastoralists. Livestock and animal products form about 65% of the exports. The Muslim Somalis would like to unite with other Somalis who live in ETHIOPIA, DJIBOUTI and KENYA. Area: 637,657 sq km; population: 3,614,000; capital: MOGADISHU.

South Africa is Africa's most developed nation. Its population is mixed. Europeans, who speak either Afrikaans or English, form 17.5% of the population.

They control South Africa's government and economy. Black Africans form 70.2%. They include the Zulus and Xhosas. Coloureds (of mixed origin) form 9.4% and Asians, 2.9%. Government policy is aimed at developing the cultures of each group separately. BANTUSTANS have been set up for the Black Africans, although over 50% of them live and work in European areas. The most valuable part of the economy is manufacturing, especially in the Witwatersrand (including JOHANNESBURG) and in CAPE TOWN,

DURBAN and Port Elizabeth. South Africa's mines produce gold, diamonds, coal, copper, iron ore, uranium and many other minerals. European farming is highly efficient, but most Black African farmers live at subsistence level. The Union of South Africa was formed in 1910. South Africa became a republic in 1961. Area: 1,221,037 sq km; population: 28,870,000; capitals: CAPE TOWN; PRETORIA.

South-West Africa was renamed NAMIBIA by the UN in 1968.

Sudan, Africa's largest

on. Radio has had, perhaps, the greatest social impact. In most parts of Africa, people can hear news, educational and entertainment broadcasts. For example, Nigeria had a listening audience of 30 millions in 1969. Television is enjoyed by comparatively few at present, but is proving useful in education.

Modern Africa

In 1945 thousands of African troops who had served in European armies returned home. Many of these ex-servicemen were no longer content to live and work as second-class citizens in foreign-ruled colonies. News from Asia, particularly the independence of British India in 1947, further encouraged nationalist movements to grow throughout the continent.

In the early 1950s, several important events occurred. First, in 1951, LIBYA became the fifth independent nation in Africa and, in 1952, Colonel Gamal Abdel Nasser (1918-70) came to power in EGYPT. He made Cairo a centre of anti-colonialism. In the same year, an armed rebellion, organized by a secret society named

Right: The 10 homelands, or Bantustans, of South Africa, shown on the map, are regions for Black African settlement. Their combined area represents 13% of the total area of South Africa. The homelands are fragmented and most people are poor farmers. Transkei and Bophuthat-swana were made independent in 1976 and 1977 respectively and, eventually, South Africa plans to make the others independent. Only South Africa recognizes their independence. The UN believes that they rely too much on South Africa and cannot be considered truly independent.

Below: The University of Nairobi in Kenya was once a college within the University of East Africa, but it became an independent university in 1970. African universities now provide the higher education that was available only overseas.

The Bantu Homelands

People	Homeland
Tswana	Bophuthat-swana
North Sotho	Lebowa
Ndebele	Ndebele
Shangaan and Tsonga	Gazankulu
Venda	Vhavenda
Swazi	Swazi
South Sotho	Basotho Qwaqwa
Zulu	Kwazulu
Xhosa	Transkei
Xhosa	Ciskei

South Africa

Mau Mau, broke out in KENYA. Mounting nationalism, together with the possibility of facing long and costly colonial wars, changed the attitudes of many people in Europe, especially as Europeans had their own problems of post-war reconstruction.

In 1956 three North African countries, SUDAN, MOROCCO and TUNISIA, became independent and, in 1957, GHANA became the first Black African country to achieve independence. Between 1957 and 1978, nearly all African nations won their independence, some by peaceful means and others after long guerilla wars. Independence, however, was only a beginning and many countries faced profound problems.

Problems of independent Africa

In 1960 the Belgian Congo (now ZAIRE) became independent. Almost immediately, law and order broke down as the army mutinied for more pay and as a protest against the fact that Belgian officers were still in command. At the same time, the people of the mineral-rich Katanga (now Shaba) province attempted to secede and establish their own country. The United Nations sent in a force to restore order, and this was finally achieved in 1964, although further revolts occurred in 1966, 1967 and 1977. Zaire is about 60 per cent of the size of Western Europe. It contains about 200 ethnic and language groups and exemplifies the problems of many African nations. In an attempt to establish national unity, Zaire became a one-party state in 1970.

country, became an independent republic in 1956. Desert covers the north and centre, but the south is wetter. The Arab and other peoples of the north and centre are Muslims, but the mainly Negroid peoples of the south practise Christianity or traditional religions. Cultural differences led to a civil war (1964-72). Cotton is the chief product. Area: 2,505,813 sq km; population: 16,126,000; capital: KHARTOUM.
Suez Canal, in EGYPT, links the Red and Mediterranean seas. It is 162 km long.

Swaziland, formerly a British protectorate, became an independent kingdom in 1968. The economy of this scenic, land-locked nation is based on farming, but there is also some mining. Area: 17,363 sq km; population: 568,000; capital: MBABANE.

T Tanganyika, Lake, between BURUNDI, TANZANIA, ZAIRE and ZAMBIA, is the world's longest freshwater lake. It has an area of 32,890 sq km.
Tanzania consists of the former British territories of Tanganyika and Zanzibar.

Tanganyika became independent in 1961 and Zanzibar in 1963. They formed the United Republic of Tanzania in 1964. This farming nation produces coffee, cotton, sisal and other crops. There are 125 Bantu-

Eland farm, Tanzania

speaking groups, and Arab, Asian and European minorities. Area: 945,087 sq km; population: 17,362,000; capital: DAR ES SALAAM.
Togo, formerly a French territory, became an independent republic in 1960. The people of this poor nation are divided into about 30 ethnic groups, including the Ewe and Cabrais. Most people are farmers and cocoa and coffee make up half of the exports. Phosphates are also important. Area: 56,000 sq km; population: 2,530,000; capital: LOME.

Various other countries, including TANZANIA and ZAMBIA, have also become one-party states, because their governments believed that multi- or two-party systems of democratic government, along European lines, were not appropriate for these countries with their diverse populations. Several countries have been taken over by military groups, some of which have been fairly benevolent, while others have maintained power by brutal and dictatorial means.

Civil wars, caused by ethnic, language, cultural and religious differences, have caused much suffering and loss of life in some places. In NIGERIA, the Igbos of the south-east tried to secede and establish their own country, Biafra, in 1967, but they were finally defeated in 1970. In SUDAN, the Nilotic, Nilo-Hamitic and Sudanic peoples of the south fought against the Muslim northerners, a mixture of Arabs, Hamitic and Negroid peoples, between 1964 and 1972. A similar cultural division between northerners and southerners bedevilled the development of CHAD in the 1970s.

Some African nations have been in conflict because of boundary problems. Many frontiers drawn by Europeans divided ethnic groups between two or more countries. For example, the lands occupied by the Somalis in the Horn of Africa were divided between Italy, Britain, France, Ethiopia and Kenya. Italian Somaliland and British Somaliland were united as SOMALIA in 1960. But Somalia has long desired to reunify its people and, in 1977–8, it supported an unsuccessful uprising of Ethiopian Somalis against the Ethiopian government.

Southern Africa

Problems of a different kind have disturbed southern Africa. In 1965 Rhodesia (now ZIMBABWE-RHODESIA), a British colony, declared itself independent. But its government was controlled by Europeans, who formed only four per cent of the population. Britain refused to accept the independence of this country until it had a government which was representative of the majority. International economic sanctions were applied against Rhodesia, but its defiance was, initially, successful. However, with the independence in 1975 of two formerly friendly nations, the Portuguese territories of Angola and Mozambique, Rhodesia's position was

Above: The Parliament buildings in Gaborone were built when it was decided to make this formerly small market town in Botswana the country's capital. Gaborone officially became the capital in 1965.

Below: The struggle for independence in Angola, as in the other Portuguese territories of Mozambique and Portuguese Guinea (now Guinea-Bissau) was preceded by a guerrilla war. These costly wars became

unpopular in Portugal and were a major factor in causing a coup to take place in Portugal in 1974. One of the first aims of the new government was to arrange a rapid hand-over of power in Africa.

Transkei, see BANTUSTANS.
Tripoli, capital of LIBYA, is also the chief port. Population: 735,000.
Tunis, capital and main port of TUNISIA, stands near the ruins of the ancient city of Carthage. Population: 944,000.
Tunisia, formerly a French territory, became an independent republic in 1956. Most people are Muslim Arabs but Berbers live in the south. The northern ATLAS region has the most rainfall and the south is largely desert. Farming is the main occupation, but the chief ex-

ports are minerals, particularly oil and phosphates. Tourism is an important source of revenue. Area: 163,610 sq km; population: 5,737,000; capital: TUNIS.

Coffee nursery, Uganda

U **Uganda,** a former British territory, became independent in 1962 and a republic in 1967. An army group, under Gen. Idi Amin, ruled from 1971 to 1979. This land-locked nation depends on farming, and coffee and cotton are the main exports. Water covers about 15% of Uganda. There are 40 ethnic groups, the largest being the Baganda. Area: 236,036 sq km; population: 13,599,000; capital: KAMPALA.
United Republic of Tanzania, see TANZANIA.
Upper Volta, formerly a French territory, became an

independent republic in 1960. The largest of the various Black African groups is the Mossi. Most people in this poor, land-locked nation are subsistence farmers. Livestock and meat are exported. Area: 274,200 sq km; population: 6,762,000; capital: OUAGADOUGOU.

V **Victoria Falls,** on the ZAMBEZI RIVER, are 108 metres high and are divided into 3 main sections.
Victoria, Lake, is Africa's largest lake. It has an area of 69,485 sq km, in parts of KENYA, TANZANIA and UGANDA.

W **Walvis Bay** is the chief seaport of NAMIBIA. It is in a small enclave which, historically, belongs to Cape Province, SOUTH AFRICA.
Western Sahara was known as Spanish Sahara until 1976, when Spain withdrew and it was partitioned between MOROCCO (taking the northern part) and MAURITANIA (the southern part). The chief resource of this desert area is the phosphate deposit at Bou Craa in the north. However, nationalists, supported by Algeria, attacked Moroccan and Mauritanian troops.

weakened. The government then sought an internal, majority-rule settlement.

SOUTH AFRICA, which helped the break-away Rhodesian regime, has special problems of its own. There, the Europeans, who first settled in South Africa in 1652, account for 17.5 per cent of the population. The others are Black Africans (70.2 per cent), Asians (2.9 per cent) and Coloureds, of mixed racial origin (9.4 per cent). The Europeans are divided into two main groups. Afrikaners form 60 per cent of the total. They are the descendants of the original Dutch settlers and they have their own language, Afrikaans. Most of the other Europeans are descendants of English-speaking British settlers. These two groups, once in conflict with each other, are now trying to maintain their own culture and to retain their control of the government and the economy. The South African government has applied a policy, called

Below: The map shows the political changes in Africa since 1951. At the start of 1951, only 4 African countries were independent, while the rest were ruled by European powers. By 1979, African countries occupied 33% of the seats in the UN General Assembly.

Above: Somalis celebrated their independence in 1960 when the former Italian and British Somalilands united to form the Somali Republic.

separate development, or apartheid, by which the Black African population has been allocated homelands which, together, form about 13 per cent of the country. In these homelands, or BANTUSTANS, the Black Africans are supposed to preserve and develop their own culture. However, more than 50 per cent of the Black Africans live and work in European areas, where they have no rights. Also the homelands have much poor land and are therefore financially dependent on South Africa. This policy has caused internal unrest and been condemned by the UN.

The way ahead

While some countries have suffered great upheavals since independence, there are others where steady progress has been made. Some countries, such as IVORY COAST and KENYA, have remained stable despite their ethnic and language diversity by following free enterprise policies. Others, such as GUINEA and TANZANIA, have favoured socialism. Whatever their ideologies, African governments have all had to shape their policies to make them relevant to African realities and traditions, which differ from those in other parts of the world. By seeking African solutions to African problems, new ideas have been thrown up and Africa has been evolving a distinctive voice which is increasingly heard in world councils.

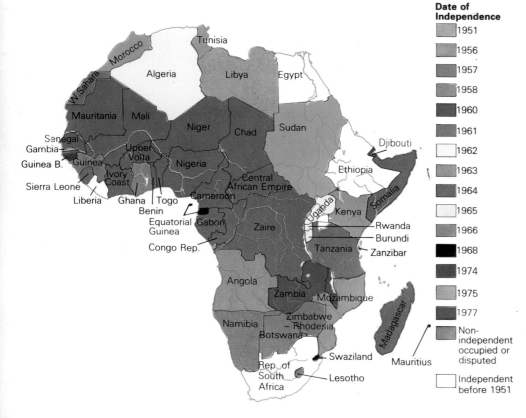

Date of Independence
1951
1956
1957
1958
1960
1961
1962
1963
1964
1965
1966
1968
1974
1975
1977
Non-independent occupied or disputed
Independent before 1951

Oceania, the smallest continent, contains two young nations, Australia and New Zealand. Both are lands of opportunity, which contrast with the beautiful but far less developed Pacific islands to the north and west.

Oceania

Oceania contains some of the world's most varied cultures and landscapes. Here, in the vast Pacific Ocean, is the huge island continent of Australia, which in 200 years has become one of the world's major suppliers of food and raw materials. It contains PAPUA NEW GUINEA, part of New Guinea, the world's second largest island, where some Stone Age tribes have never been visited but glimpsed from the air. Here also are some 10,000 coral islands, many of whose people

Below: Sandstone outcrops known as the Olgas look across the desert interior of Australia to one of the continent's major Aboriginal shrines—Ayers Rock. Jutting from the vast and arid plain, the rock glows vivid orange at sunrise and sunset. There are many very old Aboriginal rock paintings here. Today, Ayers Rock is a major tourist attraction.

have customs, languages and art forms quite different from their neighbours. Oceania had probably not been visited by man earlier than 30,000 years ago. The first settlers possibly came by boat from Asia, travelling south through the islands, and eventually reached Australia and NEW ZEALAND, where their descendants, the Aboriginals and Maoris, still live. Europeans began to explore the region in the 1600s and 1700s. While earlier peoples had accepted the vastness of Oceania and adapted themselves to live in harmony with its nature, the Europeans set about changing the environment, mining its minerals and introducing Western farming methods.

One result was to make Oceania the most ethnically mixed region of the world: more Indians live in FIJI than native Fijians; Greek language papers are published in Melbourne; and American-style policemen of Chinese origins work in HAWAII. While the Maoris of New Zealand retain some of their own farms, many

Above: Society Islanders make ready for an outrigger canoe race. Remote in their huge ocean, Polynesian islands such as these are only now beginning to become tourist playgrounds.

Reference

A **Aboriginal** is a name given to peoples who came to Australia some 30,000 years ago from the north. Skilled hunters with boomerang, spear and noose, they spread across the land in small clans. Their stories, songs, dances and paintings on rock and bark tell of the Dreamtime of their ancestors. The first white settlers hunted them for sport and killed all in Tasmania. Today, Aboriginals

Painted Aboriginal.

have full rights as citizens and few live as nomads. But their rights to own mineral resources on lands reserved for them are still argued.
Adelaide, capital of South Australia is a fast-growing industrial centre and port. It is a lively, international city whose suburbs spread 64 km across the Adelaide Plains. Skyscrapers of the inner city stand on the grid of broad streets laid down by Colonel William Light in 1836. The population is 809,000. A world famous Festival is held every two years.
Alice Springs is a remote township in the centre of Australia. Made famous by Nevil Shute's novel *A Town Like Alice* it is now a popular tourist destination. Population: 11,000.
Arnhem Land is a major

Aboriginal reserve in the Northern Territory where many sacred sites and paintings survive. The dense jungle mangrove swamps and rugged table and remain little explored.
Auckland is NEW ZEALAND's largest port, second largest city and a focus for road, rail and air links. Sited on Waitemata harbour in NORTH ISLAND, Auckland has national museums and is home to New Zealand's largest Maori community.
Australian Alps in southeast Australia are the watershed between the Murray

and Snowy rivers and include Australia's largest national park, Kosciusko, 5,376 sq km.
Australian Capital Territory is 2,332 sq km of New South Wales set aside in 1909 as the region in which CANBERRA, the national capital would be built. 50% of the region is forested. It was agreed that the capital should not stand on the land of any existing state lest that state had undue advantage in national affairs as a result.
Ayers Rock is a sandstone outcrop 333 metres high in a vast plain in Australia's

Aboriginal people have been displaced. This has frequently been by force of arms. British settlers in TASMANIA deliberately wiped out the existing Aboriginal population, hunting them with dogs for sport. During World War II, the peaceful palm-fringed coral atolls were the scene of bitter fighting between the United States and Japanese armies. It seems likely that future developments in the area will bring an increasing sense of identity to its many lands. The nations of the West are giving up their claims to the islands of Oceania, and several have begun life as independent communities. Australia and New Zealand are loosening ties with Britain, creating their own life-styles and position in world affairs.

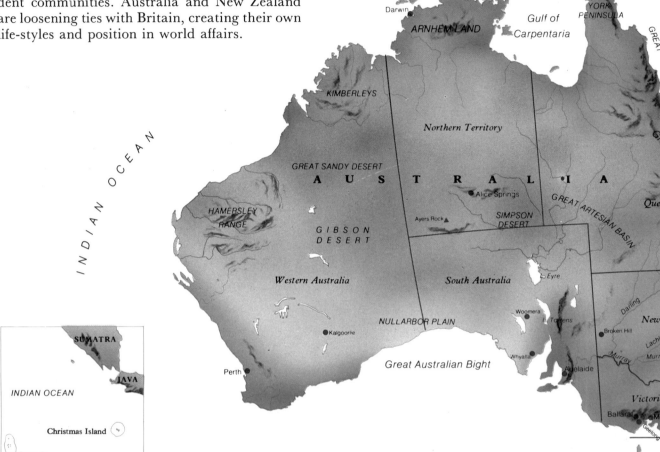

The area as a whole, with its great contrasts, beauties and opportunities has always attracted those in search of a new life. From the days of the first castaways and beachcombers, through the hectic times of the gold rushes to the present day, people from other countries all over the world have emigrated to settle anew in Australia or New Zealand.

Northern Territory. Cave dwelling Aboriginals painted mythical figures on the walls of their homes. At dawn and dusk the rock glows bright orange.

B Ballarat is the most important inland city of Victoria, a market for a fertile farming region and a sale-yard for cattle. An 1851 gold rush brought some 40,000 prospectors here – Chinese, British and Americans among them. One nugget found weighed 63 kg. In 1854 miners rebelled against licence laws, in the Eureka

Stockade incident. Government troops quelled them but they won reforms. Population: 38,910.
Barossa Valley, in South Australia, is the country's

Ballarat, Eureka monument

most famous wine growing region. German settlers put the first vines here in 1847 and German family names still survive.
Blue Mountains cover 1,400 sq km of New South Wales. They are named from the blue haze which often forms, a result of droplets of eucalyptus tree oil in the air. The City of the Blue Mountains, formed in 1947, is one of the world's largest urban areas. It is made up of 24 towns, spread through the mountains.
Botany Bay was where Europeans first landed on

Australia's east coast, on 29 April 1770. A naturalist in Captain Cook's party gave it the name because of the many wild flowers on shore. Now it is a developing commercial area 11 km north of Sydney.
Brisbane, capital of Queensland, is Australia's largest river port, 32 km from the coast on both sides of the Brisbane River. It handles some 70% of Queensland's trade. Brightly coloured shrubs in 4,000 sq km of parkland grace the city, whose commercial centre is dominated by

tower blocks and City Hall. Brisbane began as a convict settlement called Moreton Bay. It was named then after Sir Thomas Brisbane (1773–1860), a governor of New South Wales. Badly flooded in 1973, the city thrives again. Population: 986,000.
British Solomon Islands are an island chain covering 28,446 sq km in the South West Pacific. Melanesian peoples live here on low coral atolls and rugged volcanic isles. The capital is Honiara. The population is 191,000.
Broken Hill is the world's

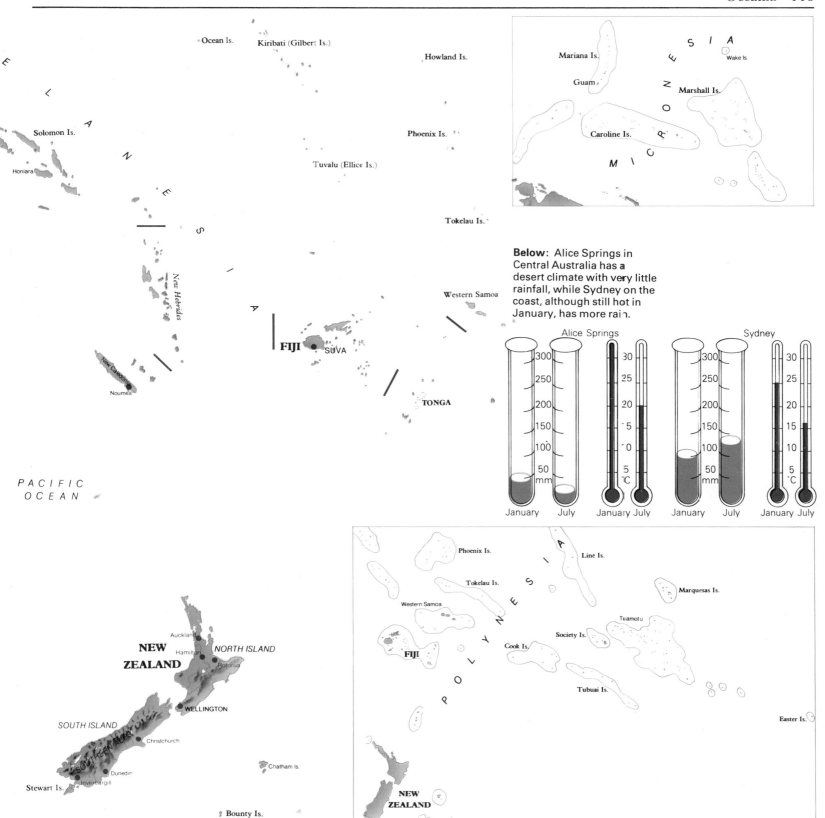

Ocean Is.
Kiribati (Gilbert Is.)
Howland Is.

Mariana Is.
Wake Is.
Guam
Marshall Is.

Solomon Is.
Phoenix Is.
Caroline Is.

Honiara

Tuvalu (Ellice Is.)

New Hebrides

Tokelau Is.

Western Samoa

FIJI
SUVA

TONGA

New Caledonia
Noumea

PACIFIC
OCEAN

Below: Alice Springs in Central Australia has a desert climate with very little rainfall, while Sydney on the coast, although still hot in January, has more rain.

Alice Springs

Sydney

January July   January July

January July   January July

NEW
ZEALAND

Auckland
Hamilton
NORTH ISLAND
Rotorua

WELLINGTON

SOUTH ISLAND

SOUTHERN ALPS

Christchurch

Dunedin
Invercargill

Stewart Is.

Chatham Is.

Bounty Is.

Auckland Is.

Phoenix Is.
Line Is.

Tokelau Is.
Marquesas Is.

Western Samoa

POLYNESIA

Tuamotu

Society Is.

FIJI
Cook Is.

Tubuai Is.
Easter Is.

NEW
ZEALAND

Bounty Is.

richest store of silver, lead and zinc. Prospectors in this part of New South Wales gave colourful names to towns they founded in the 1880s, among them, 'Terrible Dick' and 'Maggie's Secret'. Broken Hill, still known as 'the Silver City', is a base for Australia's largest business organization, Broken Hill Proprietary.

C Canberra is Australia's federal capital, a city of wide parades and avenues designed by American architect Walter Burley Griffin (1876–1937) and built this century in the AUSTRALIAN CAPITAL TERRITORY. Triangular in its design, Canberra is the setting for national occasions. More than 50% of the working population is based in government offices. The National University, Parliament House, and the broad dome of the Academy of Science are among the many fine buildings. Diplomats from the world's embassies enjoy free trout fishing in a huge artificial lake; over 50% of the city area is open space or parkland. The population is 160,000.

Caroline Islands in the West Pacific cover 1,050 sq km and are part of the UN Trust Territory of the Pacific Islands. Many nations have fought to own these islands, especially the Japanese in World War II. The capital is Saipan. The population is 60,000.

Christchurch, New Zealand, is New Zealand's largest administrative city and second most important industrial centre. Sited on the east of South Island's Canterbury Plains, it is known as the 'Garden City of the Plains'. Rail and road tunnels link it to its port at Lyttelton, 11 km to the south-east. The population is 320,530.

Cocos Islands are a group of coral islands in the Indian Ocean covering 1,359 km and forming an Australian external territory. From 1827, the Clunies Ross family dominated the islands and the copra plantations worked by Malays.

Coober Pedy, an opal mining community in South Australia, has attracted adventurers since 1915. Its church and many homes are carved underground, to avoid fierce surface heat.

D Darling River is Australia's longest, flowing 2,720 km from the Great Dividing Range to the Murray River. But much of the year it exists only as isolated water holes.

Darwin is the capital of Australia's Northern Territory.

Cocos Islands

Land, climate and vegetation

Australia is the world's flattest, most low lying and (except for Antarctica) least forested continent, with some of the world's oldest rocks. Long separated from other land masses, its flora and fauna include many found nowhere else – among them the best known are the marsupials, or pouched animals.

Ranging from the tropical swamps and forests of the far north, to the apple orchards far south in Tasmania, Australia spans many climatic zones. Its interior is a vast brown desert of scrub or pebble-strewn waste which may flower dramatically after rare but torrential rains. Over 60 per cent of Australia is too dry for farming and only two per cent of it can raise crops. Even so, Australia, with some 150 million sheep, 30 million cattle and huge wheatlands, has in 200 years become one of the world's greatest food suppliers. Some four in ten of Australia's cattle roam huge 'properties' of the far north during the 'Wet' or the months of November to March. At the beginning of the 'Dry' they are mustered, most being destined for hamburger stalls in the United States or Japanese dinner tables.

Further south, sugar cane, bananas, and pineapples flourish in Queensland's long, tropical, rainy season. South of Queensland the

Above: State education and modern settlement are available to today's Aboriginals. But for many the jump to Western lifestyles is not an easy one.
Below: Aboriginals perform a spear dance in an ancient ritual. Dance, body painting and story-telling are key art forms.

climate is more temperate, so that sheep and wheat are raised in plains that stretch to the south-east and west. 50% of Australia's cropland is devoted to wheat, while the sheep are mainly the silky haired Merinos, first bred in Spain and yielding 75 per cent of Australia's wool. On the eastern hills of the south, beef cattle thrive better than sheep. The temperate south also raises traditional European crops: fine wines are made in the BAROSSA VALLEY, and the best hops for Australian beer are grown in TASMANIA.

NEW ZEALAND is composed of NORTH ISLAND and SOUTH ISLAND and some smaller islands. It lies 1,600 kilometres from Australia, far south in the Pacific Ocean. High mountains form the backbone of both islands. In the South Island mountains rise well above the snow line. Mount Cook, the highest peak, reaches over 4,000 metres. This glaciated landscape of snowfields, lakes and fiords in the west leads down to alluvial plains in the east. The North Island landscape includes fold mountains, volcanoes, hot springs and geysers, while the coastal and valley lowlands contain most of New Zealand's rich agricultural land. The climate is temperate, with prevailing west winds. About 15 per cent of New Zealand is forested and owing to the country's isolation, certain plant species have developed in a way not found elsewhere. Tree-ferns for example, grow up to 16 metres high in the dense evergreen forest.

Built on a fine harbour, 3,200 km from other centres, Darwin is known as Australia's 'front door'. Only one road, called 'the Bitumen' links it southwards. On Christmas Day 1974, Cyclone Tracy devastated Darwin, where many homes were built on stilts. The population is 41,000.
Dunedin, far south on the east coast of New Zealand's South Island, is the nation's fourth largest city and a deep water port.

E Easter Island is dominated by some 600 huge

stone figures raised about 1,500 years ago. Set in the Pacific 3,860 km from South America, the population is 1,000 and the capital is Hangaroa.

Cyclone damage, Darwin

F Fiji is an independent dominion in the Commonwealth of Nations and consists of some 840 islands extending to 18,274 sq km in all. The capital, Suva, is on the largest island, Viti Levu. Sugar is the main export of the humid, tropical islands. The native Fijians, mostly Melanesians, lived in villages of single roomed, thatched houses. But European influence and tourism have brought changes. The Indian population, descendants of immigrants from the 1800s, outnumbers the native Fijians. Fiji became

independent in 1970. The population is 572,000.
French Polynesia is a group of many widely scattered Pacific islands, including TAHITI and TONGA. In all, the group covers 4,000 sq km. The capital is Papeete. The population is 128,000.

G Geelong is a major port and industrial centre in Victoria. Its huge wheat terminal handles much of the state's export trade. Geelong Grammar School and Geelong College are among Australia's best known schools. The population is 116,000.

Gibson Desert is an arid region of rock and stone in Western Australia. It is bounded by Lake Macdonald and Lake Disappointment.
Gilbert Islands (now Kiribati) are some 40 coral atolls in the south-west Pacific. With Tuvalu (the former Ellice Islands) they cover 744 sq km. The capital is Tarawa. Most islanders live in hut villages. Tuvalu became independent in 1978 and the Gilbert Islands in 1979. The population of the Gilbert Islands is 48,000.
Great Artesian Basin is Australia's largest source of

Above: Cricketer Jeff Thomson bowls another entry into the record books to add to Australia's fame as a nation of sportsmen.

Some 10,000 islands lie in the vast Pacific Ocean, which covers over 30 per cent of the world's surface. New Guinea, of which PAPUA NEW GUINEA is part, is the world's largest island after Greenland. It is dominated by a high chain of mountains, with tropical rain-forest as its predominant natural vegetation. The climate is equatorial with high temperatures and abundant rainfall. Most of the Pacific islands are small – either the tips of volcanoes that have risen from the sea floor or dazzling white coral atolls. Most of the islands lie in the tropics where the climate is warm with little variation in the seasons. Heavy rainfall on Hawaii contrasts with arid conditions on some of the coral atolls, such as those in Micronesia.

Peoples and ways of life

Australia has been called a desert surrounded by people. It is the most urbanized nation in the world: 82 per cent of Australians are city dwellers with 55 per cent living in the four great state capitals of the south-east, ADELAIDE, BRISBANE, MELBOURNE and SYDNEY.

In these thriving cities one can hear the languages and sample the foods of most European nations, for one in five Australians was born in Europe. In the past, nearly all new Australians

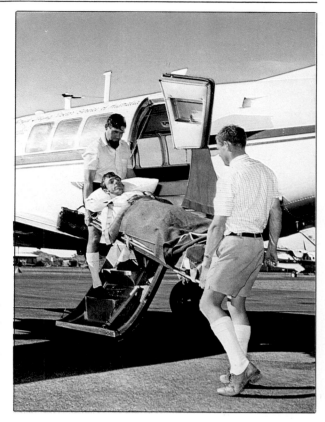

Left: Alice Springs, a remote township in central Australia, won fame from Nevil Shute's novel *A Town Like Alice.* Now it is a tourist centre. A 'regatta', run on wheels down a dry watercourse, is an annual festivity that emphasizes the blistering heat of the town's location.

Above: For patients in the Australian interior, the 'flying doctor' service remains the fastest way to medical aid. But much help is given by 2-way radio and telephone to assist emergency care on the spot. Many schoolchildren, too, receive much of their education from radio programmes.

were British, but after World War II the nation opened its doors to refugees and settlers from Italy, Greece, Yugoslavia, Poland and other countries. Though anxious to expand its population, Australia must still limit the rate of immigration; there must be sufficient manpower to raise the homes and maintain the essential services the newcomers will need. Once settled in, most think of themselves as Australians, rather than Greek or Italian, though many live in communities where their native language is spoken, and keep ties with the 'old' country.

---

underground water. Trapped deep in porous rock it gushes to the surface through bore holes, providing vital water supplies to farmers. The basin extends over 1,536,000 sq km, including over 60% of Queensland.
Great Barrier Reef is a spectacular reef formed from the skeletons of more than 300 different types of coral. The reef runs 2,000 km from Gladstone in Queensland to the Gulf of Papua, covers 204,800 sq km and includes some 700 islands. Hundreds of species of tropical fish abound. In recent

years the Crown of Thorns starfish has caused immense destruction by feeding on living coral polyps. Great efforts to destroy the starfish continue.
Guam is the largest of the Mariana Islands in the west Pacific and covers 549 sq km. It was a major US air and naval base but is now self-governing. The capital is Agana. The population is 98,000.

H Hawaii is a beautiful island group in the central Pacific. A 'crossroads' for the whole ocean, Hawaii

is a busy, tourist-conscious place. Since 1959 it has been the 50th state of the US. On 7 December 1941, its Pearl Harbor was the scene of the Japanese attack that brought the US into the war. Its capital is Honolulu. The population is 769,000.
Hobart is the capital of Tasmania and Australia's second oldest city. Splendidly sited between Mount Wellington and the River Derwent, it is 19 km from the sea but has an excellent deep water harbour. Much of the state's produce is exported through Hobart. A major

bridge, the Tasman Bridge, spans the Derwent River and was spectacularly damaged in 1975 when an ore carrier brought down three spans. One of the year's great events in Hobart is the finish of the Sydney to Hobart

Hobart, Tasman Bridge

yacht race. The population is 130,000.

K Kalgoorlie is at the centre of Australia's most important goldfield, in Western Australia. Its wide streets were laid out for the wagons of the first settlers here in the 1890s. The region is still a major gold producer. Water comes to the town in a 553-km-long pipeline from a reservoir near Perth. Its population is 21,000.
Kimberleys are a rugged region of Western Australia where rivers have carved

Australia is a very young country – over fifty per cent of its citizens are under thirty and it is fast developing its own identity and place in world affairs. Though few now live the traditional 'outback' life, where drovers still run big 'mobs' of cattle hundreds of kilometres from huge cattle stations to remote railheads, the 'Great Outdoors' is still Australia's best loved asset. Golden beaches with fine sports facilities in an ideal climate and spacious parks are the setting for Australian leisure. Australians are enthusiastic travellers: a weekend camping trip may mean driving hundreds of kilometres and air travel, more than anything, has opened Australia to the world and to itself. Some 130,000 kilometres of internal air services carry about eight million passengers cheaply round the continent each year. Railways, mainly busy with freight, also run air-conditioned expresses between Sydney and Perth and a network of national highways rings the country.

As a result, Australians are no longer isolated and although the continent's population, at just over 13 million, is only equal to that of the Netherlands (in a country 200 times larger), it commands some of the world's most valuable natural resources.

Above: Though not high in the world's table of populations, New Zealand has won world status in sport. Good food and a fine year-round climate has produced first-class performers. New Zealand's All Black rugby football team, seen in action against the British Lions, is one of the world's strongest sides.

Right: This elaborately carved building is a Maori meeting house in Rotorua, North Island, New Zealand. Although the Maoris are well integrated into New Zealand society, these traditional meeting houses are still an important focal point of local community life.

gorges deep in the sandstone. There are also huge ranges where over 60% of the state's cattle graze.
Kiribati, see GILBERT ISLANDS.

L **Lake Eyre** is Australia's largest lake. Set in South Australia, it extends 7,680 sq km after torrential rains. But usually it is a dry expanse of salt crusted mud.

M **Maoris** were the first settlers in New Zealand, arriving from Polynesia in the 1300s. Tall, brownskinned and courageous warriors, they settled their

Maoris carving, Rotorua

families and clans in villages whose wooden houses were often finely decorated with carvings. After clashing with early white settlers they agreed, under the Treaty of Waitangi of 1839, to become British subjects. But bitter wars about land ownership continued from 1845-70, reducing their numbers to some 42,000 by the early 1900s.

Marble Bar is a small township in Western Australia and known as the hottest place on the continent in summer. Temperatures of 49°C have been recorded. The population is 621.

Mariana, Caroline and Marshall Islands are in the west Pacific. The capital is Saipan. The population is 101,590.

Melanesians live in the islands north and north-east of Australia, including FIJI, NEW CALEDONIA, NEW HEBRIDES, BRITISH SOLOMON ISLANDS and the eastern part of New Guinea, now independent as PAPUA NEW GUINEA. Melanesia means 'black islands', so called because of the people's dark skins.

Melbourne is the capital of VICTORIA and is Australia's second largest port after Sydney. Over 30% of Australian manufactured goods are created in the Melbourne region, which is now one of the world's largest cities. Many parks and wide, tree-lined streets also make it one of Australia's most beautiful cities. Melbourne has a thriving cultural and leisure life, climaxing in the annual Moomba Festival (*moomba* is an Aboriginal word for 'joyful get together'). The city's Chinatown and strongly Italian suburb of Brunswick are centres for two of the many national groups that have created their own distinctive shops and restaurants. Sport plays a special part in Melbourne life. The Melbourne Cricket Ground is the site of Test matches, and, in winter, the Grand Final Match of the Australian Rules Football

Two in three New Zealanders live on North Island, where the nation's capital, WELLINGTON and the second largest city, AUCKLAND, are sited. Most MAORIS live on North Island. Fully integrated into society now, their first relations with New Zealand's white settlers were stormy.

Immigration from Britain began slowly in the mid-1800s. No convicts were sent, as they were to Australia. New Zealand became a separate colony in 1841, and an independent dominion in 1907. A short-lived gold rush in the 1860s boosted immigration, and many stayed on to farm when the gold ran out. Links of trade and affection between New Zealand and Britain remained strong and New Zealand is still a main supplier of meat and dairy produce to Britain. However, dissatisfaction with the quality and delivery of finished goods from Britain to New Zealand has grown.

New Zealanders have a prosperous life style, most people's homes being detached bungalows. Air travel has ended New Zealand's isolation and her citizens are able to afford a certain amount of foreign travel. Outdoor sports are a main leisure activity, particularly water sports, skiing and Rugby Football. The formidable All Blacks rugby team is one of the world's greatest.

Many races have moved through the Pacific islands, which are now grouped by the names given to their first inhabitants, the MELANESIANS. MICRONESIANS and POLYNESIANS. For most islanders, fishing and the growing of such crops as bananas, breadfruit and copra have been the traditional way of life. But air travel and tourism have brought many changes. Some twenty shipping lines and airlines work in the area, though a journey to the West from a remote island may take weeks. Radio and radio-telephone services bring news of the world beyond, broadcasting in the region's many languages. These include English, French and Pidgin (now the official language of independent Papua New Guinea, where hundreds of local languages, each unlike another, are spoken). A South Pacific Commission advises governments on technical and scientific affairs.

In their arts and customs, the islands are as different as the peoples that inhabit them, and are much influenced by the Western countries who long dominated different areas. The American sphere of influence covered the island region

Right: Samoa has long been studied by anthropologists intrigued by its relaxed and happy family life. In the traditional wood and thatch homes of its village communities, young and old live in harmony. In the foreground beach pebbles are for sale in woven palm-frond baskets.

north of the equator, including HAWAII, Eastern SAMOA and GUAM. The French came to FRENCH POLYNESIA and NEW CALEDONIA. The British recently gave independence to FIJI and TONGA and Australia handed control to the citizens of Papua New Guinea. In general, the countries of the West are 'moving out' of a region to which they came as traders, missionaries and colonial powers in the 1700s and 1800s. Artists and poets

Below: Headhunters of Papua dance a ritual that Western visitors are only now beginning to see as a major form of art. Such peoples living in the remote highlands developed a complex society which included inter-tribal head-hunting raids. These dancers were performing to welcome Queen Elizabeth II.

Map legend

- ◔ Iron
- ● Lead
- ■ Coal
- ● Tin
- ◔ Gold
- ○ Silver
- ◔ Opals
- ● Copper
- ◔ Uranium
- ● Zinc
- ● Aluminium
- ★ Manganese
- △ Oil and Gas

Above: The continent of Australia is a huge store of natural treasures.
Below: Living on the job, opal miners in hot Coober Pedy, Australia, have underground homes, often air conditioned. At their 'back door' may lie a fortune for the taking.

have also made their way to this beautiful part of the world – along with naturalists and anthropologists who have studied the unique social and family structures of the islands. Today, only a few tribes in Papua New Guinea keep to a life untouched by Western influences.

Economy

Skilled technology has greatly aided Australian agriculture, including the scattering of minerals from the air to render soils fertile. Bore holes have tapped the waters of the GREAT ARTESIAN BASIN and huge irrigation and hydro-electric schemes, as in the SNOWY MOUNTAINS, have made dry lands fruitful.

Alongside its agricultural wealth, a treasure-store of minerals has helped give Australia the nickname of the 'Lucky Continent'. In the 1800s the lure of gold and diamonds brought rough, tough fortune hunters here from as far away as China and the United States. Such sites as the KIMBERLEYS and BROKEN HILL have yielded untold wealth and fortunes are still made. In 1952, a miner, whose light aeroplane was forced

low by cloud en route to Perth, noticed a rust-coloured gorge that looked as if it was made of iron. It was. He became a multi-millionaire. 'New' minerals – such as bauxite, source of aluminium and nickel, vital ingredient in stainless steel – have also made (and lost) Australian fortunes. Uranium, discovered by chance in the NORTHERN TERRITORY in 1954, may prove most valuable of all, as fuel for nuclear reactors. Meanwhile, coal, natural gas and hydro-electric power are Australia's main energy sources: the world's largest brown coalfield is at Latrobe Valley, Victoria. Measuring 15 kilometres by 65 kilometres, its reserves may last 750 years.

Australian governments have made great efforts to encourage industry – so that raw materials can be turned to finished goods in Australia, rather than all exported. One in four Australians now works in industry – one in ten in the motor industry. Shipbuilding is important in a land with a 19,300-kilometre coastline and few overland routes for transporting goods, while the chemical industry is the fastest expanding, comprising more than forty large petrochemical plants. Much of industry is owned by foreign companies; American companies for example control all three car manufacturers. Foreign markets still prefer to see Australia as the world's larder and quarry, rather than supplier of finished goods, so agriculture is still the main export business of the nation. 'Living off the sheep's back' may no longer be a way of life for many, but it is still, as in the 1800s, one of the ways to wealth.

---

its capital, SYDNEY. The state has four main zones, running north to south. Sydney and many other major towns are sited on the fertile coastal strip. Inland, the tablelands include the BLUE MOUNTAINS and SNOWY MOUNTAINS. The first settlers found prosperity when a route across this barrier was made, opening up the western slopes and western plains beyond. In these regions some 50% of Australia's sheep are raised. In the far west is BROKEN HILL, for long Australia's major mineral source. New towns,

such as Albury, twin town with Wodonga, across the Victoria border, have been built to decentralize the state's economy. Covering 792,148 sq km, most of New South Wales has a temperate climate. The population is 4,955,000.
New Zealand consists of NORTH ISLAND, SOUTH ISLAND, Stewart Island, Chatham Islands and several minor islands. The capital is WELLINGTON. Over 60% of New Zealand's population is urban, but the economy is mostly dependent on farming. The main industries are those

processing farm products, but rapidly expanding industries include engineering, textiles, chemical manufacture and cars. The area is 268,665 sq km and the population is 3,142,800.
North Island, New Zealand, has broad, fertile coastal

Pohutu Geyser, Rotorua

plains and an eastern mountain range. Two in three New Zealanders dwell in North Island. WELLINGTON, the nation's capital and AUCKLAND, its largest city are sited here. So is its largest lake, Lake Taupo. Active volcanoes include Ruapehu (2,797 metres). Famous geysers around Rotorua shoot jets of steam and gas high in the air. Its area is 114,725 sq km.
Northern Territory is a huge but empty Australian state. Its capital, DARWIN, is in the monsoon zone of the far north. But, in the flat and hot interior, droughts of ten

years long are known. Some 25,000 Aboriginals live in reserves, mainly in ARNHEM LAND. Mining, cattle raising and tourism equally support the state economy. Bauxite and manganese are mined. Cattle are raised on huge stations in the outback. Tourism centres on ALICE SPRINGS. The first European settlement was in 1824, but the region was slow to develop. World War II brought many servicemen to Darwin, which was bombed by Japan. After the war many soldiers returned to live in Darwin. The population of

Over 60 per cent of the land in New Zealand can be farmed. Nine million cattle and some 57 million sheep are the main source of the country's wealth, but forestry is increasing in importance and New Zealand plans to be self-sufficient, using timber as a renewable energy source. Major hydro-electric schemes based on the high waters of South Island are also an important energy source.

It is unlikely that the Pacific islands will ever develop, as a whole, towards a thoroughly 'Western' lifestyle as they are too scattered to form large political units. Most are too small to attract the sellers of many consumer goods, and much of their produce is too perishable or too remote to export. But NEW CALEDONIA has

Below: One of the world's greatest-ever engineering projects is the Snowy Mountains HEP Scheme. Rivers running east to the sea were switched so that they would water plains to the west. Red arrows on the map show how tunnels turn the water back.

Above left: Pineapples grow well in hot Queensland, Australia. Bananas are also raised in a continent that spans a tropical far north to a cool south in Tasmania, where apples have been the traditional main crop. Today's transport costs have hurt the fruit trade.

Above: Australia grew rich 'off the sheep's back' and the plump Merinos on sale here in New South Wales still yield much of the nation's wealth. But farming is now highly mechanized, and few people live the traditional life of the outback sheep station.

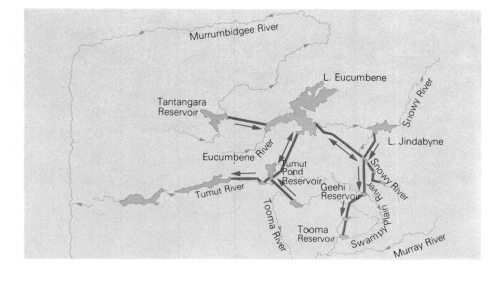

mineral reserves and exports nickel. The NEW HEBRIDES exports some manganese. And copper is the main export of PAPUA NEW GUINEA.

History and culture: Australia

For some 30,000 years, ABORIGINAL peoples had Australia to themselves. Far from the Western world, Australia was the last continent Europe colonized. In the AD 300s geographers guessed that a great southern continent might exist. They called it *Terra Australis Incognita,* the unknown southern continent.

Dutch explorers, among them Abel Tasman (1603-59), who discovered TASMANIA in 1642, led the way south. But hostile coasts and Aboriginals discouraged them. Then on 29 April 1770, the

---

the Northern Territory is 100,700.
Nullarbor Plain is a desert extending through Western Australia into South Australia and covers some 200,000 sq km. It is the world's largest limestone slab. Its name means 'no tree', but after rare rains the desert blooms dramatically.

O **Ord River Dam** in Western Australia created the country's largest artificial lake.

P **Papua New Guinea** is a tropical island country

bordering West Irian in Indonesia to the west. Papua New Guinea reached full independence on 16 September 1975. But dense rain forests, high mountains and a rainfall averaging 2,000 millimetres annually make progress to a unified nation difficult. For example, hundreds of distinct languages are spoken, so the official language is now a form of 'Pidgin' English. Some tribes have only been sighted from the air. Headhunting and cannibalism survived until recently. Timber, copra, cocoa, coffee and rubber are

staple products. A new crop is palm oil. The Bougainville copper project is the main export money winner. Papua New Guinea covers 461,691 sq km and its coastal capital is Port Moresby. The population is 2,611,000.

West New Guineans

Paramatta is west of Sydney in New South Wales. It includes engineering, motor car assembly and textile works among many industries. Elizabeth Farm House, built in 1793, is Australia's oldest surviving building.
Perth is the capital of Western Australia and lies 19 km from the mouth of the Swan River. Freemantle, the state's main port, is sited here and is one of the world's most modern shipping terminals. Perth is a lively city whose citizens are 75% Australian born. Fine

buildings include St George's (Anglican) and St Mary's (Roman Catholic) cathedrals. Spacious parks such as King's Park grace the town and night horse-trotting is a popular sport in Gloucester Park. A 3,938-km-long rail link to Sydney was completed in 1970.
Polynesians are inhabitants of Polynesia, meaning 'many islands'. Scattered in a triangle formed by New Zealand, Hawaii and EASTER ISLAND, Polynesia includes American SAMOA, the GILBERT ISLANDS and Tuvalu, and FRENCH POLYNESIA. Tall, brown-

English navigator, Captain James Cook (1728-79), landed near the site of modern SYDNEY, with orders to claim for Britain this land glimpsed by earlier explorers. He reported that it was fit for colonization.

So, on 20 January 1788 the First Fleet landed at BOTANY BAY, bringing 750 convicts to start a settlement near the world's finest natural harbour.

Above: Solomon islanders fish by night in calm seas.

Below left: Benmore Dam, New Zealand, turns the nation's high waters into a power source.

Below: Dairy herds near snow-capped Mount Egmont graze on some of the world's best pasture.

European diseases and bloodthirsty persecution by White settlers reduced the numbers of Aboriginals, who were some 700,000 strong when the first Whites arrived. The Aboriginals had never fought over land ownership, finding room for all. But the settlers squabbled – landowners versus 'squatters'. By the mid-1800s Britain gradually stopped sending convicts, partly because it was no punishment to go to a land where a man might pick up a 48-kilogram nugget of gold. Instead immigrants flooded in, increasing the population by over a million in 20 years from 1860. Many who came to seek gold went on to grow rich on Australia's true wealth, her sheep and wheatlands.

Britain agreed that the colonies should move towards self government. In 1863 the colonies began to meet to discuss whether they should join in a federation or if each should go its own way. By January 1901, federation was agreed and from that time the states have run their own internal affairs. A federal capital was transferred from Melbourne to CANBERRA in 1927 to run affairs such as defence and trade.

Australia entered the 1900s with expanding cities and prosperous farms. In World War I, Australia volunteered readily to 'stand behind the mother country' in a far distant struggle.

The war boosted Australian trade and strengthened her voice in the world. But world depression in the 1930s hit the nation hard: 500,000 were out of work. Politics were bitter. In 1931 Britain gave Australia the right to make her own foreign policy. But when war broke out

skinned peoples, the Polynesians are skilled navigators and reached New Zealand, where they are known as MAORIS.

Q Queensland is Australia's second largest state, covering 1,707,520 sq km. Its eastern coast, 5,178 km long has 14 major ports to speed produce overseas. Fine grasslands in the east and north-west of Queensland make this the leading cattle state in Australia. Sugar cane is the main crop, but manufacturing, especially from wood and paper

products, forms half the state production. The population is less concentrated on the capital (BRISBANE) than in other states. Known as the 'Sunshine State', tourism is an important activity. The population is 1,960,700.

S Samoa is the name for two countries. Eastern, or American Samoa covers 197 sq km and has Pago Pago as its capital. Western Samoa, capital Apia, became the first independent Polynesian state in 1962. Both are in the eastern Pacific. Samoan peoples are

Polynesian and tuna fishing and canning, in addition to tourism, are the main activities. The population of Eastern Samoa is 35,000, of Western Samoa 152,000.

Snowy Mountains in NEW SOUTH WALES and VICTORIA has Australia's largest snowfield and national park – and one of the world's largest engineering schemes in a huge hydro-electric and irrigation undertaking. The scheme diverts the waters of the Snowy River so that instead of wasting eastwards to the sea they now flow west, bringing 2,446 million cubic

metres to irrigate the western plains and generate 4 million Kw of electricity. Seventeen major dams and 160 km of tunnels are involved in a scheme first planned in the 1880s and completed in the mid 1970s.

South Australia is the nation's major agricultural and industrial producer-state and the fastest growing in population. Half the population works in manufacturing industries, mainly centred on ADELAIDE, the state capital. The fertile Murray River basin has vineyards and other orchards. The semi-

arid Western Plateau includes a major Aboriginal reserve and the rocket range at Woomera. In the highland chain of mountains is the dramatic landscape of the Flinders Ranges. For South Australians, shark and fresh-

Vineyards, S. Australia

expression in their homeland, for example through Australia's own fine ballet, opera and theatre companies. In the past, too, many Australian writers and artists struggled self-consciously to break away from European traditions and create arts that would be specially Australian. Now, increasingly, they feel more free to choose personal subjects and styles.

One symbol of the new spirit is the world famous Sydney Opera House. The bold design of a young Danish architect, the Opera House was opened in 1973 after twenty years of problems and delay. At one stage it seemed that its soaring sail-like roofs could never be built. Now it is host to international stars of opera, ballet and drama.

Among Australia's opera stars are Dame Joan Sutherland (1926-) and Harold Blair (1924-). The dancer, choreographer and actor Sir Robert Helpmann (1909-) directed the Australian Ballet Company until 1975, while other leading ballet companies in Australia include the Australian Dance Theatre of South Australia, and the Queensland Ballet. Famous actors have included Judith Anderson (1893-1962) and Peter Finch

Above: Bora Bora island epitomizes an image of the world's southern oceans—the cone of an extinct volcano, its coral-crowned rim, and a blue lagoon. For centuries, adventurers, castaways, artists and traders have made this region one of the most mixed and exotic of earthly paradises.

Right: Coral reefs are formed from the stony skeletons of millions of tiny coral polyps (*far right*) continuously budding. Atolls are formed by coral reefs growing around an active volcano. Eruptions cause the volcano to sink below the level of the reef, leaving it exposed as islands.

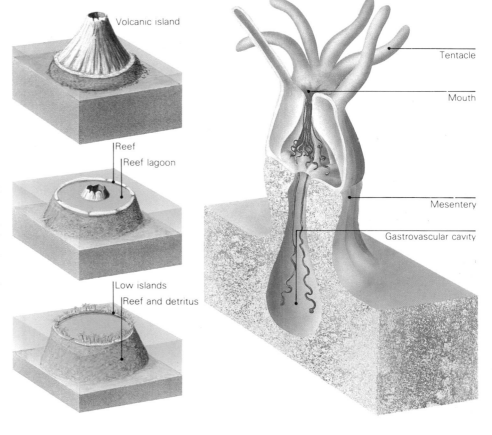

Volcanic island

Reef
Reef lagoon

Low islands
Reef and detritus

Tentacle

Mouth

Mesentery

Gastrovascular cavity

again in 1939 Australia once more sent men. They fought bravely in the Western Desert, but this time there was an enemy closer at hand. Fifteen thousand Australians went into harsh Japanese captivity at Singapore. And Japan, by raiding DARWIN on 19 February 1942, brought war to the doorstep.

After World War II, Australia opened her doors to many nations and foreign investors. The country boomed. It has become the world's fifth most prosperous nation. Trade with Britain declined and increased in turn with the United States and Japan. The arts in Australia have reflected the history of a fast-developing nation. In the past, many creative people left Australia to make their careers abroad. Now they can find

---

water fishing are popular sports. SA, first colonized in the 1830s, got its own constitution in 1856. Many migrants arrived in the 1960s and 1970s. The population is 1,217,600.

South Island, New Zealand, is dominated by the Southern Alps, where 17 peaks top 3,000 metres. Fast flowing rivers from the Alps generate electricity through hydro-electric schemes. In the lowlands the Canterbury Plains are among many fertile eastern areas on which sheep are raised. Its area is 153,940 sq km.

Sydney, capital of New South Wales, is Australia's largest and oldest city. A bridge, built in 1932 and 1,149 metres long, is a world famed landmark, as are the white concrete 'sails' of Sydney Opera House — home to the Sydney Symphony Orchestra and the Australian Ballet. Sydney and its vast suburbs, home to 59% of the state's peoples, is a thriving place with 25,000 factories, a major business and banking centre, and a port that handles some 4,000 vessels a year in the world's finest

natural harbour. Ferries bring commuters to work in the inner city, dominated by high buildings and fine parklands. Nearby are 34 beaches, including Bondi and Manley which are famed for surfing. Inner suburbs have a lively, international air, with Greek and Italian communities and the well restored historical areas such as Paddington's terraced houses. Among many academic centres is the University of Sydney, Australia's first, founded in 1850. Captain Cook landed nearby at BOTANY BAY in 1770.

The town became a city in 1840. Its population is 2,717,000.

T Tahiti, largest island of the Windward Group in French Polynesia, lies in the central south Pacific. The

Convict barracks, Hobart

artist Paul Gauguin made it his home. The mountains and coral fringes of its fertile coast, from which cocoa, sugar, copra and coffee are exported, make it an important tourist centre.

Tasmania is Australia's smallest state — an island about the size of Ireland. Long known as the 'Apple State', and supplier of 75% of Australia's apples, this crop has declined rapidly in the 1970s owing to the costs of packing and shipping overseas. But the mild climate favours other crops, such as hops. Tasmania is

Above: Kiri Te Kanawa, a Maori New Zealander, gained world fame as one of the foremost opera singers of the 1970s. Her success highlighted the problem for artists in small countries like New Zealand: those with great talent must take it abroad in order to win fame.

(1916-1978), best known for his film roles.

Australia's film industry has recently been given much financial support from the Australian Film Development Corporation, and a 'new wave' of Australian films began to win prizes worldwide in the 1970s. They include *Picnic at Hanging Rock, Caddie, Newsfront* and *The Chant of Jimmy Blacksmith.* Many films were based on the novels of Australian writers. Patrick White (1912-) is the major Australian writer of the century, and won a Nobel Prize in 1973 for his novel, *The Solid Mandala.* The novelist Morris West (1916-) wrote the best-selling *The Shoes of the Fisherman.* Alan Moorehead (1910-) is the author of many novels, and was a distinguished war correspondent. Australia's dramatists include David Williamson (1942-), author of *Don's Party.* Major poets include Judith Wright (1915-) and Alec Hope (1907-).

Above: White sails of the Sydney Opera House match those of the yachts in the world's best harbour. But, for a time, it seemed that nobody could build this dream planned by a young Danish architect. Perseverance by the city fathers finally saw this national home of opera, ballet and drama through to completion.

In the visual arts Sidney Nolan (1917-) is the best known painter, particularly for his pictures of Leda and the swan, and the outlaw Ned Kelly. Sir Russell Drysdale (1912-) has painted the harsh landscape of the Australian interior.

The work of individual creative workers and of national artistic companies is aided by the Australia Council of the Arts, and the Australian Broadcasting Commission is the major patron of music in Australia. Arts festivals encourage the new vigour of Australian cultural life, most notably those at Adelaide and Perth.

History and culture: New Zealand

The native Maoris of New Zealand occupied the country for about 400 years before its discovery by Europeans in 1642. Later, sealers, whalers and Kauri seekers established settlements along the coast. These people had a devastating effect

also one of the world's most mountainous islands – and as a result is rich in hydro-electric power potential for industry. Though only 3% of Australia's population lives here, the state produces 8% of all Australia's electricity. Forests of pine, eucalyptus and myrtle cover half the state's area (67,540 sq km). Tasmanians are of 97% British stock. Keen yachtsmen, they held the first Hobart Regatta in 1838. Today, the capital, HOBART is still the destination of one of the world's great races, from Sydney to Hobart. The fact

that this island separated from the mainland some 11,000 years ago has preserved unique animals and plants such as the Tasmanian Tiger and Tasmanian Devil. A Dutch explorer, Abel Tasman, first sighted Tasmania on 24 November 1642 and named it Van Diemen's Land. It was claimed for England in 1802 and won its own local government in 1856. The population is 400,700.

Tonga, a Pacific island kingdom also known as the Friendly Islands, has been independent from Britain

since 1970. More than 150 islands make up the group, whose capital is Nuku 'alofa. Polynesian peoples live in Tonga, respecting since the AD 900s a line of sacred monarchs called the Tu'i Tonga. Queen Salote Tupous III, who reigned from

Queen Salote, Tonga

1918 to 1965, was a popular visitor in Britain. Tongatapu, extending to 260 sq km, is the largest island in the group which, in all, covers 699 sq km. Coconuts, copra and bananas are exported. The population is 96,000.

V **Victoria** is Australia's second smallest state but second highest in population. 70% of the land is farmed, but in so mechanized a way that only 7% of the population works on the land. Thirty per cent of the workforce is engaged in manufacturing industries,

mostly based in the region of Melbourne. Manufacturing earns twice as much revenue for the state as agriculture. Victoria, in Australia's far south-east, is temperate in climate and has four main regions. Gippsland lies behind the Ninety Mile Beach coastline and is a prosperous dairy farm region. Its northern parts are mountainous. Westward lies the central district where Melbourne stands on the Yarra River, with orchards, forests and plains nearby. Next in the western district, cattle raising and dairy farm-

Zealand began to trade with other nations, notably those of the Pacific Basin.

New Zealand's remoteness and small population has meant that organized cultural life cannot be on a large scale. The cost of bringing orchestras or stage productions from abroad is too high, for example. Many New Zealanders have had to make their artistic careers abroad, among them the world famous Maori singer, Kiri Te Kanawa.

There is, however, a national orchestra, three professional theatre companies, and in the 1970s a 'new wave' of New Zealand film-making began paralleling that in Australia. Important authors of this century have included the short-story writer Katherine Mansfield (1888-1923). The short story is a commonly practised medium among New Zealand writers.

A new development in New Zealand's cultural life is the fact that the Maoris are now creating a written tradition, recording stories and folklore previously passed down by word of mouth.

Left: A 'new wave' of fine Australian films was one of the nation's most important contributions to world culture in the 1970s. *Picnic at Hanging Rock* was based on a novel that told of mysterious disappearances from a girls' school early in the century.

Below: Tuvalu celebrates independence day in colourful dance. One of several South Sea communities to reach independence recently, Tuvalu faces a future with the problems confronted by all small nations.

on the Maori population by bringing European diseases into the country. They also provoked inter-tribal wars with the sale of muskets in the 1820s. New Zealand was annexed to Britain in 1840 and the Treaty of Waitangi was signed, guaranteeing the Maoris undisturbed possession of their lands. Land titles were, however, disputed and hostile Maori chiefs crushed before order was established in the 1800s. The Maoris now have four representatives in government, are four times as numerous as in 1900 and take an increasing part in their country's affairs.

New Zealand became an independent dominion in 1907, but its economy still entirely depended on Britain. It was greatly affected by the depression of the 1920s and 30s. Since World War II, an increased demand for food exports has boosted New Zealand's economy. When Britain joined the Common Market in 1973, New

ing are the major activities. The north region includes mountains, but also plains watered by tributaries of the Murray River. Most of the state's wheat is raised in this region. Irrigation projects in the north-west, based on the township of Mildura, have created a world-known dried fruit industry. European settlements began with a convict colony in 1803, which was quickly abandoned. Three expeditions, organized by Tasmanians, staked claims here in the early 1830s. By 1850 much of the state was occupied. Victoria's constitution dates from 1855. Its population is 3,647,500.

W **Wellington** is the capital city of NEW ZEALAND. Sited at the far south of NORTH ISLAND on a fine natural harbour, it is the country's major port and commercial centre. Road and rail links make it the hub of the nation's communication network. The population is 140,000.

Western Australia is the nation's largest state, covering 2,498,355 sq km. Because much of Western Aus-

tralia is dry, it has been the nation's slowest state to develop, but has prospered since World War II. Half the state's population live in the conurbation of the state capital, PERTH and its port at Fremantle. And 75% of the

Goldminers of Kalgoorlie

state's workforce dwell in these or other towns. But huge sheep stations prosper in the central and southern part of Western Australia. Gold, coal, oil, iron ore and nickel (found in huge deposits at Kambalda in 1966) enrich the state. The 'Golden Mile' of KALGOORLIE has been in production since the 1880s – and in 1979 world wide interest was raised among speculators at news of new mineral treasures in the KIMBERLEYS. The first settlement in Western Australia was in 1826. The population is 1,095,300.

Whyalla is the third largest city of South Australia and base of the Whyalla Shipbuilding and Engineering Works. From here in May 1972 the largest ship built in Australia to date, the *Clutha Capricorn* (a 78,000 tonne carrier) was launched.

Woomera in central South Australia has since 1947 been a base for testing guided missiles for the UK and Australia. Australia's first satellite was launched here in 1967. Woomera derives from an Aboriginal word meaning 'spear thrower'.

The polar regions offer hostile environments for people. But the Arctic and, possibly, the ice-covered continent of Antarctica contain resources which may assume great importance in the future.

Polar regions

Below: Although Antarctica is the world's most barren continent, it has huge riches not yet explored. The seas around it teem with life, in a complex chain that runs from minute organisms up to mighty whales. Many kinds of penguin flourish on the coast and its icebergs, which break continually from the huge ice cap.

Below right: For centuries Lapplanders followed the reindeer on their travels and found in them a source of meat, clothing, tools and—from their hide—shelter. The reindeer are still important in the life of this remote Arctic region, and their meat is still exported southwards. But few Lapplanders now lead the traditional hard life of the true nomad.

Both polar regions are the planet's radiators, drawing heat from warmer zones and reflecting it skywards. Both are regions of ice and snow, scenes of epic journeys of discovery. But in fact the poles differ greatly.

The Arctic is a small sea surrounded by continents. Nuclear submarines regularly pass 'below' the thin ice of the North Pole. Passenger aeroplanes fly 'above' it daily. The Antarctic is a huge continent surrounded by oceans. Though ancient Greeks guessed it was there, and Maori legend told of it, no one is known to have set foot on Antarctica until the 1800s. Today, some 800 scientists who brave its savage and sunless winter have many secrets still to find.

Antarctica

It is the world's most remote, highest and only treeless continent. Forming a rough circle around the Pole, the size of the United States plus Mexico, it lies buried beneath 90 per cent of all the world's snow and ice – to an average depth of 2,134 metres. If it melted, the world's sea level would rise 60 metres, drowning London, New York and Sydney. Yet Antarctica's climate is as dry as the Sahara's – fire is the hazard most feared by its explorers. Huge winds race clockwise round the continent, topping 160 kilometres per hour. The coldest temperature known on Earth, –88·3°C, was recorded in the Antarctic.

Huge mineral wealth must lie beneath the ice cap of Antarctica, but no technology yet known can reach it. Partly for this reason Antarctica is known as the 'peaceful continent' where no man has ever been killed in anger. The Antarctic Treaty, signed in 1959 by 14 nations, scrapped older maps that show the region sliced like a cake

better planned expedition had won its way, without loss of life, to the heart of the last continent to be explored.

Its exploration continues and today, tourist cruises from New Zealand ply to a land through seas so dangerous that any sailor, in the days of sailing ships, could claim the right of putting both feet on the table after dinner if he had been to the Antarctic.

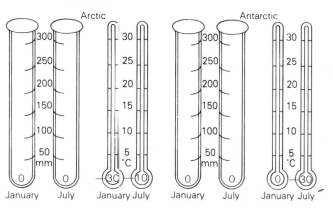

Above: The Arctic and Antarctic have light snow instead of rain and their temperatures never rise above 0°C.

(with the pole as centre) between various claimant nations.

Since 1957 (the International Geophysical Year) it has been a 'continent for science' where all may move freely and military activity is banned. The Treaty runs out in 1989; then earlier claims, particularly on the ANTARCTIC PENINSULA, may be revived. Meanwhile, important research on the world's climate and magnetic field has been done. Air conditioning and nuclear power plants make life comfortable for scientists on Antarctica's bases today. But near the modern McMURDO STATION is the wooden hut raised by Captain Scott, whose doomed expedition to the pole began here in 1911. The bodies of his dogs and hay for his ponies will lie here for ever in Antarctica's great refrigerator. Scott reached the Pole, via the BEARDMORE GLACIER, to find a Norwegian flag, raised by Roald Amundsen (1872–1928) on 14 December 1911 – a month earlier. Amundsen's

of which Australia and Antarctica were once part.
Greenland is the world's largest island. Its 2,175,600 sq km lie mostly in the Arctic circle and only some 5% of the surface is ice free. On the southern coast, summers are cool but pleasant and some sheep are raised. But the sea's wealth of seals and whales has been Greenland's main source of livelihood, though mineral resources may be exploited in future. Greenland was an integral part of Denmark from 1953 to 1979. Then its own parliament, the *Landst-*

ing, was established. Greenland was a remote and little developed society until

Packing reindeer meat, Greenland

World War II, when its strategic position between the US and Russia brought

radar and weather stations there. Now air travel and an ultra modern telephone network of 90 stations has opened up the country.
Greenlanders are by race a mix of European and Eskimo peoples. There are few pure Eskimos.
Gunnbjorn's Mountain on the east coast is the tallest in Greenland, rising to 3,700 metres.

Icebergs, the chunks of ice that break off from ice shelves in polar regions, may drift far; regular patrols chart their course in north-

ern shipping waters. One iceberg 145 km long was sighted in Antarctica. But most are about 1.6 km long and rectangular.
Ice shelves occur where polar ice spreads from the land over the sea. Ross ice shelf in Antarctica is larger than France.

Lapps dwell on the arctic edges of Scandinavia. Some 30,000 strong, they are the last survivors of the people who lived in Europe in the Ice Age and went north with the ice as it retreated. The reindeer has

The Arctic

Northern Russia, Scandinavia, Alaska and the world's largest island, GREENLAND, border the North Pole located in the frozen Arctic Ocean. The Indians who settled in America came this way from east to west. Some stayed in the far north and are known as ESKIMOS. Later, when reindeer herds retreated north with the snows of the Ice Age, LAPPS followed them to the Arctic.

It is now one of the world's fastest developing regions. Modern technology can tap its oil and gas resources. Greenland, for long an undevelopable country, is now prospecting its mineral wealth. Russia even raises strawberries under glass within the Arctic Circle. US military bases have brought some prosperity, but also such problems as alcoholism to many Eskimos.

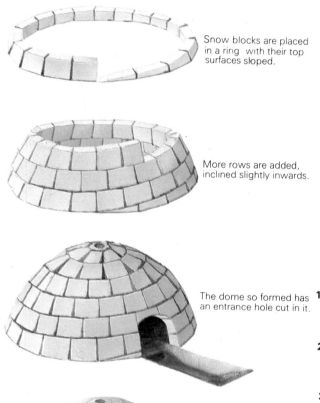

Snow blocks are placed in a ring with their top surfaces sloped.

More rows are added, inclined slightly inwards.

The dome so formed has an entrance hole cut in it.

The entrance to the igloo is protected by blocks.

Below: The kayak is still used by Eskimos for fishing and hunting.

Modern exploration began with a search for a North West Passage – a trade route from east to west. Explorers like William Baffin (1584–1622), Henry Hudson (c.1600s) and Martin Frobisher (c.1535–94) left their names on the map, but failed to find a viable route. There are now plans to build a massive icebreaker to open one up. Less severe in climate than Antarctica, the north polar region is rich in wild life: seals, walrus and polar bears can approach the neighbourhood of the pole itself across the pack ice. No lives were lost on the two great polar expeditions; in the first, Fridtjof Nansen (1861–1930) a Norwegian, attempted to reach the pole by allowing his ship to freeze into the ice and drifting with it. The successful assault on the pole was by Americans, Robert Peary (1856–1920) and Matthew Henson, on 6 April 1909.

Far Left: Stages in the construction of a temporary igloo.

Below: The umiak, made of walrus skin stretched over a frame, is still used, often with an outboard motor.

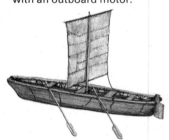

Below: Stages in the construction of a kayak. The open design of the framework (**1–3**) makes the craft light and manoeuvrable. Sealskin is stretched tightly across the frame and hunting tools are attached (**4**).

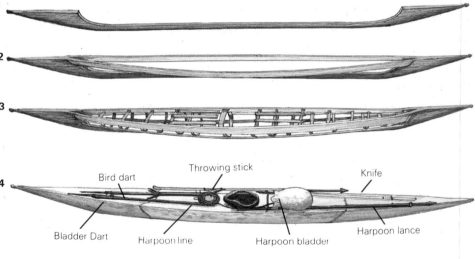

1

2

3

4

Bird dart
Throwing stick
Knife
Bladder Dart
Harpoon line
Harpoon bladder
Harpoon lance

---

always been their source of food, clothing, and shelter. Few now follow the herds, but instead trade reindeer products to southern lands. **Little America** was the name of five bases established in Antarctica by the US.

M **McMurdo Station** is now the main US base on Antarctica, and is sited on the southern end of Ross Island. It is a sprawling, 100 hut village powered by a nuclear reactor and obtains fresh water from the sea through a desalination plant.

Nearby, Robert Scott's first hut is maintained by New Zealand as an historical monument. **Mount Erebus** is the only recently active volcano in Antarctica. Always topped by a white plume of gases, it is 1,140 metres high. **Mount Terror,** extinct neighbour of Mount Erebus in Ross Island, Antarctica, is 994 metres high.

N **North Pole** was first reached by Robert Peary (1856-1920), the American explorer, on 6 April 1909.

S **South Pole** was first reached by Roald

North Pole – 13 base

Amundsen the Norwegian polar explorer (1872-1928) on 14 December 1911. There is now a US base here. A striped pole, topped by a globe and surrounded by the flags of the nations that signed the Antarctic Treaty, marks the pole. Also in Antarctica is the Pole of Relative Inaccessibility, marking the region least accessible from the coast. A Russian base, Sovetskaya, was built here.

T **Thule** is a major US air base on Cape Athol in north-west Greenland. Origi-

nally a World War II base, it developed in 1952 as a stop on the transpolar route from the US to Europe. There is a 365-metre-high radio and radar tower and a ballistic early warning station. **Transantarctic Mountains** form one of the world's greatest mountain chains, stretching 4,800 km from Oates Land to the Filchner ice shelf.

V **Vostock** is a Russian base established at the Geomagnetic Pole in 1958.

Index

Acknowledgements

Contributing artists
Creative Cartography, Nick Cudworth, Howard Dyke, Sue and Dave Holmes, Cathy James, Dave Mallett, Ralph Stobbart, Tony Yates.

The publishers also wish to thank the following:
Adespoton Film Services 17C, 55C, 111T.
Bryan & Cherry Alexander 126TR
Associated Press 32C, 109TR
Australian News and Information 113B, 115B, 116B, 117TR, 117B, 119B
Barnaby's 12B, 13B, 64T
Barnaby's/Ken Lambert 5B
Barnaby's/H. Sibley 18B
Barnaby's/Ian D. Walker 10B
Bo Bojesen 25B, 50C, 51TL, 63T, 89T
Anne Bolt 49B, 57B, 63B, 64B, 105B
British Aerospace 14TC
British Gas 14CB
Camera Press 16T, 22T, 33T, 47T, 80C
Camera Press/J. Carnemolla/P. Prenzel 120T
Camera Press/M. Kaplan 107C
Camera Press/David Moore 113TR, 122T, 123T
Canada House 43B
J. Allan Cash 9C, 17T, 61B, 71T, 80T
Colorpix 77C, 109TL
Colorsport 117TL, 118T
C. T. O. Films/Denis Davidson Associates 125T
Daily Telegraph Colour Library 19T, 73T, 124TL
Daily Telegraph Colour Library/Nicholas Guppy 126TL
Daily Telegraph Colour Library/L. L. T. Rhodes 37TL
Jesse Davies 31TL
Douglas Dickins 72T, 76B, 77B, 78C, 78B, 80B, 81B, 82B, 83T, 84B, 86B, 88B, 89B, 91T, 92B, 94T, 94B, 95T, 95B, 110C
Robert Estall 38T, 44T, 47C
Mary Evans Picture Library 8B, 34B, 39B, 44B, 48B, 123B
Peter Frankel 97T, 98TL, 100T, 101T, 104C, 105T, 111T
Michael Freeman 53T
Sonia Halliday 70C
Robert Harding Associates 7T, 25TR, 35B, 37TR, 39T, 40TR, 48T, 50T, 57T, 62T, 76T, 78T, 79T, 82TR, 88C, 89T, 93T, 95C, 117C
Robert Harding Associates/ G. & P. Corrigan 9C
Robert Harding Associates/A. Mather 58T
Robert Harding Associates/Sybil Sassoon 98C
Anwar Hussein 125C
Alan Hutchison Library 51TR, 54B, 59B, 60B, 64C, 70T,B, 75T,C, 85B, 96T, 97B, 98B, 100B, 101B, 102B, 103T, 106B, 107T, 108B, 110B, 112T
Alan Hutchison Library/Sarah Errington 109B
Alan Hutchison/Brian Moser 56C
Alan Hutchison Library/C. Nairn/Granada Disappearing World 119C
Alan Hutchison Library/Granada Disappearing World 58B
Imperial War Museum 32T
Louis-Yves-Loirat/C-D Tetrel 72C
Macdonald Educational 14b, 111B
Macquitty Collection 68B
Tony & Marion Morrison 59T, 60T, 68T
Musee De L'Homme, Paris 36T
National Film Board of Canada 41B
High Commissioner for New Zealand 118B, 120B
Chris Niedenthal 24T,C, 26T, 27T
Novosti 20B, 22B, 24B, 26B, 27B, 28B, 29T,B, 30B, 31B, 32B, 128B
Photographers Library 18CR
Photri 33B, 37B, 38B, 40B, 42B, 46B, 47B
Judith Platt 25TL
Popperfoto 15T, 36B, 40C, 45B, 50B, 52B, 55B, 73B, 96C, 104B, 114B, 119T, 122B, 125B
Rex Features 19B, 28T
Rex Features/Fotos International 46TL
Rex Features/Sipa 4BR, 46C
G. R. Roberts 113TL, 118C, 121TL,TR, 122CL,CR
Servizio Editorial Fotografico 3C, 14T, 31TR
Swiss National Tourist Office 8C
Homer Sykes 4T
John Topham Picture Library 3BL,BR, 4BL, 6B, 7BL, 8B, 9BC, 11B, 15B, 16B, 17B, 18T, 18CL, 21B, 22B, 23B, 25C, 51B, 53B, 56B, 61B, 62B, 67B, 69B, 71B, 72B, 74B, 75B, 77T, 79B, 83B, 87B, 90B, 91B, 93B, 96B, 99B, 103B, 107B, 121B, 124B, 126B, 127B
John Topham Picture Library/Bente Fasmer 116T
John Topham Picture Library/Fotogram 56T
John Topham Picture Library/Harvey 8T
Mireille Vautier 52T, 55T, 57C, 59C, 62C, 63C, 69C, 86T, 87T, 92T
D. C. Williamson 82TL
Woodfin Camp/Ira Block 43T
Woodfin Camp/Dan Budnik 34C
Woodfin Camp/George Hall 34T
Woodfin Camp/Sylvia Johnson 45C
Woodfin Camp/Leroy Woodson 37CL
Woodfin Camp/Adam Woolfitt 42T
Jerry Young 69T
Zefa 44C
Zefa/Baglin 116C
Zefa/Biedermann 23T
Zefa/Franscnia 98TR
Zefa/Pierer 11T
Zefa/Scholtz 7T
Zefa/Seider 3T
Zefa/Strauss 54T